Fodor's 96

Las Vegas, Reno, Tahoe

"When it comes to information on regional history, what to see and do, and shopping, these guides are exhaustive."

—*USAir Magazine*

"Usable, sophisticated restaurant coverage, with an emphasis on good value."

—Andy Birsh, *Gourmet Magazine* columnist

"Valuable because of their comprehensiveness."

—*Minneapolis Star-Tribune*

"Fodor's always delivers high quality...thoughtfully presented...thorough."

—*Houston Post*

"An excellent choice for those who want everything under one cover."

—*Washington Post*

Fodor's Travel Publications, Inc.
New York • Toronto • London • Sydney • Auckland

Fodor's Las Vegas, Reno, Tahoe

Editors: Anto Howard, Kristen Perrault

Editorial Contributors: Robert Andrews, Robert Blake, Deke Castleman, Janet Foley, Mary Ellen Schultz, M. T. Schwartzman (Gold Guide editor), Dinah Spritzer

Creative Director: Fabrizio La Rocca

Cartographer: David Lindroth

Cover Photograph: R. Llewellyn/Superstock, Inc.

Text Design: Between the Covers

Copyright

ISBN 0-679-03036-0

Special Sales

Fodor's Travel Publications are available at special discounts for bulk purchases for sales promotions or premiums. Special editions and corporate imprints can be created in large quantities for special needs. For more information, contact your local bookseller or write to Special Markets, Fodor's Travel Publications, 201 East 50th Street, New York, NY 10022. Inquiries from Canada should be directed to your local Canadian bookseller or sent to Random House of Canada, Ltd., Marketing Department, 1265 Aerowood Drive, Mississauga, Ontario L4W 1B9. Inquiries from the United Kingdom should be sent to Fodor's Travel Publications, 20 Vauxhall Bridge Road, London SW1V 2SA, England.

PRINTED IN THE UNITED STATES OF AMERICA

10 9 8 7 6 5 4 3 2 1

CONTENTS

Maps

ON THE ROAD WITH FODOR'S

A GOOD TRAVEL GUIDE is like a wonderful traveling companion. It's charming, it's brimming with sound recommendations and solid ideas, it pulls no punches in describing lodging and dining establishments, and it's consistently full of fascinating facts that make you view what you've traveled to see in a rich new light. In the creation of *Las Vegas, Reno, Tahoe '96,* we at Fodor's have gone to great lengths to provide you with the very best of all possible traveling companions—and to make your trip the best of all possible vacations.

About Our Writers

The information in these pages is largely the work of one extraordinary writer. Deke Castleman lives in Las Vegas and is the managing editor of the *Las Vegas Advisor,* a monthly consumer newsletter. He has just finished updating the fourth edition of his *Compass American Guide to Las Vegas* and he is also author of the *Nevada Handbook*. Deke has worked for Fodor's for a number of years and, to put it simply, Deke knows just about everything you need to know about Las Vegas, Reno, and Tahoe.

Many thanks go to the following Las Vegans for their help, direct or indirect, with the preparation of this book: Myram Borders; Virginia, Adam, and Jonathan Castleman; Anthony Curtis; Mara Fierstein; Jackie Joniec; Katie Rose; Max Rubin; and Phyllis Snyder.

What's New

A New Design

If this is not the first Fodor's guide you've purchased, you'll immediately notice our new look. More readable and easier to use than ever? We think so—and we hope you do, too.

New Takes on Traveling with Children

Deke Castleman has added to this edition a chapter on traveling to Vegas with children. Vegas has a lot more to offer than just gambling and nightlife. As gambling becomes legal in more and more states and casinos spring up just about everywhere, Las Vegas knows that it has to change with the times. With Walt Disney World as the obvious model, Vegas has realized that family entertainment may be the way of the future. In practical terms that means bigger and better amusement parks, spectacular kiddies shows, and dining and lodging geared toward the whole family, not just the high rollers.

Let Us Do Your Booking

Our writers have scoured Las Vegas to come up with an extensive and well-balanced list of the best resorts, motels, and hotels, both small and large, new and old. But you don't have to beat the bushes to come up with a reservation. Now we've teamed up with an established hotel-booking service to make it easy for you to secure a room at the property of your choice. It's fast, it's free, and confirmation is guaranteed. If your first choice is booked, the operators can line up your second right away. Just call 800/FODORS-1 or 800/363-6771 (0800/89-1030 when in Great Britain; 0014/800-12-8271 when in Australia; 1800/55-9101 when in Ireland).

Travel Updates

In addition, just before your trip, you may want to order a Fodor's Worldview Travel Update. From local publications all over Las Vegas, the lively, cosmopolitan editors at Worldview gather information on concerts, plays, opera, dance performances, gallery and museum shows, sports competitions, and other special events that coincide with your visit. See the order blank at the back of this book, call 800/799-9609, or fax 800/799-9619.

And in Las Vegas

With nine of the country's 10 largest resort hotels, Las Vegas accommodates nearly 30 million tourists a year, attracted by the hotels, the large variety of gambling opportunities, the inexpensive rooms and food, the world-class entertainment, the growing number of amusement parks, the neon lights of the city, and the spectacular scenery of the American Southwest surrounding it all.

This year's edition of *Fodor's Las Vegas, Reno, Tahoe* will help prepare you for the casinos and suggest other activities and excursions to tear you away from the slot and video poker machines. But it will also attune you to the essence of Las Vegas, which is often obscured by the steamrolling, surface level stimulation of the town.

Las Vegas has been a boomtown on and off for the past 40 years, but continuously for the past six years, and there's no end in sight. With the opening of Circus Circus's Luxor, the Mirage's Treasure Island, and Kirk Kerkorian's MGM Grand, all in late 1993, Las Vegas now not only boasts nine of the top 10 hotels in the country, but 12 of the 16 largest hotels in the world.

The corner of Tropicana and the Strip alone claims three of the top 12 hotels in the world. But that's just for starters. A partnership between the MGM Grand and Primadonna (which owns three casinos at the state line on I–15) is building a **new 2,400-room megaresort on Tropicana Avenue.** The hotel rooms will be housed in reproductions of the Big Apple's greatest skyscrapers, including a 350-foot-tall Empire State Building. Visitors will stream into the casino on a replicated Brooklyn Bridge under the watchful gaze of a 200-foot-tall Statue of Liberty. Theme areas inside will include Greenwich Village and Grand Central Station.

And that's not all. Circus Circus, which owns and operates Excalibur and Luxor, recently bought the Hacienda Hotel (next door to Luxor) for $80 million, along with a vacant 73-acre lot, on which it plans to build a $600 million megaresort, currently dubbed **"Project H."** The four casinos-in-a-row will give Circus a miracle-mile-type monopoly on the south end of the Strip.

Never one to sit idly by while the competition builds bigger and better tourist traps, main Las Vegas juiceman Steve Wynn of Mirage Resorts is adding another 3,000-room high-roller hotel to the Las Vegas skyline. The $900 million **Bellagio** is rising on the ashes of the Dunes hotel and golf course. It will feature a 15-acre bay fronting the Strip, a 48-story hotel tower (tallest in town), and a magnificent water theater to house a new production of Cirque du Soleil.

The **Stratosphere Hotel and Tower** will finally be completed in spring 1996, and at 1,149 feet, it will have one of the tallest observation towers in the world. Planned for the deck of the tower are a 450-seat revolving restaurant, four wedding chapels, a floor of high-roller suites, and—hold onto your hats—a roller coaster that gives you the sensation of going off the edge of the tower and a "sling shot" ride that gives you the sensation of going off the edge of the planet! With its 1,500-room, fully renovated hotel and 100,000-square-foot casino next door, the Stratosphere Hotel and Tower could win the intense battle to become the premier attraction in Las Vegas.

Long in decline due to competition from the megaresorts on the Strip, downtown Las Vegas will sustain a major boost from the completion of the **Fremont Street Experience.** This four-block, 100-foot-high awning over Glitter Gulch will turn downtown into a covered pedestrian mall and a unified attraction of its own: seven major and five minor casinos, with dozens of restaurants, hundreds of table games, and thousands of slots, all within a short, climate-controlled stroll.

Bally's is building a 2,500-room, as-yet-unnamed resort next door to its existing 2,814-room hotel. A partnership between Circus Circus and the Mirage is building the 3,000-room **Victoria** resort on part of the vast old Dunes property. Small, neighborhood hotel-casinos are being thrown up all over the valley: Texas and Kactus Kates on El Rancho Road in North Las Vegas, New Orleans and Sundance in west Las Vegas, two Lone Stars in east Las Vegas, Grand Victoria, Sunset Station, and Safari on Boulder Highway in southeast Las Vegas. If all goes according to plan, by 1997 Las Vegas will top the 100,000-room mark.

Las Vegas remains, for the seventh year in a row, the fastest-growing city in the country. The population of the Metropolitan Statistical Area (MSA) surpassed the 1 million mark in mid-1995. Las Vegas is growing so fast, in fact, that it's the only city in the country that requires two editions of the Yellow Pages every year, one in January, the other in July. McCarran International Airport jumped from 11th busiest in the world in 1993 to eighth busiest in 1994, with half a million arrivals and departures carrying 27.5 million passengers. The visitor volume for 1994 reached 28.2 million, by many estimates tying Disney World for the position of number-one vacation destination in the country.

Amid all this change, one thing about Las Vegas remains the same. The people keep gambling and the casinos keep profiting. In 1994 all the casinos in Nevada took a little more than $7 billion from gamblers, of which $5.5 billion (nearly 80%) went to Las Vegas casinos. That was $700 million more than the year before. To give you an idea of how much visitors are losing in Las Vegas casinos, $5.5 billion divides out to $15 million a day, or $175 every second of every day of the year.

How to Use This Book

Organization

Up front is the **Gold Guide,** comprising two sections on gold paper that are chock-full of information about traveling within your destination and traveling in general. Both are in alphabetical order by topic. **Important Contacts A to Z** gives addresses and telephone numbers of organizations and companies that offer destination-related services and detailed information or publications. Here's where you'll find information about how to get to Las Vegas from wherever you are. **Smart Travel Tips A to Z,** the Gold Guide's second section, gives specific tips on how to get the most out of your travels, as well as information on how to accomplish what you need to in Las Vegas, Reno, and Tahoe.

Stars

Stars in the margin are used to denote highly recommended sights, attractions, hotels, and restaurants.

Credit Cards

The following abbreviations are used: **AE,** American Express; **D,** Discover; **DC,** Diners Club; **MC,** MasterCard; and **V,** Visa.

Please Write to Us

Everyone who has contributed to *Las Vegas, Reno, Tahoe '96* has worked hard to make the text accurate. All prices and opening times are based on information supplied to us at press time, and Fodor's cannot accept responsibility for any errors that may have occurred. The passage of time will bring changes, so it's always a good idea to call ahead and confirm information when it matters—particularly if you're making a detour to visit specific sights or attractions. When making reservations at a hotel or inn, be sure to mention if you have a disability or are traveling with children, if you prefer a private bath or a certain type of bed, or if you have specific dietary needs or any other concerns.

Were the restaurants we recommended as described? Did our hotel picks exceed your expectations? Did you find a museum we recommended a waste of time? We would love your feedback, positive and negative. If you have complaints, we'll look into them and revise our entries when the facts warrant it. If you've happened upon a special place that we haven't included, we'll pass the information along to the writers so they can check it out. So please send us a letter or postcard (we're at 201 East 50th Street, New York, NY 10022). We'll look forward to hearing from you. And in the meantime, have a wonderful trip!

Karen Cure
Editorial Director

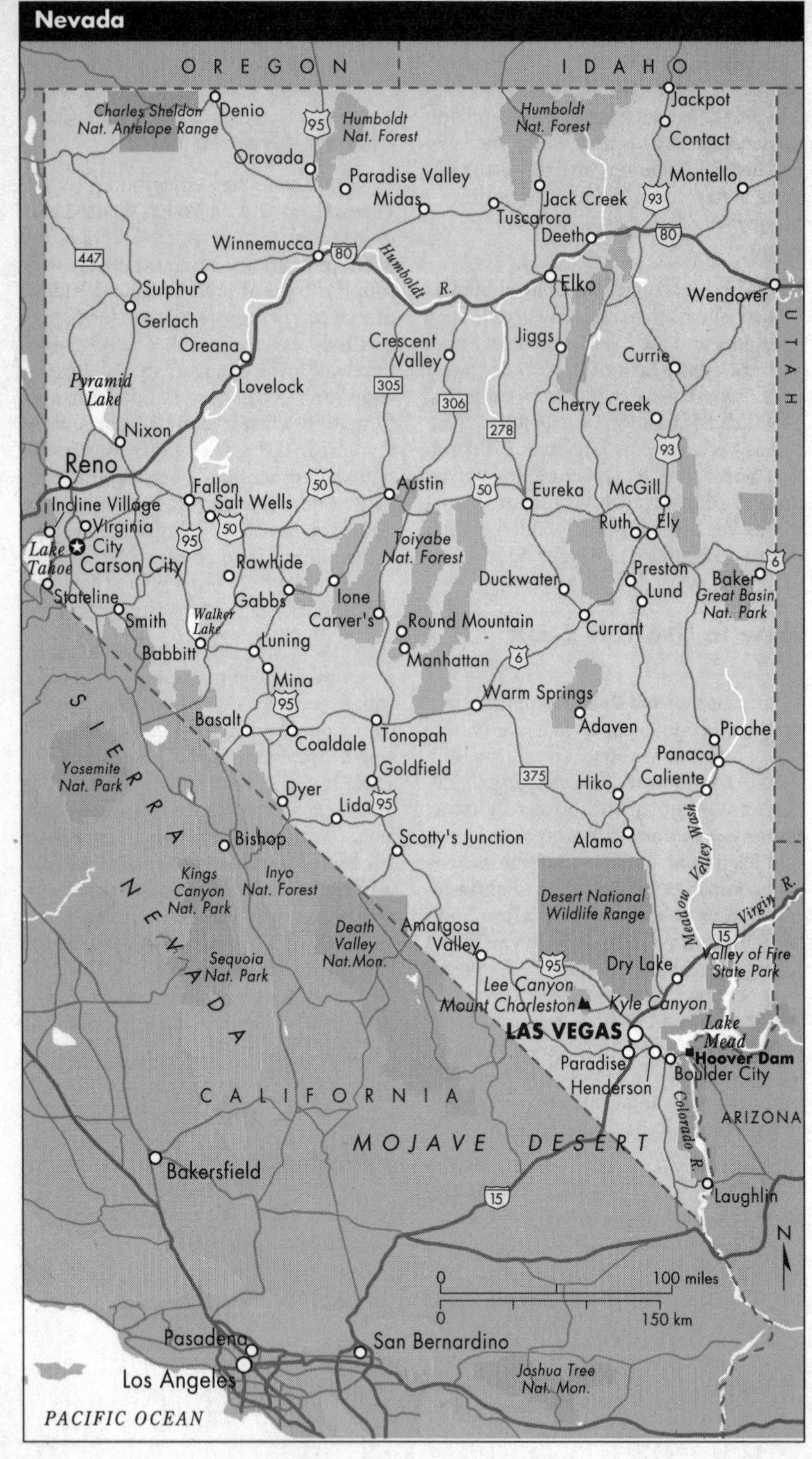
Nevada
OREGON
IDAHO
UTAH
ARIZONA
CALIFORNIA
SIERRA NEVADA
MOJAVE DESERT
PACIFIC OCEAN
Charles Sheldon Nat. Antelope Range
Denio
Humboldt Nat. Forest
Jackpot
Contact
Montello
Orovada
Paradise Valley
Midas
Tuscarora
Jack Creek
Deeth
Winnemucca
Humboldt R.
Elko
Wendover
Sulphur
Gerlach
Oreana
Lovelock
Crescent Valley
Jiggs
Currie
Pyramid Lake
Nixon
Cherry Creek
Reno
Fallon
Salt Wells
Austin
Eureka
McGill
Ely
Ruth
Incline Village
Virginia City
Lake Tahoe
Carson City
Stateline
Smith
Rawhide
Gabbs
Ione
Toiyabe Nat. Forest
Duckwater
Preston
Lund
Baker
Great Basin Nat. Park
Walker Lake
Babbitt
Luning
Mina
Carver's
Round Mountain
Manhattan
Currant
Warm Springs
Adaven
Basalt
Coaldale
Tonopah
Goldfield
Pioche
Panaca
Caliente
Hiko
Yosemite Nat. Park
Dyer
Lida
Scotty's Junction
Alamo
Bishop
Kings Canyon Nat. Park
Inyo Nat. Forest
Meadow Valley Wash
Virgin R.
Desert National Wildlife Range
Death Valley Nat. Mon.
Amargosa Valley
Valley of Fire State Park
Sequoia Nat. Park
Dry Lake
Lee Canyon
Mount Charleston
Kyle Canyon
LAS VEGAS
Lake Mead
Hoover Dam
Paradise
Henderson
Boulder City
Colorado R.
Laughlin
Bakersfield
Pasadena
Los Angeles
San Bernardino
Joshua Tree Nat. Mon.
0 100 miles
0 150 km
N
95
80
93
447
305
306
278
50
6
375
15

Las Vegas

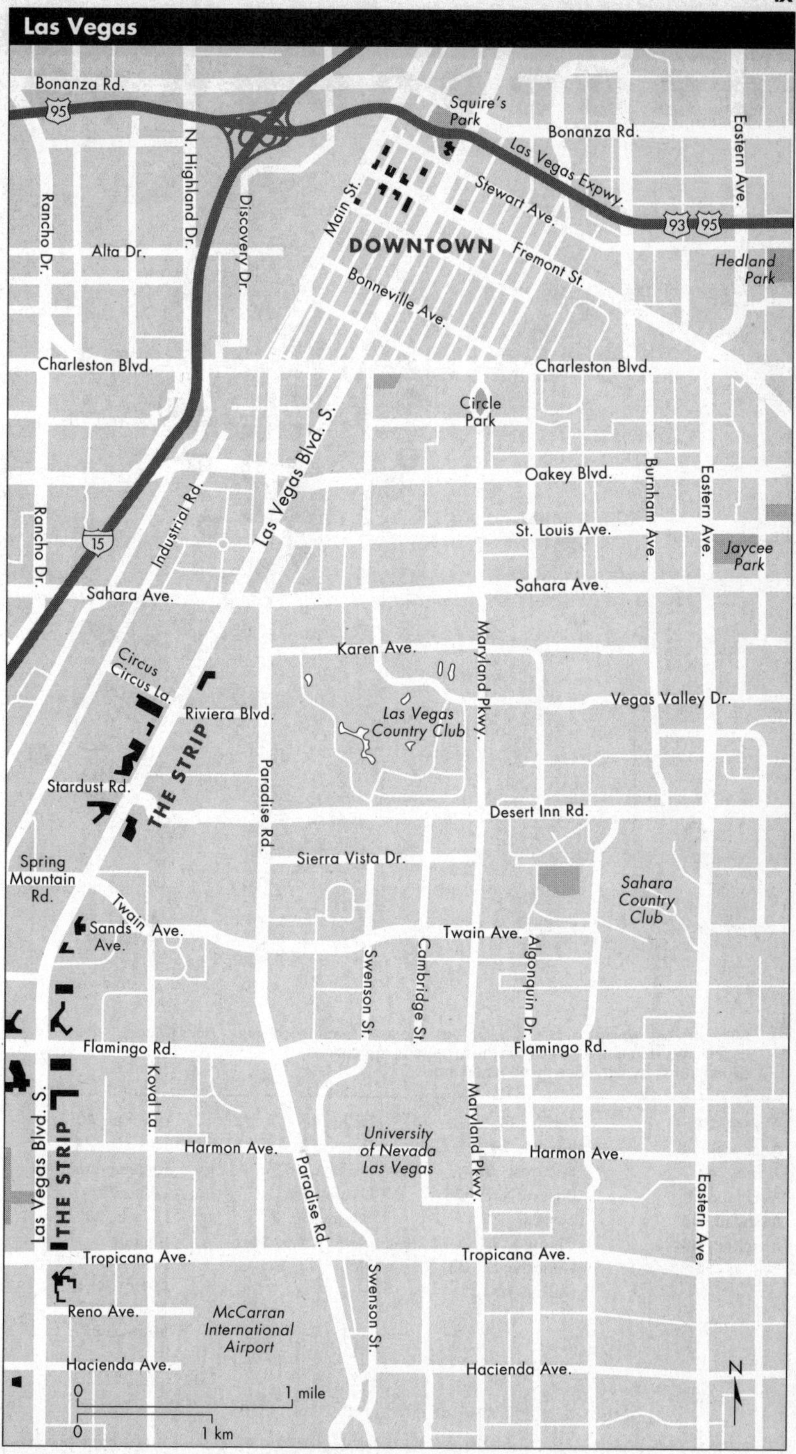

Bonanza Rd.
95
Squire's Park
Bonanza Rd.
Eastern Ave.
Las Vegas Expwy.
Stewart Ave.
93
95
Rancho Dr.
N. Highland Dr.
Discovery Dr.
Main St.
DOWNTOWN
Fremont St.
Hedland Park
Alta Dr.
Bonneville Ave.
Charleston Blvd.
Charleston Blvd.
Circle Park
Oakey Blvd.
Burnham Ave.
Eastern Ave.
Industrial Rd.
Las Vegas Blvd. S.
St. Louis Ave.
Jaycee Park
Rancho Dr.
15
Sahara Ave.
Sahara Ave.
Karen Ave.
Maryland Pkwy.
Circus Circus La.
Vegas Valley Dr.
Riviera Blvd.
Las Vegas Country Club
THE STRIP
Paradise Rd.
Stardust Rd.
Desert Inn Rd.
Spring Mountain Rd.
Sierra Vista Dr.
Sahara Country Club
Twain Ave.
Sands Ave.
Twain Ave.
Swenson St.
Cambridge St.
Algonquin Dr.
Flamingo Rd.
Flamingo Rd.
Koval La.
Maryland Pkwy.
University of Nevada Las Vegas
Harmon Ave.
Harmon Ave.
Paradise Rd.
Eastern Ave.
Las Vegas Blvd. S.
THE STRIP
Tropicana Ave.
Tropicana Ave.
Reno Ave.
McCarran International Airport
Swenson St.
Hacienda Ave.
Hacienda Ave.
0
1 mile
0
1 km
N

World Time Zones

Numbers below vertical bands relate each zone to Greenwich Mean Time (0 hrs.). Local times frequently differ from these general indications, as indicated by light-face numbers on map.

Algiers, **29**
Anchorage, **3**
Athens, **41**
Auckland, **1**
Baghdad, **46**
Bangkok, **50**
Beijing, **54**
Berlin, **34**
Bogotá, **19**
Budapest, **37**
Buenos Aires, **24**
Caracas, **22**
Chicago, **9**
Copenhagen, **33**
Dallas, **10**
Delhi, **48**
Denver, **8**
Djakarta, **53**
Dublin, **26**
Edmonton, **7**
Hong Kong, **56**
Honolulu, **2**
Istanbul, **40**
Jerusalem, **42**
Johannesburg, **44**
Lima, **20**
Lisbon, **28**
London (Greenwich), **27**
Los Angeles, **6**
Madrid, **38**
Manila, **57**

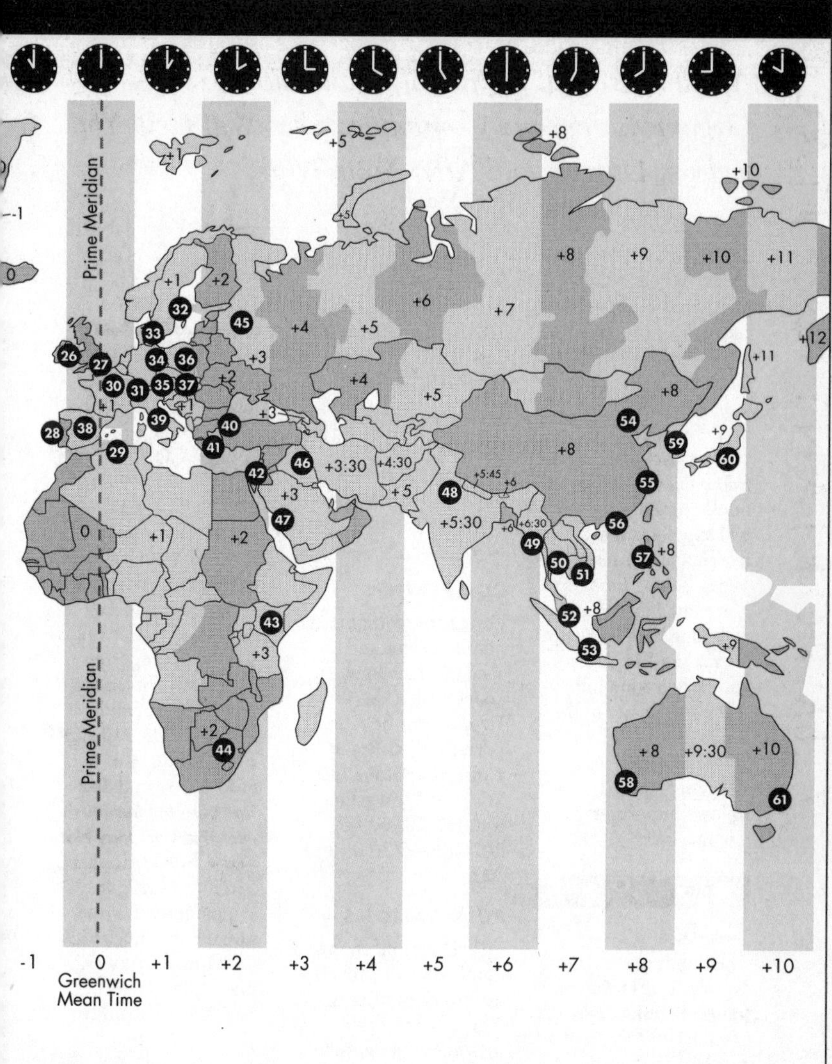

Mecca, **47**
Mexico City, **12**
Miami, **18**
Montréal, **15**
Moscow, **45**
Nairobi, **43**
New Orleans, **11**
New York City, **16**
Ottawa, **14**
Paris, **30**
Perth, **58**
Reykjavík, **25**
Rio de Janeiro, **23**
Rome, **39**
Saigon (Ho Chi Minh City), **51**
San Francisco, **5**
Santiago, **21**
Seoul, **59**
Shanghai, **55**
Singapore, **52**
Stockholm, **32**
Sydney, **61**
Tokyo, **60**
Toronto, **13**
Vancouver, **4**
Vienna, **35**
Warsaw, **36**
Washington, D.C., **17**
Yangon, **49**
Zürich, **31**

IMPORTANT CONTACTS A TO Z

An Alphabetical Listing of Publications, Organizations, and Companies That Will Help You Before, During, and After Your Trip

No single travel resource can give you every detail about every topic that might interest or concern you at the various stages of your journey—when you're planning your trip, while you're on the road, and after you get back home. The following organizations, books, and brochures will supplement the information in *Las Vegas, Reno, Tahoe '96.* For related information, including both basic tips on visiting Las Vegas and background information on many of the topics below, study Smart Travel Tips A to Z, the section that follows Important Contacts A to Z.

A

AIR TRAVEL

The major gateway to Las Vegas is **McCarran International Airport** (☎ 702/261–5743), 5 miles south of the business district and immediately east of the southern end of the Strip. Flying time is 4½ hours from New York, 3¼ hours from Chicago, and one hour from Los Angeles.

CARRIERS

Carriers serving Las Vegas include **American Airlines** (☎ 800/433–7300), **America West** (☎ 800/235–9292), **Continental** (☎ 702/383–8291 or 800/231–0856), **Delta** (☎ 800/221–1212), **Northwest** (☎ 800/225–2525), **Southwest** (☎ 800/435–9792), **TWA** (☎ 702/385–1000 or 800/221–2000), **United** (☎ 800/241–6522), and **USAir** (☎ 800/428–4322).

For inexpensive, no-frills flights, contact **Midwest Express** (☎ 800/452–2022) and **Reno Air** (☎ 800/736–6247).

COMPLAINTS

To register complaints about charter and scheduled airlines, contact the U.S. Department of Transportation's **Office of Consumer Affairs** (400 7th St. NW, Washington, DC 20590, ☎ 202/366–2220 or 800/322–7873).

PUBLICATIONS

For general information about charter carriers, ask for the Office of Consumer Affairs' brochure **"Plane Talk: Public Charter Flights."** The Department of Transportation also publishes a 58-page booklet, **"Fly Rights"** ($1.75; Consumer Information Center, Dept. 133B, Pueblo, CO 81009).

For other tips and hints, consult the Consumers Union's monthly **"Consumer Reports Travel Letter"** ($39 a year; Box 53629, Boulder, CO 80322, ☎ 800/234–1970) and the newsletter **"Travel Smart"** ($37 a year; 40 Beechdale Rd., Dobbs Ferry, NY 10522, ☎ 800/327–3633); ***The Official Frequent Flyer Guidebook,*** by Randy Petersen ($14.99 plus $3 shipping; 4715-C Town Center Dr., Colorado Springs, CO 80916, ☎ 719/597–8899 or 800/487–8893); ***Airfare Secrets Exposed,*** by Sharon Tyler and Matthew Wonder (Universal Information Publishing; $16.95 plus $3.75 shipping from Sandcastle Publishing, Box 3070-A, South Pasadena, CA 91031, ☎ 213/255–3616 or 800/655–0053); and ***202 Tips Even the Best Business Travelers May Not Know,*** by Christopher McGinnis ($10 plus $3 shipping; Irwin Professional Publishing, 1333 Burr Ridge Parkway, Burr Ridge, IL 60521, ☎ 800/634–3966).

AIRPORT TRANSFERS

BY TAXI

Metered taxicab service awaits your arrival at the airport. The fare is $2.20 on the meter when you get in, plus $1.50 for every mile. The trip to most hotels on the Strip should cost less than $9–$12; the trip downtown should be about $15–$18.

BY LIMOUSINE

A limo from the airport to your hotel, shared

with other riders, costs $3–$4 per person to the Strip, $4–$5 to downtown. The limos wait for passengers outside the terminal, along with the cabs. Private limousine service is available from **Bell Trans** (☎ 702/739–7990), **Presidential** (☎ 702/731–5577), and **Rancho** (☎ 702/645–7634).

B

BETTER BUSINESS BUREAU

Contact the **Better Business Bureau of Las Vegas** (1022 E. Sahara Ave., Las Vegas, NV 89104, ☎ 702/735–6900).

BUS TRAVEL

Greyhound/Trailways Lines (200 S. Main St., ☎ 800/231–2222), one block south of the Plaza Hotel, has nationwide service.

WITHIN LAS VEGAS

Local bus lines are operated by **Citizen Area Transit** (☎ 702/228–7433) and the **Las Vegas Strip Trolley** (☎ 702/382–1404).

C

CAR RENTAL

Major car-rental companies represented in Las Vegas include **Alamo** (☎ 800/327–9633, 0800/272–2000 in the U.K.), **Avis** (☎ 800/331–1212, 800/879–2847 in Canada), **Budget** (☎ 800/527–0700, 0800/181–181 in the U.K.), **Dollar** (known as Eurodollar outside North America, ☎ 800/800–4000, 0181/952–6565 in the U.K.), **Hertz** (☎ 800/654–3131, 800/263–0600 in Canada, 0181/679–1799 in the U.K.), and **National** (☎ 800/227–7368, 0181/950–5050 in the U.K., where it is known as Europcar). Rates in Las Vegas begin at $23 a day and $106 a week for an economy car with unlimited mileage. This does not include 6% state tax; if you rent your car at the airport, an additional 8% tax applies.

CHILDREN AND TRAVEL

FLYING

Look into **"Flying With Baby"** ($5.95 plus $1 shipping; Third Street Press, Box 261250, Littleton, CO 80126, ☎ 303/595–5959), cowritten by a flight attendant. **"Kids and Teens in Flight,"** free from the U.S. Department of Transportation's Office of Consumer Affairs, offers tips for children flying alone. Every two years the February issue of ***Family Travel Times*** (*see* Know-How, *below*) details children's services on three dozen airlines.

GAMES

The gamemeister, Milton Bradley, has games to help keep little (and not so little) children from getting fidgety while riding in planes, trains, and automobiles. Try packing the *Travel Battleship* sea battle game ($7), *Travel Connect Four,* a vertical strategy game ($8), the *Travel Yahtzee* dice game ($6), the *Travel Trouble* dice and board game ($7), and the *Travel Guess Who* mystery game ($8).

KNOW-HOW

Family Travel Times, published four times a year by Travel With Your Children (annual subscription $40; TWYCH, 45 W. 18th St., New York, NY 10011, ☎ 212/206–0688), covers destinations, types of vacations, and modes of travel.

The ***Family Travel Guides*** catalogue ($1 postage; Box 6061, Albany, CA 94706, ☎ 510/527–5849) lists about 200 books and articles on family travel. From Globe Pequot Press (Box 833, 6 Business Park Rd., Old Saybrook, CT 06475, ☎ 203/395–0440 or 800/243–0495) are ***The 100 Best Family Resorts in North America,*** by Jane Wilford with Janet Tice ($12.95), and the two-volume (eastern and western editions) set of ***50 Great Family Vacations in North America*** ($18.95 each plus $3 shipping).

LODGING

The **Nevada Commission on Tourism**'s accommodation guide lists Las Vegas hotels that have a children's game room (Capitol Complex, Carson City, NV 89710, ☎ 800/638–2328). An especially comprehensive child-care program can be found at **MGM Grand's King Looey's Youth Center** (3700 Las Vegas Blvd. S, ☎ 702/891–1111).

TOUR OPERATORS

Contact **Grandtravel** (6900 Wisconsin Ave., Suite 706, Chevy Chase, MD 20815, ☎ 301/986–0790 or 800/247–

7651), which has tours for people traveling with grandchildren ages seven to 17.

CUSTOMS

CANADIANS

Contact **Revenue Canada** (2265 St. Laurent Blvd. S, Ottawa, Ontario K1G 4K3, ☎ 613/993–0534) for a copy of the free brochure **"I Declare/Je Déclare"** and for details on duties that exceed the standard duty-free limit.

U.K. CITIZENS

HM Customs and Excise (Dorset House, Stamford St., London SE1 9NG, ☎ 0171/202–4227) can answer questions about U.K. customs regulations and publishes **"A Guide for Travellers,"** detailing standard procedures and import rules.

D

FOR TRAVELERS WITH DISABILITIES

COMPLAINTS

To register complaints under the provisions of the Americans with Disabilities Act, contact the U.S. Department of Justice's **Public Access Section** (Box 66738, Washington, DC 20035, ☎ 202/514–0301, FAX 202/307–1198, TTY 202/514–0383).

LODGING

Generally, the layouts of most hotels and casinos require that you walk long distances to get around in them. The following hotels provide wheelchair-accessible accommodations: **Bally's Casino Resort** (3645 Las Vegas Blvd. S, ☎ 702/739–4111), **Barbary Coast Hotel and Casino** (3595 Las Vegas Blvd. S, ☎ 702/737–7111), **Caesars Palace** (3570 Las Vegas Blvd. S, ☎ 702/731–7110), **Excalibur** (3850 Las Vegas Blvd. S, ☎ 702/597–7777), the **Flamingo Hilton and Tower** (3555 Las Vegas Blvd. S, ☎ 702/733–3111), **Four Queens Hotel and Casino** (202 E. Fremont St., ☎ 702/385–4011), **Golden Nugget Hotel and Casino** (129 E. Fremont St., ☎ 702/385–7111), **Hacienda Hotel and Casino** (3950 Las Vegas Blvd. S, ☎ 702/739–8911), **Lady Luck Casino and Hotel** (206 N. 3rd St., ☎ 702/477–3000), **Las Vegas Club Hotel and Casino** (18 E. Fremont St., ☎ 702/385–1664), **Las Vegas Hilton** (3000 W. Paradise Rd., ☎ 702/732–5111), **Plaza Hotel** (1 Main St., ☎ 702/386–2110), and **Sam's Town Hotel and Casino** (5111 W. Boulder Hwy., ☎ 702/456–7777). The **Imperial Palace** (3535 Las Vegas Blvd. S, ☎ 702/731–3311) has the most facilities for accommodating people with disabilities, including a hydraulic lift at the pool, an Amigo chair in the pit, and more than 100 accessible rooms, many of which feature roll-in showers and transfer chairs.

ORGANIZATIONS

Several local organizations provide information to visitors with disabilities. **HELP of Southern Nevada** (☎ 702/369–4357) refers callers to the proper social agency. **Nevada Association for the Handicapped** (6200 W. Oakey Blvd., Las Vegas 89102, ☎ 702/870–7050) refers callers to agencies serving people with disabilities. **Southern Nevada Sightless** (1001 N. Bruce St., Las Vegas 89101, ☎ 702/642–0100) provides general information and transportation assistance.

FOR TRAVELERS WITH HEARING IMPAIRMENTS➢ Contact the **American Academy of Otolaryngology** (1 Prince St., Alexandria, VA 22314, ☎ 703/836–4444, FAX 703/683–5100, TTY 703/519–1585).

FOR TRAVELERS WITH MOBILITY PROBLEMS➢ Contact the **Information Center for Individuals with Disabilities** (Fort Point Pl., 27–43 Wormwood St., Boston, MA 02210, ☎ 617/727–5540, 800/462–5015 in MA, TTY 617/345–9743); **Mobility International USA** (Box 10767, Eugene, OR 97440, ☎ and TTY 503/343–1284, FAX 503/343–6812), the U.S. branch of an international organization based in Belgium (*see below*) that has affiliates in 30 countries; **MossRehab Hospital Travel Information Service** (1200 W. Tabor Rd., Philadelphia, PA 19141, ☎ 215/456–9603, TTY 215/456–9602); the **Society for the Advancement of Travel for the Handicapped** (347 5th Ave., Suite 610, New York, NY 10016, ☎ 212/447–7284, FAX 212/725–8253); the **Travel Industry and Disabled Exchange** (TIDE, 5435 Donna

Ave., Tarzana, CA 91356, ☎ 818/344-3640, FAX 818/344-0078); and **Travelin' Talk** (Box 3534, Clarksville, TN 37043, ☎ 615/552-6670, FAX 615/552-1182).

FOR TRAVELERS WITH VISION IMPAIRMENTS➤ Contact the **American Council of the Blind** (1155 15th St. NW, Suite 720, Washington, DC 20005, ☎ 202/467-5081, FAX 202/467-5085) or the **American Foundation for the Blind** (15 W. 16th St., New York, NY 10011, ☎ 212/620-2000, TTY 212/620-2158).

IN THE U.K.

Contact the **Royal Association for Disability and Rehabilitation** (RADAR, 12 City Forum, 250 City Rd., London EC1V 8AF, ☎ 0171/250-3222) or **Mobility International** (Rue de Manchester 25, B1070 Brussels, Belgium, ☎ 00-322-410-6297), an international clearinghouse of travel information for people with disabilities.

PUBLICATIONS

Several publications for travelers with disabilities are available from the Consumer Information Center (Box 100, Pueblo, CO 81009, ☎ 719/948-3334). Call or write for a free catalogue of current titles.

Fodor's ***Great American Vacations for Travelers with Disabilities*** ($18; available in bookstores, or call 800/533-6478) details accessible attractions, restaurants, and hotels in U.S. destinations. The 500-page ***Travelin' Talk Directory*** ($35; Box 3534, Clarksville, TN 37043, ☎ 615/552-6670) lists people and organizations who help travelers with disabilities. For specialist travel agents worldwide, consult the ***Directory of Travel Agencies for the Disabled*** ($19.95 plus $2 shipping; Twin Peaks Press, Box 129, Vancouver, WA 98666, ☎ 206/694-2462 or 800/637-2256). The Sierra Club publishes ***Easy Access to National Parks*** ($16 plus $3 shipping; 730 Polk St., San Francisco, CA 94109, ☎ 415/776-2211 or 800/935-1056).

TRAVEL AGENCIES AND TOUR OPERATORS

The Americans with Disabilities Act requires that travel firms serve the needs of all travelers. However, some agencies and operators specialize in making group and individual arrangements for travelers with disabilities, among them **Access Adventures** (206 Chestnut Ridge Rd., Rochester, NY 14624, ☎ 716/889-9096), run by a former physical-rehab counselor. In addition, many general-interest operators and agencies (*see* Tour Operators, *below*) can also arrange vacations for travelers with disabilities.

FOR TRAVELERS WITH MOBILITY IMPAIRMENTS➤ A number of operators specialize in working with travelers with mobility impairments, including **Hinsdale Travel Service** (201 E. Ogden Ave., Suite 100, Hinsdale, IL 60521, ☎ 708/325-1335 or 800/303-5521), a travel agency that will give you access to the services of wheelchair traveler Janice Perkins, and **Wheelchair Journeys** (16979 Redmond Way, Redmond, WA 98052, ☎ 206/885-2210), which can handle arrangements worldwide.

FOR TRAVELERS WITH DEVELOPMENTAL DISABILITIES➤ Contact the nonprofit **New Directions** (5276 Hollister Ave., Suite 207, Santa Barbara, CA 93111, ☎ 805/967-2841), as well as the general-interest operators above.

DISCOUNT CLUBS

Options include **Entertainment Travel Editions** (fee $28-$53, depending on destination; Box 1068, Trumbull, CT 06611, ☎ 800/445-4137), **Great American Traveler** ($49.95 annually; Box 27965, Salt Lake City, UT 84127, ☎ 800/548-2812), **Moment's Notice Discount Travel Club** ($25 annually, single or family; 163 Amsterdam Ave., Suite 137, New York, NY 10023, ☎ 212/486-0500), **Privilege Card** ($74.95 annually; 3391 Peachtree Rd. NE, Suite 110, Atlanta, GA 30326, ☎ 404/262-0222 or 800/236-9732), **Travelers Advantage** ($49 annually, single or family; CUC Travel Service, 49 Music Sq. W, Nashville, TN 37203, ☎ 800/548-1116 or 800/648-4037), and **Worldwide Discount Travel Club** ($50 annually for family, $40 single; 1674 Meridian Ave., Miami Beach, FL 33139, ☎ 305/534–2082).

E

EMERGENCIES

Police, fire, ambulance (☎ 911).

DENTISTS

Clark County Dental Society (☎ 702/255–7873) offers referral service.

DOCTORS

Clark County Medical Society (☎ 702/739–9989) will make referrals.

HOSPITAL EMERGENCY ROOM

University Medical Center (1800 W. Charleston Blvd. at Shadow La., ☎ 702/383–2000) has a 24-hour emergency service with outpatient and trauma-care facilities. **Sunrise Hospital** (3186 S. Maryland Pkwy., near Desert Inn Rd., ☎ 702/731–8000) has an emergency room.

LATE-NIGHT PHARMACY

White Cross Drug (1700 Las Vegas Blvd. S, ☎ 702/382–1733) is near Vegas World Hotel on the Strip and is open 24 hours a day.

G

GAY AND LESBIAN TRAVEL

ORGANIZATIONS

The **International Gay Travel Association** (Box 4974, Key West, FL 33041, ☎ 800/448–8550), a consortium of 800 businesses, can supply names of travel agents and tour operators.

PUBLICATIONS

The premier international travel magazine for gays and lesbians is ***Our World*** ($35 for 10 issues; 1104 N. Nova Rd., Suite 251, Daytona Beach, FL 32117, ☎ 904/441–5367). The 16-page monthly **"Out & About"** ($49 for 10 issues; ☎ 212/645–6922 or 800/929–2268) covers gay-friendly resorts, hotels, cruise lines, and airlines.

TOUR OPERATORS

Cruises and resort vacations are handled by **Toto Tours** (1326 W. Albion, Suite 3W, Chicago, IL 60626, ☎ 312/274–8686 or 800/565–1241), which has group tours worldwide.

TRAVEL AGENCIES

The largest agencies serving gay travelers are **Advance Travel** (10700 Northwest Freeway, Suite 160, Houston, TX 77092, ☎ 713/682–2002 or 800/695–0880), **Islanders/Kennedy Travel** (183 W. 10th St., New York, NY 10014, ☎ 212/242–3222 or 800/988–1181), **Now Voyager** (4406 18th St., San Francisco, CA 94114, ☎ 415/626–1169 or 800/255–6951), and **Yellowbrick Road** (1500 W. Balmoral Ave., Chicago, IL 60640, ☎ 312/561–1800 or 800/642–2488). **Skylink Women's Travel** (746 Ashland Ave., Santa Monica, CA 90405, ☎ 310/452–0506 or 800/225-5759) works with lesbians.

I

INSURANCE

Travel insurance covering baggage, health, and trip cancellation or interruptions is available from **Access America** (Box 90315, Richmond, VA 23286, ☎ 804/285–3300 or 800/284–8300), **Carefree Travel Insurance** (Box 9366, 100 Garden City Plaza, Garden City, NY 11530, ☎ 516/294–0220 or 800/323–3149), **Near Travel Services** (Box 1339, Calumet City, IL 60409, ☎ 708/868–6700 or 800/654–6700), **Tele-Trip** (Mutual of Omaha Plaza, Box 31716, Omaha, NE 68131, ☎ 800/228–9792), **Travel Insured International** (Box 280568, East Hartford, CT 06128-0568, ☎ 203/528–7663 or 800/243–3174), **Travel Guard International** (1145 Clark St., Stevens Point, WI 54481, ☎ 715/345–0505 or 800/826–1300), and **Wallach & Company** (107 W. Federal St., Box 480, Middleburg, VA 22117, ☎ 703/687–3166 or 800/237–6615).

IN THE U.K.

The **Association of British Insurers** (51 Gresham St., London EC2V 7HQ, ☎ 0171/600–3333; 30 Gordon St., Glasgow G1 3PU, ☎ 0141/226–3905; Scottish Provident Bldg., Donegall Sq. W, Belfast BT1 6JE, ☎ 01232/249176; and other locations) gives advice by phone and publishes the free **"Holiday Insurance,"** which sets out typical policy provisions and costs.

L

LODGING

APARTMENT AND VILLA RENTALS

If you want a home base that's roomy enough for a family and comes with cooking facilities, a furnished rental may be the solution. It's generally costwise, too, although not always—some rentals are luxury properties (economical only when your party is large). Home-exchange directories do list rentals—often second homes owned by prospective house swappers—and some services search for a house or apartment for you and handle the paperwork. Some send an illustrated catalogue and others send photographs of specific properties, sometimes at a charge; up-front registration fees may apply. Among the companies is **Rent-a-Home International** (7200 34th Ave. NW, Seattle, WA 98117, ☎ 206/789-9377 or 800/488-7368).

HOME EXCHANGE

You can find a house, apartment, or other vacation property to exchange for your own by becoming a member of a home-exchange organization, which then sends you its annual directories listing available exchanges and includes your own listing in at least one of them. Arrangements for the actual exchange are made by the two parties to it, not by the organization. Principal clearinghouses include **Intervac International** ($65 annually; Box 590504, San Francisco, CA 94159, ☎ 415/435-3497), which has three annual directories.

M

MONEY MATTERS

ATMS

For specific **Cirrus** locations in the United States and Canada, call 800/424-7787. For U.S. **Plus** locations, call 800/843-7587 and enter the area code and first three digits of the number you're calling from (or of the calling area where you want an ATM).

WIRING FUNDS

Funds can be wired via **American Express MoneyGram**[SM] (☎ 800/926-9400 from the U.S. and Canada for locations and information) or **Western Union** (☎ 800/325-6000 for agent locations or to send using MasterCard or Visa, 800/321-2923 in Canada).

P

PASSPORTS AND VISAS

U.K. CITIZENS

For fees, documentation requirements, and to get an emergency passport, call the **London Passport Office** (☎ 0171/271-3000). For visa information, call the **U.S. Embassy Visa Information Line** (☎ 0891/200-290; calls cost 48p per minute or 36p per minute cheap rate) or write the **U.S. Embassy Visa Branch** (5 Upper Grosvenor St., London W1A 2JB). If you live in Northern Ireland, write the **U.S. Consulate General** (Queen's House, Queen St., Belfast BTI 6EQ).

PHOTO HELP

The **Kodak Information Center** (☎ 800/242-2424) answers consumer questions about film and photography.

R

RAIL TRAVEL

Amtrak (☎ 800/872-7245) offers nationwide service to Las Vegas's **Union Station** (1 N. Main St., ☎ 702/386-6896).

S

SENIOR CITIZENS

EDUCATIONAL TRAVEL

The nonprofit **Elderhostel** (75 Federal St., 3rd Floor, Boston, MA 02110, ☎ 617/426-7788), for people 60 and older, has offered inexpensive study programs since 1975. The nearly 2,000 courses cover everything from marine science to Greek myths and cowboy poetry. Fees for programs in the United States and Canada, which usually last one week, run about $300, not including transportation.

ORGANIZATIONS

Contact the **American Association of Retired Persons** (AARP, 601 E St. NW, Washington, DC 20049, ☎ 202/434-2277; $8 per person or couple annually). Its Purchase

Privilege Program gets members discounts on lodging, car rentals, and sightseeing, and the AARP Motoring Plan furnishes domestic trip-routing information and emergency road-service aid for an annual fee of $39.95 per person or couple ($59.95 for a premium version).

For other discounts on lodgings, car rentals, and other travel products, along with magazines and newsletters, contact the **National Council of Senior Citizens** (membership $12 annually; 1331 F St. NW, Washington, DC 20004, ☎ 202/347–8800) and ***Mature Outlook*** (subscription $9.95 annually; 6001 N. Clark St., Chicago, IL 60660, ☎ 312/465–6466 or 800/336–6330).

PUBLICATIONS

The 50+ Traveler's Guidebook: Where to Go, Where to Stay, What to Do, by Anita Williams and Merrimac Dillon ($12.95; St. Martin's Press, 175 5th Ave., New York, NY 10010, ☎ 212/674–5151 or 800/288–2131), offers many useful tips. **"The Mature Traveler"** ($29.95; Box 50400, Reno, NV 89513, ☎ 702/786–7419), a monthly newsletter, covers travel deals.

SIGHTSEEING

BOAT TOURS

Lake Mead Cruises (Lake Mead Marina, ☎ 702/293–6180) offers narrated tours of the lower portion of the lake and the Hoover Dam on a 250-passenger sternwheeler, the *Desert Princess*. Cruises last 1½ to three hours; some are sightseeing only, while others include breakfast, dinner, or dinner and live entertainment. Prices range from $14.50 to $43 for adults, $6 to $15 for children 3–12.

HELICOPTER TOURS

Sundance Helicopter (135 E. Reno Ave., ☎ 702/597–5505) has a 10-minute helicopter tour of the Las Vegas Strip for $45 per person, as well as a 2½-hour tour into the Grand Canyon (with a champagne landing) for $295 per person.

HOT-AIR BALLOONING

Reno's **Zephyr Hot Air Balloons** (☎ 702/329–1700) take you on 35-minute flights over the region.

ORIENTATION TOURS

Gray Line (1550 S. Industrial Rd., ☎ 702/384–1234 or 800/634–6579) offers a variety of bus, rafting, and flight-seeing tours of Las Vegas and its environs. Itineraries include the Strip, Hoover Dam, and the Grand Canyon. City tours last 5½ hours; tours beyond the area are all-day affairs. Gray Line will pick you up at your hotel and return you to it at the end of the tour. Tours run from $17.50 (city tour) to $95 (Grand Canyon, air only). Reservations can be made by telephone at any hour.

Ray and Ross Transport Inc. (300 W. Owens Ave., ☎ 702/646–4661) has six-hour city tours for $23.40. Hotel pickup and return are included.

Key Tours (3305 W. Spring Mountain, ☎ 702/362–9355) offers trips from Las Vegas to Laughlin, a gambling town that is about 90 miles from Las Vegas on the Colorado River at the Arizona state line, from $5 a person; a four-hour Hoover Dam tour for $14.50; and a six-hour Hoover Dam plus the city and desert tour for $25.

RAFTING TOURS

Black Canyon Raft Tours (1297 Nevada Hwy., Boulder City, NV 89005, ☎ 702/293–3776, 602/767–3311, or 800/696–7238) offers float trips along an 11-mile stretch of the Colorado River from the Hoover Dam to Willow Beach.

STUDENTS

HOSTELING

Contact **Hostelling International–American Youth Hostels** (733 15th St. NW, Suite 840, Washington, DC 20005, ☎ 202/783–6161) in the United States, **Hostelling International–Canada** (205 Catherine St., Suite 400, Ottawa, Ontario K2P 1C3, ☎ 613/237–7884) in Canada, and the **Youth Hostel Association of England and Wales** (Trevelyan House, 8 St. Stephen's Hill, St. Albans, Hertfordshire AL1 2DY, ☎ 01727/855215 or 01727/845047) in the United Kingdom. Membership ($25 in the U.S., C$26.75 in Canada, and £9 in the U.K.) gets you access to 5,000 hostels worldwide that charge $7–$20 nightly per person.

I.D. CARDS

To get discounts on transportation and admissions, get the **International Student Identity Card** (ISIC) if you're a bona fide student or the **Go 25 Card** if you're under 26. In the United States, the ISIC and Go 25 cards cost $18 each and include basic travel accident and illness coverage, plus a toll-free travel hot line. Apply through the Council on International Educational Exchange (*see* Organizations, *below*). Cards are available for $15 each in Canada from **Travel Cuts** (187 College St., Toronto, Ontario M5T 1P7, ☎ 416/979–2406 or 800/667–2887) and in the United Kingdom for £5 each at student unions and student travel companies.

ORGANIZATIONS

A major contact is the **Council on International Educational Exchange** (CIEE, 205 E. 42nd St., 16th Floor, New York, NY 10017, ☎ 212/661–1450) with locations in Boston (729 Boylston St., 02116, ☎ 617/266–1926), Miami (9100 S. Dadeland Blvd., 33156, ☎ 305/670–9261), Los Angeles (10904 Lindbrook Dr., 90024, ☎ 310/208–3551), 43 other college towns nationwide, and the United Kingdom (28A Poland St., London W1V 3DB, ☎ 0171/437–7767). Twice a year, it publishes *Student Travels* magazine. The CIEE's Council Travel Service offers domestic air passes for bargain travel within the United States and is the exclusive U.S. agent for several student-discount cards.

Campus Connections (325 Chestnut St., Suite 1101, Philadelphia, PA 19106, ☎ 215/625–8585 or 800/428–3235) specializes in discounted accommodations and airfares for students. The **Educational Travel Centre** (438 N. Frances St., Madison, WI 53703, ☎ 608/256–5551) offers rail passes and low-cost airline tickets, mostly for flights departing from Chicago.

In Canada, also contact **Travel Cuts** (*see above*).

T

TAXI TRAVEL

Desert Cab (☎ 702/376–2687), **Whittlesea Blue Cab** (☎ 702/384–6111), and **Yellow and Checker Cab** (☎ 702/873–2000) are the principal taxi operators in Las Vegas.

TOUR OPERATORS

Among the companies selling tours and packages to Las Vegas, the following have a proven reputation, are nationally known, and offer plenty of options.

GROUP TOURS

For a deluxe escorted tour to Las Vegas, contact **Maupintour** (Box 807, Lawrence, KS 66044, ☎ 800/255–4266 or 913/843–1211) and **Tauck Tours** (11 Wilton Rd., Westport, CT 06880, ☎ 800/468–2825 or 203/226–6911). Another operator falling between deluxe and first class is **Globus** (1 S. Federal Circle, Littleton, CO 80123-2980, ☎ 800/221–0090 or 303/797–2800). In the first-class and tourist range, try **Mayflower Tours** (1225 Warren Ave., Downers Grove, IL 60515, ☎ 708/960–3430 or 800/323–7064), **Brendan Tours** (15137 Califa St., Van Nuys, CA 91411, ☎ 818/785–9696 or 800/421–8446), and **Collette Tours** (162 Middle St., Pawtucket, RI 02860, ☎ 800/832–4656 or 401/728–3805). For budget and tourist class programs, try **Cosmos** (*see* Globus, *above*).

PACKAGES

Independent vacation packages are available from major airlines and tour operators. Contact **American Airlines Fly AAway Vacations** (☎ 800/321–2121), **America West Vacations** (☎ 800/356–6611), **Continental Airlines' Grand Destinations** (☎ 800/634–5555), **Delta Dream Vacations** (☎ 800/872–7786), **SuperCities** (☎ 800/333–1234), and **United Airlines Vacation Planning Center** (☎ 800/328–6877). **Gogo Tours** sells packages to Las Vegas only through travel agents.

FROM THE U.K.

Tour operators offering package tours to Las Vegas, often in conjunction with visits to the surrounding region, or other U.S. cities, include: **Americana Vaca-**

tions Ltd. (Morley House, 320 Regent St., London W1R 5AD, ☎ 0171/637–7853), **Jetsave** (Sussex House, London Rd., East Grinstead, Sussex RH19 1LD, ☎ 01342/ 312033), **Key to America** (1–3 Station Rd., Ashford, Middlesex TW15 2UW, ☎ 01784 /248777), **Kuoni Travel** (Kuoni House, Dorking, Surrey RH5 4AZ, ☎ 01306/742222), and **Premier Holidays** (Premier Travel Centre, Westbrook, Milton Rd., Cambridge CB4 1YG, ☎ 01223/516–688).

Travel agencies that offer cheap fares to Las Vegas include **Trailfinders** (42–50 Earl's Court Rd., London W8 6FT, ☎ 0171/937–5400), **Travel Cuts** (295a Regent St., London W1R 7YA, ☎ 0171/637–3161; *see* Students, *above*), and **Flightfile** (49 Tottenham Court Rd., London W1P 9RE, ☎ 0171/700–2722).

ORGANIZATIONS

The **National Tour Association** (546 E. Main St., Lexington, KY 40508, ☎ 606/ 226–4444 or 800/755–8687) and **United States Tour Operators Association** (USTOA, 211 E. 51st St., Suite 12B, New York, NY 10022, ☎ 212/750–7371) can provide lists of member operators and information on booking tours.

PUBLICATIONS

Consult the brochure **"On Tour"** and ask for a current list of member operators from the National Tour Association (*see* Organizations, *above*). Also get a copy of the **"Worldwide Tour & Vacation Package Finder"** from the USTOA (*see* Organizations, *above*) and the Better Business Bureau's **"Tips on Travel Packages"** (publication No. 24-195, $2; 4200 Wilson Blvd., Arlington, VA 22203).

TRAVEL AGENCIES

For names of reputable agencies in your area, contact the **American Society of Travel Agents** (1101 King St., Suite 200, Alexandria, VA 22314, ☎ 703/739–2782).

V

VISITOR INFORMATION

Contact the **Las Vegas Convention and Visitors Authority** (3150 Paradise Rd., Las Vegas, NV 89109, ☎ 702/ 892–0711, FAX 702/ 226–9011) or the **Las Vegas Chamber of Commerce** (711 E. Desert Inn Rd., Las Vegas, NV 89109, ☎ 702/735–1616, FAX 702/735–2011). For maps and brochures on Las Vegas and the rest of Nevada, contact the **Nevada Commission on Tourism** (Capitol Complex, Carson City, NV 89710, ☎ 702/687–4322 or 800/237–0774, FAX 702/687–6779).

The Las Vegas Convention and Visitors Authority is next door to the Las Vegas Hilton and can provide brochures and general information. Hotels and gift shops on the Strip have maps, brochures, pamphlets, and free events magazines—***What's On in Las Vegas, Las Vegas Today,*** and ***Tourguide***—that list shows and buffets and offer discounts to area attractions.

In the United Kingdom, also contact the **United States Travel and Tourism Administration** (Box 1EN, London W1A 1EN, ☎ 0171/ 495–4466). For a free USA pack, write the USTTA at Box 170, Ashford, Kent TN24 0ZX. Enclose stamps worth £1.50.

The **"Las Vegas Advisor"** ($5 for a sample issue; 5280 S. Valley View, Suite B-3F, Las Vegas, NV 89118, ☎ 702/597–1884), a 12-page monthly newsletter, keeps up-to-the-minute track of the constantly changing Las Vegas landscapes of gambling, accommodations, dining, entertainment, Top Ten Values, complimentaries, and more. It is indispensable for any Las Vegas visitor.

W

WEATHER

For current conditions and forecasts, plus the local time and helpful travel tips, call the **Weather Channel Connection** (☎ 900/932–8437; 95¢ per minute) from a touch-tone phone.

SMART TRAVEL TIPS A TO Z

Basic Information on Traveling in Las Vegas and Savvy Tips to Make Your Trip a Breeze

The more you travel, the more you know about how to make trips run like clockwork. To help make your travels hassle-free, Fodor's editors have rounded up dozens of tips from our contributors and travel experts all over the world, as well as basic information on visiting Las Vegas. For names of organizations to contact and publications that can give you more information, *see* Important Contacts A to Z, *above.*

A

AIR TRAVEL

If time is an issue, **always look for nonstop flights,** which require no change of plane. If possible, **avoid connecting flights,** which stop at least once and can involve a change of plane, although the flight number remains the same; if the first leg is late, the second waits.

CUTTING COSTS

The Sunday travel section of most newspapers is a good source of deals.

MAJOR AIRLINES➤ The least-expensive airfares from the major airlines are priced for round-trip travel and are subject to restrictions. You must usually **book in advance and buy the ticket within 24 hours** to get cheaper fares, and you may have to **stay over a Saturday night.** The lowest fare is subject to availability, and only a small percentage of the plane's total seats are sold at that price. It's good to **call a number of airlines, and when you are quoted a good price, book it on the spot**—the same fare on the same flight may not be available the next day. Airlines generally allow you to change your return date for a $25 to $50 fee, but most low-fare tickets are nonrefundable. However, if you don't use it, you can apply the cost toward the purchase price of a new ticket, again for a small charge.

CONSOLIDATORS➤ Consolidators, who buy tickets at reduced rates from scheduled airlines, sell them at prices below the lowest available from the airlines directly—usually without advance restrictions. Sometimes you can even get your money back if you need to return the ticket. Carefully read the fine print detailing penalties for changes and cancellations. If you doubt the reliability of a consolidator, **confirm your reservation with the airline.**

ALOFT

AIRLINE FOOD➤ If you hate airline food, **ask for special meals when booking.** These can be vegetarian, low cholesterol, or kosher, for example; commonly prepared to order in smaller quantities than standard catered fare, they can be tastier.

SMOKING➤ Smoking is banned on all flights within the United States of less than six hours' duration and on all Canadian flights; the ban also applies to domestic segments of international flights aboard U.S. and foreign carriers. Delta has banned smoking system-wide.

B

BOOKS

It's always a good idea to read about a place before you go there, but not just in the usual travel publications. Fiction can be the most incisive source of information about a destination. Here are a few books that offer some enlightenment of the Vegas way of life.

Hunter S. Thompson's *Fear and Loathing in Las Vegas* is probably the most notorious book ever written about the city. In it, Thompson, the creator of "gonzo journalism," chronicles his trip from Los Angeles to Las Vegas—in a drug-filled red Cadillac convertible, with a 300-pound Samoan attorney—to cover the now-defunct Mint 400 desert motorcycle race.

Mario Puzo's novel *The Godfather* describes the

building of Las Vegas in the 1940s by the mob and the Corleone family's rub-out of Moe Green, the character modeled on Bugsy Siegel.

Ovid Demaris and Ed Reid's *The Green Felt Jungle* shocked the nation in the early 1960s with its account of how the mob built Las Vegas and had a hand in virtually every hotel and casino built during the 1940s and 1950s.

Max Rubin's *Comp City—A Guide to Free Las Vegas Vacations* is the most important gambling book published in the past 30-odd years. Akin to Edward Thorp's *Beat the Dealer,* the first serious book on blackjack, *Comp City* is the first book on comps, up till now the most mystery-shrouded system in the casino. Rubin, a former pit boss, tells all.

BUS TRAVEL

The municipally operated Citizen Area Transit runs local buses up and down the Strip, between the Hacienda Hotel and the Downtown Transportation Center, stopping on the street in front of all the major hotels every 15 minutes (in a perfect world) 24 hours a day. An express Strip service stops at Circus Circus and Caesars Palace southbound, Harrah's and the Riviera northbound between 5:30 AM and 1 AM. The fare for both is $1.50 (exact change required).

If you plan to get on and off the bus, **buy a discounted commuter card** from the driver. Other routes serve the Meadows and Boulevard shopping malls, and Sam's Town Hotel and Casino and the Western Emporium gift shop on Boulder Highway.

From 9:30 AM to 2 AM, the Las Vegas Strip Trolley travels every 30 minutes among Strip hotels, with stops at Fashion Show Mall and Wet 'N Wild. An exact fare of $1 is required.

BUSINESS HOURS

Banks are generally open Monday to Friday 10–4.

Most stores are open Monday to Friday 10–9, Saturday 9–6, and Sunday 11–6. The souvenir shops on the Strip remain open until midnight.

C

CAMERAS, CAMCORDERS, AND COMPUTERS

LAPTOPS

Before you depart, **check your portable computer's battery,** because you may be asked at security to turn on the computer to prove that it is what it appears to be. At the airport, you may prefer to **request a manual inspection,** although security X-rays do not harm hard-disk or floppy-disk storage.

PHOTOGRAPHY

If your camera is new or if you haven't used it for a while, **shoot and develop a few rolls of film** before you leave. Always **store film in a cool, dry place**—never in the car's glove compartment or on the shelf under the rear window.

Every pass through an X-ray machine increases film's chance of clouding. To protect it, carry it in a clear plastic bag and **ask for hand inspection at security.** Such requests are virtually always honored at U.S. airports. Don't depend on a lead-lined bag to protect film in checked luggage—the airline may increase the radiation to see what's inside.

VIDEO

Before your trip, **test your camcorder, invest in a skylight filter to protect the lens, and charge the batteries.** (Airport security personnel may ask you to turn on the camcorder to prove that it's what it appears to be.)

Videotape is not damaged by X-rays, but it may be harmed by the magnetic field of a walk-through metal detector, so **ask that videotapes be hand-checked.**

CHILDREN AND TRAVEL

BABY-SITTING

For recommended local sitters, **check with your hotel desk.** Independent local agencies typically charge $6 to $7 an hour, with a four-hour minimum.

DRIVING

If you are renting a car, **arrange for a car seat when you reserve.** Sometimes they're free.

FLYING

On domestic flights, children under two not

occupying a seat travel free, and older children currently travel on the lowest applicable adult fare.

BAGGAGE➢ In general, the adult baggage allowance applies for children paying half or more of the adult fare.

SAFETY SEATS➢ According to the Federal Aviation Administration, it's a good idea to **use safety seats aloft.** Airline policy varies. U.S. carriers allow FAA-approved models, but airlines usually require that you buy a ticket, even if your child would otherwise ride free, because the seats must be strapped into regular passenger seats.

FACILITIES➢ When making your reservation, **ask for children's meals or a freestanding bassinet** if you need them; bassinets are available only to those with seats at the bulkhead, where there's enough legroom. If you don't need a bassinet, **think twice before requesting bulkhead seats**—the only storage for in-flight necessities is in the inconveniently distant overhead bins.

LODGING

Most hotels allow children under a certain age to stay in their parents' room at no extra charge, while others charge them as extra adults; be sure to **ask about the cut-off age.**

In addition to offering family discounts and special rates for children, many hotels and resorts arrange for baby-sitting services and run a variety of special children's programs. Check with your travel agent for more information, or ask a hotel representative about children's programs when you make your reservations.

Many Las Vegas hotels, such as Circus Circus and Excalibur, offer activities to keep children occupied while their parents play their own games, but an especially comprehensive child-care program can be found at MGM Grand's King Looey's Youth Center. Guests of the Grand take precedence, but guests at any hotel can take advantage of this large day-care facility if space is available. Children ages 3–12 play, snack, and eat meals from 8 AM till midnight starting at $5 an hour per child (up to $8 an hour for nonguests 5–11 PM). Activities include basketball, Foosball, Nintendo, arts and crafts, and air hockey; there are also two six-hour supervised amusement-park excursions a day.

CUSTOMS AND DUTIES

IN LAS VEGAS

British visitors aged 21 or over may import the following into the United States: 200 cigarettes or 50 cigars or 2 kilograms of tobacco; 1 U.S. liter of alcohol; gifts to the value of $100. Restricted items include meat products, seeds, plants, and fruits. Never carry illegal drugs.

BACK HOME

IN CANADA➢ Once per calendar year, when you've been out of Canada for at least seven days, you may bring in C$300 worth of goods duty-free. If you've been away less than seven days but more than 48 hours, the duty-free exemption drops to C$100 but can be claimed any number of times (as can a C$20 duty-free exemption for absences of 24 hours or more). You cannot combine the yearly and 48-hour exemptions, use the C$300 exemption only partially (to save the balance for a later trip), or pool exemptions with family members. Goods claimed under the C$300 exemption may follow you by mail; those claimed under the lesser exemptions must accompany you.

Alcohol and tobacco products may be included in the yearly and 48-hour exemptions but not in the 24-hour exemption. If you meet the age requirements of the province through which you reenter Canada, you may bring in, duty-free, 1.14 liters (40 imperial ounces) of wine or liquor *or* 24 12-ounce cans or bottles of beer or ale. If you are 16 or older, you may bring in, duty-free, 200 cigarettes, 50 cigars or cigarillos, and 400 tobacco sticks or 400 grams of manufactured tobacco. Alcohol and tobacco must accompany you on your return.

An unlimited number of gifts valued up to C$60

each may be mailed to Canada duty-free. These do not count as part of your exemption. Label the package "Unsolicited Gift—Value Under $60." Alcohol and tobacco are excluded.

IN THE U.K.➢ From countries outside the European Union, including the United States, you may import duty-free 200 cigarettes, 100 cigarillos, 50 cigars or 250 grams of tobacco; 1 liter of spirits or 2 liters of fortified or sparkling wine; 2 liters of still table wine; 60 milliliters of perfume; 250 milliliters of toilet water; plus £136 worth of other goods, including gifts and souvenirs.

D

FOR TRAVELERS WITH DISABILITIES

When discussing accessibility with an operator or reservationist, **ask hard questions.** Are there any stairs, inside *or* out? Are there grab bars next to the toilet *and* in the shower/tub? How wide is the doorway to the room? To the bathroom? For the most extensive facilities, meeting the latest legal specifications, **opt for newer accommodations,** which more often have been designed with access in mind. Older properties or ships must usually be retrofitted and may offer more limited facilities as a result. Be sure to **discuss your needs before booking.**

DISCOUNT CLUBS

Travel clubs offer members unsold space on airplanes, cruise ships, and package tours at as much as 50% below regular prices. Membership may include a regular bulletin or access to a toll-free hot line giving details of available trips departing from three or four days to several months in the future. Most also offer 50% discounts off hotel rack rates. Before booking with a club, **make sure the hotel or other supplier isn't offering a better deal.**

DRIVING

The best way to experience Las Vegas may be to drive it. A car gives you easy access to the attractions on the Strip as well as to those that are several blocks away, it lets you make excursions to Lake Mead and elsewhere at your leisure, and it gives you the chance to cruise the Strip and bask in its neon glow.

Las Vegas is an easy city to drive in, even for those who are terrible navigators. The principal north–south artery is Las Vegas Boulevard (I–15 runs roughly parallel to it, less than a mile to the west). A 3½-mile stretch of Las Vegas Boulevard South is the Strip, where a majority of the city's hotels and casinos are clustered. Many of the major streets running east–west (Tropicana Avenue, Flamingo Road, Desert Inn Road, Sahara Avenue) are named for the casinos built at their intersections with the Strip.

Free parking is available at virtually every hotel, although the parking area can be far from the hotel, and you may have to hunt for a space. To avoid this, simply **make use of valet parking.** You can't park anywhere on the Strip itself, and parking spaces on Fremont Street downtown are nearly always taken. Parking in the high-rise structures downtown is free, as long as you **validate your parking ticket at the casino cashier.**

Because the capacity of the streets of Las Vegas has not kept pace with the city's incredible growth, traffic can be heavy in the late afternoons, in the evenings, and on the weekends. At those times, you may prefer to drive the streets that parallel Las Vegas Boulevard: Paradise Road and Maryland Parkway to the east, and Industrial Road to the west. The Industrial Road shortcut (from Tropicana Avenue almost all the way to downtown) will save you an enormous amount of time. You can enter the parking lots at Caesars Palace, the Mirage, Treasure Island, the Stardust, and Circus Circus from Industrial Road (but there's no intersection with West Flamingo Avenue).

ARRIVING BY CAR

Approximately half of the visitors to Las Vegas arrive by automobile. The principal highway is I–15, which brings motorists from southern California to the southwest and Utah to the northeast. U.S. 93

(Boulder Highway and Fremont Street in Las Vegas) extends into Arizona to the southeast, where it connects with I–40. U.S. 95 brings traffic from northern California, Reno, and I–80 to the northwest.

Drivers en route to Las Vegas should keep in mind, when there's an opportunity to fill up, that the next gas station can be an hour away.

I

INSURANCE

BAGGAGE

Airline liability for your baggage is limited to $1,250 per person on domestic flights. On international flights, the airlines' liability is $9.07 per pound or $20 per kilogram for checked baggage (roughly $640 per 70-pound bag) and $400 per passenger for unchecked baggage. Insurance for losses exceeding the terms of your airline ticket can be bought directly from the airline at check-in for about $10 per $1,000 of coverage; note that it excludes a rather extensive list of items, shown on your airline ticket.

FLIGHT

You should **think twice before buying flight insurance.** Often purchased as a last-minute impulse at the airport, it pays a lump sum when a plane crashes, either to a beneficiary if the insured dies or sometimes to a surviving passenger who loses eyesight or a limb. Supplementing the airlines' coverage described in the limits-of-liability paragraphs on your ticket, it's expensive and basically unnecessary. Charging an airline ticket to a major credit card often automatically entitles you to coverage and may also embrace travel by bus, train, and ship.

FOR U.K. TRAVELERS

According to the Association of British Insurers, a trade association representing 450 insurance companies, it's wise to **buy extra medical coverage when you visit the United States.** You can buy an annual travel-insurance policy valid for most vacations during the year in which it's purchased. If you go this route, make sure it covers you if you have a preexisting medical condition or are pregnant.

TRIP

Without insurance, you will lose all or most of your money if you must cancel your trip due to illness or any other reason. Especially if your airline ticket, cruise, or package tour is nonrefundable and cannot be changed, it's essential that you **buy trip-cancellation-and-interruption insurance.** When considering how much coverage you need, look for a policy that will cover the cost of your trip plus the nondiscounted price of a one-way airline ticket should you need to return home early. Read the fine print carefully, especially sections defining "family member" and "preexisting medical condition." Also **consider default or bankruptcy insurance,** which protects you against a supplier's failure to deliver. However, such policies often do not cover default by a travel agency, tour operator, airline, or cruise line if you bought your tour and the coverage directly from the firm in question.

L

LODGING

HOME EXCHANGE

If you would like to find a house, an apartment, or other vacation property to exchange for your own while on vacation, **become a member of a home-exchange organization,** which will send you its annual directories listing available exchanges and will include your own listing in at least one of them. Arrangements for the actual exchange are made by the two parties to it, not by the organization.

M

MONEY AND EXPENSES

ATMS

Chances are that you can **use your bank card at ATMs** to withdraw money from an account and get cash advances on a credit-card account if your card has been programmed with a personal identification number, or PIN. Before leaving home, **check in on frequency limits** for withdrawals and cash advances.

On cash advances you are charged interest from the day you receive the money from ATMs as well as from tellers. Transaction fees for ATM withdrawals outside your home turf may be higher than for withdrawals at home.

TRAVELER'S CHECKS

Whether or not to buy traveler's checks depends on where you are headed; **take cash to rural areas and small towns, traveler's checks to cities.** The most widely recognized are American Express, Citicorp, Thomas Cook, and Visa, which are sold by major commercial banks for 1% to 3% of the checks' face value—it pays to **shop around.** Both American Express and Thomas Cook issue checks that can be countersigned and used by you or your traveling companion. Record the numbers of the checks, cross them off as you spend them, and keep this information separate from your checks.

WIRING MONEY

You don't have to be a cardholder to send or receive funds through MoneyGram[SM] from American Express. Just go to a MoneyGram agent, located in retail and convenience stores and in American Express Travel Offices. Pay up to $1,000 with cash or a credit card, anything over that in cash. The money can be picked up within 10 minutes in cash or check at the nearest MoneyGram agent. There's no limit, and the recipient need only present photo identification. The cost, which includes a free long-distance phone call, runs from 3% to 10%, depending on the amount sent, the destination, and how you pay.

You can also send money using Western Union. Money sent from the United States or Canada will be available for pickup at agent locations in 100 countries within 15 minutes. Once the money is in the system, it can be picked up at any one of 25,000 locations. Fees range from 4% to 10%, depending on the amount you send.

P

PACKAGES AND TOURS

A package or tour to Las Vegas can make your vacation less expensive and more convenient. Firms that sell tours and packages purchase airline seats, hotel rooms, and rental cars in bulk and pass some of the savings on to you. In addition, the best operators have local representatives to help you out at your destination.

A GOOD DEAL?

The more your package or tour includes, the better you can predict the ultimate cost of your vacation. Make sure you know exactly what is included, and **beware of hidden costs.** Are taxes, tips, and service charges included? Transfers and baggage handling? Entertainment and excursions? These can add up.

Most packages and tours are rated deluxe, first-class superior, first class, tourist, and budget. The key difference is usually accommodations. If the package or tour you are considering is priced lower than in your wildest dreams, **be skeptical.** Also, **make sure your travel agent knows the hotels** and other services. Ask about location, room size, beds, and whether it has a pool, room service, or programs for children, if you care about these. Has your agent been there or sent others you can contact?

BUYER BEWARE

Each year consumers are stranded or lose their money when operators go out of business—even very large ones with excellent reputations. If you can't afford a loss, take the time to **check out the operator**—find out how long the company has been in business, and ask several agents about its reputation. Next, **don't book unless the firm has a consumer-protection program.** Members of the United States Tour Operators Association and the National Tour Association are required to set aside funds exclusively to cover your payments and travel arrangements in case of default. Nonmember operators may instead carry insurance; look for the details in the operator's brochure—and the name of an underwriter with a solid reputation. Note: When it comes to tour operators, **don't trust escrow accounts.** Although there are laws governing those of charter-flight operators, no governmental body prevents tour operators from raiding the till. Next, **contact your local Better Business Bureau and the attorney general's office** in both your own state and the operator's; have any complaints been filed? Last, **pay with a major credit card.** Then you can cancel payment, provided that you can document your complaint. Always **consider trip-cancellation insurance** (*see* Insurance, *above*).

BIG VS. SMALL➢ An operator that handles several hundred thousand travelers annually can use its purchasing power to give you a good price. Its high volume may also indicate financial stability. But some small companies provide more personalized service; because they tend to specialize, they may also be experts on an area.

USING AN AGENT

Travel agents are an excellent resource. In fact, large operators accept bookings only through travel agents. But it's good to **collect brochures from several agencies,** because some agents' suggestions may be skewed by promotional relationships with tour and package firms that reward them for volume sales. If you have a special interest, **find an agent with expertise in that area**; the American Society of Travel Agents can give you leads in the United States. (Don't rely solely on your agent, though; agents may be unaware of small-niche operators, and some special-interest travel companies only sell direct.)

SINGLE TRAVELERS

Prices are usually quoted per person, based on two sharing a room. If traveling solo, you may be required to pay the full double-occupancy rate. Some operators eliminate this surcharge if you agree to be matched up with a roommate of the same sex, even if one is not found by departure time.

PACKING FOR LAS VEGAS

Ever since the Last Frontier opened on the Los Angeles Highway, which later became the Strip, visitors have been invited to "Come as You Are." The warm weather and informal character of Las Vegas render casual clothing appropriate day and night. Some people like to spruce up for the evening—the women wearing cocktail dresses and the men donning jacket and tie. But only a handful of the fanciest restaurants in town require such attire. Shorts and sundresses can be worn from April through October. November through March, it's sweaters and overcoats.

Comfortable shoes for walking are a must; no matter what your intentions may be, you'll find yourself covering a lot of ground on foot. If you pack light you'll avoid long waits for the transfer of luggage to and from hotel rooms on arrival and departure.

Bring an extra pair of eyeglasses or contact lenses in your carry-on luggage, and if you have a health problem, **pack enough medication** to last the trip. In case your bags go astray, **don't put prescription drugs or valuables in luggage to be checked.**

LUGGAGE

Free airline baggage allowances depend on the airline, the route, and the class of your ticket; ask in advance. In general, on domestic flights you are entitled to check two bags—neither exceeding 62 inches, or 158 centimeters (length + width + height), or weighing more than 70 pounds (32 kilograms). A third piece may be brought aboard; its total dimensions are generally limited to less than 45 inches (114 centimeters), so it will fit easily under the seat in front of you or in the overhead compartment. In the United States, the FAA gives airlines broad latitude to limit carry-on allowances and tailor them to different aircraft and operational conditions. Charges for excess, oversize, or overweight pieces vary.

SAFEGUARDING YOUR LUGGAGE➢ Before leaving home, **itemize your bags' contents** and their worth, and label them with your name, address, and phone number. (If you use your home address, cover it so that potential thieves can't see it.) Inside your bag, **pack a copy of your itinerary.** At check-in, **make sure that your bag is correctly tagged** with the airport's three-letter destination code. If your bags arrive damaged or not at all, file a written report with the airline before leaving the airport.

PASSPORTS AND VISAS

CANADIANS

No passport is necessary to enter the United States.

U.K. CITIZENS

British citizens need a valid passport. If you are staying fewer than 90 days and traveling on a vacation, with a return or onward ticket, you will probably not need a visa. However, you will need to fill out the Visa Waiver Form, 1-94W, supplied by the airline.

While traveling, **keep one photocopy of the data page** separate from your wallet and leave another copy with someone at home. If you lose your passport, promptly call the nearest embassy or consulate, and the local police; having the data page can speed replacement.

PHOTOGRAPHY

Though Las Vegas is one of the top tourist destinations in the United States, it's the only one whose major attractions discourage photography. At Disney World; the Grand Canyon; Washington, D.C.; or anywhere in California, your camera is as welcome as your kids. But walk into a Vegas casino with a camera hanging from your neck, and the security guard will give you stares. Start to pull off the lens cap, and the guard will tell you sternly, "No pictures in the casino." (You can, in fact, take pictures in the Excalibur, Harrah's, and Four Queens casinos, but these are the only exceptions.)

The practice goes back to the 1940s and 1950s, when men who had been criminals outside Nevada for most of their lives were making the rules in Las Vegas. In New York, Miami, Chicago, most of them had always gone to great lengths to avoid being photographed, especially while gambling, which was illegal in every other state in the country. And even though it was legal in Nevada, their old habits and phobias died hard. Remember the scene at Don Corleone's daughter's wedding in *The Godfather,* when a photo is taken of one of the dons and he orders that the film be exposed and the camera broken?

Although gambling in Las Vegas no longer has a stigma attached to it, the current no-photo policy might be rationalized as follows: If a guy is sitting at a 21 table with a woman at his side who is not his wife, and a photograph is taken, the guy might get angry and leave. Or certain people who handle other peoples' funds—a banker, say, or politician—might feel that a photo could be (or at least look) incriminating. And others may simply not want folks to think they were dropping a bunch of money in a casino.

There are consolations, however: Outside the casinos, Las Vegas is a great city to photograph, and for the most part, all you have to do is point and shoot. During the day, the desert light is flat; at sunrise and sunset it's magical. At night Las Vegas is brighter than any other city in America. Subjects abound: the big picture, the small details, the people, the signs, the statues. And if you're a little crafty, you can always whip out a camera and shoot a casino. The worst that'll happen is you'll be 86ed.

CAMERAS AND FILM➤ An ordinary point-and-shoot camera will do fine, but if you have 35mm equipment and a wide-angle lens, your pictures will look even better. With so much to take in when shooting Las Vegas, the wide-angle (28mm or 35mm) really pays off by fitting as much as possible into the picture. When you're shooting video, you'll probably want to leave your lens set at the widest point of view and zoom in only for the occasional close-up.

If you're shooting color-print film (as most of us do), get the 100 ISO film; it's cheaper, and it offers the best color reproduction. In Las Vegas you won't have much need for high-speed film (400 or 1000 ISO) because most of your subjects will be outdoors, under the bright desert sun.

Those who want the best possible color will go for slide film. Fuji 50 produces hues so rich you won't believe it; the bright colors of Las Vegas will look surreal.

When you shoot neon signs at night, and when you shoot slides, the low-ISO films are a must. High-speed films dilute the colors and give you a bland photo. Signs will photograph best when you mount your camera on a tripod and make exposures of up to half a second. You can still get decent color prints of signs by using 100 ISO print film; the important thing to remember is not to shoot them at night. The best time is immediately after the sun has gone down, when the sky is still blue and a desert haze has fallen, leaving strands of reds and yellows in the sky. At that time, the neon signs have been turned on, giving you full-strength "signage" against a blue sky, which will be far more photogenic than a black sky. Take a look at any hotel's promotional brochures, and you'll notice that every one of the marquee pictures has been shot this way.

Shooting immediately after sunset is the best time for people pictures, too, because the light adds a nice warm tone to the skin. If you're shooting with a flash, you can easily light the person posed in front of the sign and not have to worry about the sign being overexposed.

All of the above applies to video as well. Just after sunset, you'll get the flickering of the signs against a blue rather than a black sky—and a much more pleasing picture. But keep in mind that these signs are very large; it'll take steady camera work to get everything into the frame. Rest the camcorder on your shoulder, not on your hand, take a deep breath, and move your body up and down to pan across the sign.

SUBJECTS➢ Go downtown for the best neon photos; there's simply more neon here than anywhere else. At the corner of Fremont and 3rd, place your subject on the street during a red light, and you've got either the Fremont and the Horseshoe, or the Vegas Vic and Vicky signs as backdrops.

A few of the neon signs on the Strip (Circus Circus, Sahara) are so large that they are quite difficult to photograph. The manageable ones are those of the Stardust, Riviera, and the Flamingo Hilton.

Overhead shots of the Strip are pretty easy to get. Most hotels have hallways with picture windows overlooking the Strip; all you need to do is to take an elevator to the floor of your choice, aim your camera out the window, and shoot.

How about a photo of your subject out in the desert with all the big hotels of Vegas in the background? There are still a few vacant lots on and at either end of the Strip, and many a few blocks to the east and west. You can also head over to the airport (the circular parking structure is a good spot) or up the Sunrise Mountains (drive east on Lake Mead Boulevard). These photos should also be taken just after sundown, with the light still on the sand and the colorful signs in the background.

R

RENTING A CAR

CUTTING COSTS

To get the best deal, **book through a travel agent and shop around.** When pricing cars, **ask where the rental lot is located.** Some off-airport locations offer lower rates—even though their lots are only minutes away from the terminal via complimentary shuttle. You may also want to **price local car-rental companies,** whose rates may be lower still, although service and maintenance standards may not be up to those of a national firm. Also **ask your travel agent about a company's customer-service record.** How has it responded to late plane arrivals and vehicle mishaps? Are there often lines at the rental counter, and, if you're traveling during a holiday period, does a confirmed reservation guarantee you a car?

INSURANCE

When you drive a rented car, you are generally responsible for any damage or personal injury that you cause as well as damage to the vehicle. Before you rent, **see what coverage you already have** by means of your personal auto-insurance policy and credit cards. For about $14 a day, rental companies sell insurance, known as a collision damage waiver (CDW), that eliminates your liability for damage to the car; it's always optional and should never be automatically added to your bill.

FOR U.K. CITIZENS

In the United States you must be 21 to rent a car; rates may be higher for those under 25. Extra costs cover child seats, compulsory for children under five (about $3 per day), and additional drivers (about $1.50 per day). To pick up your reserved car you will need the reservation voucher, a passport, a U.K. driver's license, and a travel policy covering each driver.

SURCHARGES

Before picking up the car in one city and leaving it in another, **ask about drop-off charges or one-way service fees,** which can be substantial. Note, too, that some rental agencies charge extra if you return the car before the time specified on your contract. To avoid a hefty refueling fee, **fill the tank just before you turn in the car.**

S

SENIOR-CITIZEN DISCOUNTS

To qualify for age-related discounts, **mention your senior-citizen status up front** when booking hotel reservations, not when checking out, and before you're seated in restaurants, not when paying your bill. Note that discounts may be limited to certain menus, days, or hours. When renting a car, **ask about promotional car-rental discounts**—they can net lower costs than your senior-citizen discount.

STUDENTS ON THE ROAD

To save money, **look into deals available through student-oriented travel agencies.** To qualify, you'll need to have a bona fide student I.D. card. Members of international student groups also are eligible. *See* Students *in* Important Contacts A to Z, *above.*

T

TAXIS

You'll find cabs waiting at the airport and at every hotel in town (*see* Airport Transfers *in* Important Contacts A to Z, *above,* for rates). If you take a cab to a restaurant off the Strip, the restaurant will call a taxi to take you home.

TELEPHONES

LONG DISTANCE

The long-distance services of AT&T, MCI, and Sprint make calling home relatively convenient and let you avoid hotel surcharges; typically, you dial an 800 number in the United States.

W

WHEN TO GO

Las Vegas is a year-round destination. Except for the first three weeks in December and weekdays during July, you can assume that Las Vegas will be running at full bore. Weekends, always crowded, are especially jam-packed for the Super Bowl, Valentine's Day, the NCAA Final Four, Easter, Cinco de Mayo, Memorial Day, July 4th, and Labor Day. The week between Christmas and New Year's is about the most crowded week of the year. In addition, nearly 50 conventions of more than 10,000 participants are held here every year; prices skyrocket, availability plummets, and the hordes fill every open space. Sporting events, such as boxing matches, golf tournaments, and the National Finals Rodeo, also have a major impact on the crowd situation. It's a good idea to **call the Las Vegas Convention and Visitors Authority** (*see* Visitor Information *in* Important Contacts A to Z, *above*) to find out who or what will be in town at the time you're planning to visit.

During a "normal" week—no conventions, holidays, title fights, or local events—you can count on the weekdays, Sunday through Thursday, to be less crowded, less expensive, and less stressful than the weekends. During even a routine weekend, however, traffic jams, along with competition for rooms, restaurant and show reservations, and spots at the slots or tables, can be ferocious.

Weatherwise, the most comfortable times to be in Las Vegas are the spring and fall. In April and May, daytime temperatures are delightful, in the 70s and 80s. The Las Vegas you see pictured in the ads—women lying by the pools, saxophone players performing on the street, visitors dressed in shorts and T-shirts, but not sweating like pigs—begins when the pools open in April.

In September and October, the summer heat has abated, and the pools remain open.

Winter is a distinctly different season, with snowcapped mountains in the distance, windy and chilly days, and surprisingly cold nights. The two weeks before Christmas find Las Vegas nearly deserted, with rooms going for bargain rates, and hardly a traffic jam on the Strip.

Summer is a time of dry, uncomfortably hot weather (sometimes literally 110 degrees in the shade), when lounging at an outdoor pool requires protection from the relentless desert sun. You'll probably find yourself thirstier than you can remember ever being. At the height of the heat, however, hotels offer their lowest rates.

What follows are the average daily maximum and minimum temperatures for Las Vegas.

Climate

Jan.	60F	16C	May	89F	32C	Sept.	95F	35C
	28	– 2		51	11		57	14
Feb.	66F	19C	June	98F	37C	Oct.	84F	29C
	33	1		60	16		46	8
Mar.	71F	22C	July	102F	39C	Nov.	71F	22C
	39	4		68	20		35	2
Apr.	80F	27C	Aug.	102F	39C	Dec.	60F	16C
	44	7		66	19		30	– 1

1 Destination: Las Vegas, Reno, Tahoe

VEGAS: THE FAMILY RESORT?

THE NAME LAS VEGAS is instantly recognized around the world as a fantasyland for adults, a place that exists for one reason and one reason only: gambling. But Las Vegas is currently changing faster than its image's ability to keep pace, as this traditionally X-rated city strives for the big "G" of general admittance, trying to attract adults, children, friends, baby-sitters, grandparents, nongamblers, and nonsmokers—in short, everybody. Fabulous theme hotels such as Excalibur, Treasure Island, and Luxor, and amusement parks such as Wet 'N Wild, Grand Slam Canyon, and MGM Grand Adventures all provide a minivacation's worth of excitement—without visitors ever having to step up to a slot machine or blackjack table.

Why is Las Vegas seemingly abandoning its adults-only image in favor of appealing to a wholesome family market? For one thing, gambling is proliferating around the country and the world at such a furious pace that Las Vegas must broaden its appeal to maintain its edge. Secondly, the demographically powerful baby boomers are now having their own baby bulge, which has changed the shape of their vacation demands. Finally, a few years ago, Las Vegas cast its wanton gaze toward the number-one tourist destination in the country, Walt Disney World. In 1995, for the first time ever, Vegas glitter outpulled Mickey Mouse.

Still, a substantial, though underpublicized, contingent of Las Vegas boosters is content to let the family bandwagon parade by, and continues to embrace adults and gamblers. After all, Las Vegas hasn't exactly been transformed. Yes, there are pyramids and water slides and towers, along with museums and galleries, but tens of millions of visitors still come to Las Vegas for the traditional reason, to seduce the goddess of chance. You are constantly reminded of this fact as you walk or drive along the Strip or stroll the new pedestrian mall on Fremont Street. There are no supermarkets, post offices, movie theaters, or other familiar businesses of everyday life, only places where you can buy a hamburger or a souvenir, get married, and lay a bet.

The Las Vegas of the Strip and downtown is Tom Jones, David Copperfield, Michael Crawford, and Steve and Eydie. It's cards, dice, roulette wheels, and slots. It's harried keno runners and leggy cocktail waitresses, grizzled pit bosses and nervous break-in dealers. It's cab and limo drivers, valets and bellmen. Las Vegas is showgirls with smiles as white as spotlights and headwear as big and bright as fireworks. It's a place where thousands of people earn their living counting billions in chips, change, bills, checks, and markers. The big bosses in this town, which has never had a widely known political leader, have always been the flamboyant casino owners: the late Moe Dalitz of the Desert Inn; Kirk Kerkorian of the MGM Grand; Steve Wynn of the Golden Nugget, Mirage, and Treasure Island; Jackie Gaughan of the Plaza and El Cortez; Michael Gaughan of the Barbary Coast and Gold Coast; Bob Stupak of Vegas World; Bill Boyd of the Fremont, California, and Stardust; and Jack Binion of the Horseshoe.

While the strip and downtown are the best known and principal tourist areas of the city, a million people live—and lead "normal" lives—within 10 miles of them. Endless subdivisions enclose rows and rows of pink-stuccoed and red-tiled, three-bedroom and two-bath houses, most of them less than five years old and occupied by recent transplants hoping to cash in on the fulsome boom. "Lost Wages" is a city of dreamers: gamblers hoping to beat the odds and get rich; dancers, singers, magicians, acrobats, and comedians praying to make it in the Entertainment Capital of the World; realtors, supermarket cashiers, shoe salesmen, and librarians seeking a better way of life.

For all the local talk about Las Vegas citizens being average people who just happen to live and work in an unusual city, living here is undeniably different. For example, two out of every four locals have a direct connection to the hospitality industry; the town is full of people whose jobs are to cater to strangers 24 hours a day, 365 days a year. Las Vegas probably has the largest graveyard shift in the world. And the notion that locals never gamble and rarely see a show or eat at a buffet is also largely mythic. Las Vegas residents are a large and active part of the total market that relishes in 99¢ breakfasts and $5 prime ribs, slot clubs, and gambling promotions. Indeed, the casinos that cater primarily to locals (Palace Station, the Rio, Gold Coast, Santa Fe, and Arizona Charlie's) are among the most successful in town. Surprisingly, Las Vegas is also a religious town—about a third of the 450 congregations here are Latter-day Saint—which adds a somewhat incongruous conservative dimension to local politics and morals.

GAMBLING AND TOURISM are not the only games in town. Nellis Air Force Base employs upwards of 10,000 people. The construction industry is huge, and the warehousing business is major. Large corporations and small manufacturing firms frequently relocate to southern Nevada, which offers tax incentives as well as a lower cost of living. But local life is merely a curiosity to the tens of millions of tourists whose primary concern is choosing among 50 major hotel-casinos, several dozen shows, a mind-boggling variety of gambling options, limitless dining, and spectacular day trips.

To get the full impact of the neon spectacle, it's best to drive into Las Vegas at night. Fifty miles out, the great desert glow is discernible; 30 miles away, it begins to resolve into pinpoints of light. In another 10 miles you can start to make out the skyline, surrounded by the brilliance of a billion bulbs. Ten miles from Las Vegas you're finally in it: amber streetlights, harsh like the desert. If you stop, get out of the car, and listen, you can hear the hum of the shine.

The largest city in Nevada, Las Vegas is 2,030 feet above sea level. It's one of the most remote large cities in the country: The nearest major population center to the west is Barstow, California, 2½ hours away; St. George, Utah, is two hours to the east. Over the years, Las Vegas has wrested the political and economic power of Nevada away from Reno, 448 miles to the northwest, the city where legalized gambling first became popular and where the early casinos were built.

Las Vegas is surrounded by the Mojave Desert, and Las Vegas Valley is flanked by mountain ranges. Among them are the Spring Mountains, including Mt. Charleston (11,918 feet), which features downhill skiing, and Red Rock Canyon, characterized by stunning Southwest sandstone. The Las Vegas Wash drains the valley to the southeast into Lake Mead and the Colorado River system.

Average high temperatures in Las Vegas rise to 105°F in July and August; lows drop to 30°F in January and February. The heat is saunalike throughout the summer, except during electrical storms that can dump an inch of rain an hour and cause dangerous flash floods. Heavy rains any time of year exacerbate two of Las Vegas's major problems: lack of water drainage and surplus of traffic. The summer blaze often makes it very uncomfortable to be outside for any length of time. Winters can be surprisingly chilly during the day, and especially cold after the sun goes down. The weather doesn't get any better here than in September and October, and April and May, but the crowds are aware of it.

Las Vegas is the largest U.S. city founded in the 20th century—1905 to be exact. Some might argue that the significant year was 1946, when Bugsy Siegel's Fabulous Flamingo opened for business. But the beginnings of modern Las Vegas can be traced back to 1829, when Antonio Armijo led a party of 60 on the Old Spanish Trail to Los Angeles. While his caravan camped about 100 miles northeast of the present site of Las Vegas, a scouting party set out to look for water. Rafael Rivera, a young Mexican scout who left the main party and headed due west over the unexplored desert, discovered an oasis. The abundance of artesian spring water here shortened the Spanish trail to Los Angeles by allowing travelers to go directly through, rather than around, the desert and eased the rigors of travel for the Spanish traders who used the route. They named the oasis Las Vegas, Spanish for "the Meadows."

The next major visitor to the Las Vegas Springs was John C. Fremont, who in 1844 led one of his many explorations of the Far West. Today he is remembered in the name of the principal downtown thoroughfare.

Ten years later, a group of Mormon settlers were sent by Brigham Young from Salt Lake City to colonize the valley. They built a 150-square-foot, adobe-brick fort, a small remnant of which still stands today; it's the oldest building in Las Vegas. The Mormons spent two years growing crops, mining lead, and converting the local Paiute Indians, but the rigors of the desert defeated their ambitions and by 1857 the fort was abandoned.

THINGS DIDN'T START HOPPING here until 1904, when the San Pedro, Los Angeles, and Salt Lake Railroad laid its tracks through Las Vegas Valley, purchased the prime land and water rights from the handful of homesteaders, and surveyed a town site for its railroad servicing and repair facilities. In April 1905, the railroad held an auction and sold 700 lots. Las Vegas became a dusty railroad watering stop with a few downtown hotels and stores, a saloon and redlight district known as Block 16, and a few thousand residents—and remained just that for the next 23 years. It all changed, however, in 1928, when the Boulder Canyon Project Act was signed into law, appropriating $165 million for the building of the world's largest antigravity dam 40 miles from Las Vegas.

Construction of the dam began in 1931, a historic year for Nevada. This was the year Governor Fred Balzar approved the "wide-open" gambling bill that had been introduced by a Winnemucca rancher, Assemblyman Phil Tobin. Gambling had been outlawed several times since Nevada became a state in 1864, but it had never been completely eliminated. Back-room gambling, brothels, and easy divorces continued regardless of laws that attempted to curtail these activities. Tobin maintained that controlled gaming would be good for tourism and the state's economy; people were going to gamble anyway, so why shouldn't the state tax the profits? Thus, he was able to convince lawmakers to make gambling permanently legal.

The early 1930s marked the height of the Depression and Prohibition. The construction of the dam on the Colorado River (bordering Arizona and Nevada) brought thousands of job seekers to southern Nevada. Because the federal government didn't want dam workers to be distracted by the temptations of Las Vegas, it created a separate government town, Boulder City—still the only community in the state where gambling is illegal.

At this time, Nevada's political and economic power resided in the northern part of the state: the capital in Carson City and the major casinos (notably Harold's Club and Harrah's) in Reno. But the completion of the dam in 1935 turned southern Nevada into a magnet for federal appropriations, thousands of tourists and new residents, and a seemingly inexhaustible supply of electricity and water. In addition, as the country mobilized for World War II, tens of thousands of pilots and gunners trained at the Las Vegas Aerial Gunnery School, opened by the federal government on 3 million acres just north of town. Today, this property is home to Nellis Air Force Base and the Nevada Test Site.

By the early 1940s, downtown Las Vegas boasted several luxury hotels and a dozen small but successful gambling clubs. In 1941, Thomas Hull, who owned a chain of California motor inns, decided to build a place on a plot of land in the desert just outside the city limits on Highway 91, the road from Los Angeles. El Rancho Vegas opened with 100 motel rooms, a western-motif casino, and, right off the highway, a large parking lot with an inviting swimming pool in the middle. El Rancho's quick success led to the opening a year later of the Last Frontier Hotel, a mile down the road. Thus the Las Vegas Strip was founded.

Benjamin "Bugsy" Siegel, who ran the New York mob's activities on the West Coast, began to see the incredible potential of a remote oasis where land was cheap and gambling was legal. He visualized a swank resort showplace with Hollywood entertainment, neon, palm trees, and a big bright casino. He struggled for two years to build his Fabulous Flamingo even farther from town than the Last Frontier, alienating both his local partners and silent investors with his lavish overspending. He opened the joint prematurely, on a rainy night, the day after Christmas 1946. Although movie stars attended and headliners Jimmy Durante, Xavier Cugat, and Rose Marie performed, the Flamingo flopped; the casino paid out more money than it took in. This made Siegel's partners not only unhappy, but also suspicious, and six months later Bugsy was dead. Ironically, once he had been bumped off, business at the Flamingo boomed. Siegel's gangland assassination had made front-page news across the country, and people flocked to see the house that Bugsy built.

THE SUCCESS OF THE FLAMINGO paved the way for gamblers and gangsters from all over the country to invest in Las Vegas hotel-casinos, one after another. The Desert Inn, Horseshoe, Sands, Sahara, Riviera, Dunes, Fremont, Tropicana, and Stardust were all built in the 1950s, financed with mob money. Every new hotel came on like a theme park opening for the summer with a new ride. Each was bigger, better, more unusual than the last. The Sahara had the tallest freestanding neon sign. The Riviera was the first high-rise building in town. The Stardust had 1,000 rooms and the world's largest swimming pool.

That the underworld owned and ran the big joints was a proverbial worst-kept secret, but only added to the allure of Las Vegas. And the town's great boom in the 1950s couldn't have happened without the mob's access to millions of dollars in cash. Under the circumstances, no bank, corporation, or legitimate investor would have touched the gambling business.

In time, however, the state began to take steps to weed out the most visible undesirables. The federal government assisted in the crackdown, using its considerable resources to hound the gangsters out of business. And, finally, an old man arrived on a train and soon revolutionized the nation's image of Las Vegas.

Howard Hughes had just sold TWA for $546 million and he either had to spend half the money or turn it in as taxes. During a four-year stay in Las Vegas, he bought the Desert Inn, Frontier, Sands, Landmark, and Silver Slipper hotels, a television station, an airfield, and millions of dollars' worth of real estate. His presence in Las Vegas gave gambling its first positive image: As a former pilot and aviation pioneer, Hollywood mogul, and American folk hero, Hughes could in no way be connected with gangsters.

Hughes's presence also opened the door to corporate ownership of hotel-casinos. In 1971, Hilton Corporation purchased the International (now the Las Vegas Hilton) and the Flamingo, becoming the first major hotel chain to step onto the Las Vegas playing field. Ramada, Holiday Inn, Hyatt, and others have since followed suit. Las Vegas felt the effects of both the legalization of gambling in the late 1970s and of the national recession of the early 1980s—but not for very long. Over the years, the city has carved a secure niche for itself as a destination for national and international tourists, a winter sojourn for snowbirds from the north, and a weekend getaway for gamblers and families from California, Arizona, and Utah. Las Vegas has expanded at a ferocious pace for the past seven or eight years, during which upwards of 35,000 hotel rooms have been added and 300,000 people have moved in.

And why not? Room costs are 50% to 90% lower than in any other major city. Restaurant and buffet dining here can be cheaper than preparing a meal at home. Entertainment is abundant and reasonably priced. Las Vegas is possibly the easiest place in the world to receive freebies—the ubiquitous "comps." And best of all, gambling promotions such as coupons, slot clubs, paycheck bonuses, and drawings provide a fighting chance to win in the casino. In the back of everyone's mind is the idea that a trip to Las Vegas can be free or even a money-making vacation. That kind of thinking keeps the Las Vegas bosses smiling as they add the finishing touches to their new multimillion-dollar hotels.

WHAT'S WHERE

Hot Spots

NEW FOUR CORNERS➢ The junction of Las Vegas Boulevard and Tropicana Avenue is fast becoming the prime tourist intersection in the country. The world's biggest hotel, the MGM Grand, is located here, as is the fantasy Tropicana Resort and Casino and Excalibur.

OLD FOUR CORNERS➢ The intersection of Las Vegas Boulevard and Flamingo Road has Caesars Palace on the northwest corner, Bally's on the southeast corner, and the Flamingo Hilton and Tower on the northeast corner. The area was once dominated by the Dunes Hotel on the southwest corner, but the Dunes was leveled in 1993 to make way for two new megaresorts that are currently under construction at the site.

FREMONT STREET➢ You'll find the heart of downtown Vegas where Fremont Street meets Las Vegas Boulevard. It's also the epicenter of the world's greatest collection of neon signs. The hotels and casinos on Fremont tend to be older than those on the Strip, and perhaps a little classier.

THE STRIP➢ Officially titled Las Vegas Boulevard, the Strip runs north–south through the heart of the city. Without leaving this street you could sample all that's best in Vegas; the food, the shows, and of course the gambling. Almost all the major casinos are either on or just off the Strip, 30 in all—that's more than 2 million square feet of gambling fever.

Excursions

BOULDER CITY➢ Built in the early 1930s to house workers on the Hoover Dam, Boulder City is really just a small Nevada town which is famous because it's the only place in Nevada where it's illegal to gamble—the perfect reason to go there!

BRYCE CANYON NATIONAL PARK➢ A hike through Bryce Canyon is like a trip back to a prehistoric age. As with much of this area, red is the dominant color here, but reds like you've never seen them before, dancing and glinting in the desert sun. This is a Nevada far from the hue and cry of the casino, a necessary reminder in the land of the developer that the glories of the world are not all man-made.

HOOVER DAM➢ About 35 miles east of Vegas lies one of the seven man-made wonders of the world, the monster Hoover Dam. Guided tours take visitors right into the heart of this concrete beast, all 4.4 million cubic yards of it.

LAKE MEAD➢ Covering an area of over 229 square miles, Lake Mead is the largest man-made lake in the country. Its water supply comes from the Colorado River backed up behind the Hoover Dam. Fishing and water sports are permitted on the lake, and a large ferry takes visitors on daylong cruises.

LAUGHLIN➢ This is a major gambling center right in the middle of the Mojave Desert. Laughlin is about 90 miles southeast of Vegas on the Arizona state line. If the pace of Vegas gets to you, you might try the low-pressure, low-minimum tables, and low-cost rooms of this riverside town.

LOST CITY MUSEUM➢ About 8 miles southeast of the Valley of Fire is the Lost City Museum, with its displays of early Pueblo Indian crafts, weapons, and jewelry.

MT. CHARLESTON➢ The fifth-highest peak in Nevada, Mt. Charleston is the perfect mountain retreat if you want a couple of days away from the madness of Vegas. In wintertime it's a local ski haven, and in the summer visitors like to hike, bike, and camp on the slopes. The famous Mount Charleston Hotel and Mount Charleston Restaurant and Lounge offer the best in food and lodging in the most serene of environments. You might not want to go back to Vegas at all.

OLD NEVADA➢ Old Nevada is a western theme park with staged gunfights and hangings right there in the streets. It has everything an old western town might have had, plus a few extras, including a movie theater and a minitrain that runs around the grounds.

RED ROCK CANYON➢ You have probably seen Red Rock in the movies; this 13-mile scenic loop through the red rock formations and unusual high-desert scenery of southern Nevada is a very popular location spot for Hollywood.

ST. GEORGE➢ Over a hundred miles north of Las Vegas you'll find the picturesque town of St. George. Its Victorian-style streets are home to low-price lodging and dining as well as a number of Mormon historical sites and some magnificent red rocks.

SPRING MOUNTAIN RANCH STATE PARK➢ The perfect place to drive to from the city (about 20 miles west) with a blanket and some vittles. Spring Mountain Ranch is a picnickers' paradise, with long green lawns and a stunning mountain backdrop.

VALLEY OF FIRE STATE PARK➢ Nevada's first state park is about 55 miles northeast of Las Vegas. It takes its name from its distinctive coloration, which ranges from lavender to tangerine to bright red. Visitors flock to see the incredible rock formed by the desert winds.

ZION NATIONAL PARK➢ If monstrous red rocks and stunning vistas are your thing, you can't miss the 6-mile drive through this park. When the Mormons first saw the area they believed they had found God's country, and after your spectacular drive you might be tempted to agree with them.

PLEASURES & PASTIMES

Winning and Losing

Times are changing but gambling is still the thing to do in Las Vegas. The visitor is faced with a terrifying choice of possible bets; a thousand and one different ways to part with your hard-earned dollars. If you're going to gamble you should ensure that you suck all the fun out of it you can, and maybe even win in the process. Blackjack, craps, and baccarat are all thrilling games and they happen to offer the best odds for winning of any gambling attraction in Vegas. The average bankroll of a Vegas gambler is $500, but you can experience the thrill of losing for a lot less. The smaller casinos off the Strip are often the best bet for the amateur gambler; the pressure is less intense, the minimums are reasonable, and the staff are more patient.

Wining and Dining

Dining out in Las Vegas is an adventure in variety. The fun lies in choosing from the vast array of styles and price ranges, from cheap Chinese to pricey Portuguese. Every major hotel has four or five eating places (the Las Vegas Hilton has eight), and independent restaurants are scattered about town. The fabulous buffets are a traditional treat, where you find yourself, plate in hand, standing before a mountain of all-you-can-eat food, and all for as little as $5. Because plenty of big-spending high rollers come to Vegas, there is no shortage of gourmet dining, with European chefs, silver service, and JACKET AND TIE REQUIRED signs.

Magic and Song

Nobody ever came to Vegas to see Shakespeare. The city has made famous a certain brand of entertainment based on big names, spectacular production values, sex, and magic. Siegfried and Roy remain the biggest draw here, old reliable Wayne Newton packs them in, and you can still catch a scantily dressed chorus line if you want. But a new breed of show, the production spectacular, is popping up in all the major hotels and each one is competing with the other for even more amazing special effects. "EFX" at the MGM combines the Broadway talent of Michael Crawford with crazy special effects in a 90-minute spectacular that includes singing, battling dragons, a cast of 70, and mind-boggling sets. Bally's "Jubilee" is one of the largest shows in town, with a cast of more than 100 performing in a showroom with 1,100 seats and effects that include the sinking of the *Titanic.* "Mystere" at Treasure Island is a new-age circus that combines haunting music and high-tech lighting with incredible human feats of daring.

Other Pleasures

DOWNTOWN NEON➢ It is a simple (and free) pleasure in Las Vegas to stand on the corner of Las Vegas Boulevard and Fremont Street in the evening and behold a testament to the extraordinary powers of mankind, who has turned day into night. The area is home to a collection of neon signs that only downtown Toyko can claim to match. The 50-foot-tall neon cowboy (Vegas Vic) and cowgirl (Vegas Vicky) are perhaps the most famous signs, as they endlessly wave a welcome to the city's visitors.

THE HIGH ROLLERS➢ If you get a chance—that is, if it happens in one of the casinos' public rooms—just stand (in Vegas, chairs are for gamblers only) and watch one of the bigger "players" or high rollers take on the tables at Vegas. You have nothing to lose, but if the player hits a big streak and those chips start piling up, you can ride his adrenaline rush for free.

THE LAS VEGAS BUZZ➢ Besides the renowned enticements of Las Vegas, there are other, more subtle ones. There's the twisting of time, noticeable, for example, in coffee shops, when at any hour some people are having breakfast, others lunch or dinner, and still others snacks or coffee. There's the unmistakable air—sounds, smells, sights—of a casino. And there's the phenomenon of a city that never closes or seems to sleep, that galvanizes and emblazons the familiar activities of daily life.

FODOR'S CHOICE

Activities

★ Watch the **free pirate show at Treasure Island's Buccaneer Bay** from the safety of the shore as the pirate schooner *Hispaniola* sinks the Navy frigate H.M.S *Britannia* seven times a day!

★ Experience air-conditioned terror on **the roller coaster at Grand Slam Canyon,** the largest indoor amusement ride in the world.

★ See movies for the next century at the **high-tech theaters at Luxor,** a three-part motion, video, and 3-D movie extravaganza.

Moments

★ There are two possible responses to **standing outside Luxor, right at the base, and looking up** at the giant pyramid, "Look what they've done" or "Oh my God! Look what they've done."

★ Enjoy your **first coffee-shop comp for two** after a couple of hours at a $5 blackjack table.

★ A wall of synchronized video monitors leaps up before you as you **enter the MGM Grand's lobby,** welcoming you to the world's largest hotel.

Sights

★ **The light show within the Fremont Street Experience is an** umbrella of light that turns night into day.

★ The **Hoover Dam** was one of the seven man-made wonders of the world when it was completed in 1935, and it still impresses today.

★ The 56,000-acre **Valley of Fire** is home to wondrous rock formations that have been weathered into unusual shapes that suggest elephants, domes, and beehives.

★ The computer-driven **volcano in front of the Mirage Hotel** erupts every 30 minutes and sends a tower of flame into the sky.

Hotels

★ The opulent Roman theme at **Caesars Palace,** including marble fountains, statues, bas-reliefs, and handmaidens, hints of the decadent treatment you'll receive at this quality Vegas standout. *$$$$*

★ You get two vacations for one at the **Mirage** as you find yourself in a South-Sea paradise—including 3,000 tropical plants and seven dolphins in the world's largest saltwater pool—in the middle of a major metropolis. *$$$$*

★ Modeled on the grand castles of Europe, the **Excalibur Hotel and Casino**'s Arthurian wonderland includes some of the best value accommodation in Las Vegas. *$$*

★ In the 1960s **Sands** was the headquarters for Sinatra and the rest of the Rat Pack when they were in town. The place is steeped in Vegas history and it feels like it when you stay here. *$$*

★ You might be forgiven for thinking that the **Gold Spike Hotel and Casino,** with penny slots, $1 blackjack tables, and $20 rooms, was stuck in some kind of weird time warp. *$*

Restaurants

★ The business of eating meets big-time showbiz at **Bacchanal, Caesars,** where toga-clad "wine goddesses," a lighted pool in the center of the dining room, and gluttonous prix fixe dinners evoke the atmosphere of a Roman feast. *$$$$*

★ The best white-glove restaurant in Las Vegas is **Palace Court, Caesars.** A stained-glass skylight domes the rotunda-style dining room and the caviar is famous. *$$$$*

★ You could easily forget that you were in Vegas when you eat at **Le Montrachet, Las Vegas Hilton.** The menu changes with the seasons and the atmosphere is serene and restful, with fresh flowers the only ostentation. *$$$*

★ A new hot ticket in Las Vegas dining is the **Xanadu, Sands,** where for a fixed price you can enjoy a top-class hearty meal with a dash of style. *$$$*

★ Believe it or not, the **Steak House, Circus Circus,** manages to maintain a quiet, comfortable dining room in the middle of one of Las Vegas's busiest hotels. Sturdy meat dishes amid warm wood and brass surroundings make it the perfect place to decompress after a day at the slots. *$$*

★ The epitome of the famous Las Vegas buffet can be found at the **Carnival World Buffet, Rio.** The variety and volume of food defy description, and the price is just right. *$*

FESTIVALS AND SEASONAL EVENTS

Las Vegas is not known for specific celebrations—the Strip is the venue for a never-ending parade. Still, a number of annual events do attract wide attention.

WINTER

EARLY DEC.➢ **National Finals Rodeo,** the Super Bowl of rodeos, brings together 15 finalists to compete in each of seven events; there are 10 performances in nine days at the Thomas and Mack Center. When the rodeo comes to town, the showrooms all feature country music, and it seems as though everyone on the street is wearing jeans, boots, and a cowboy hat. ☎ 702/731–2115.

DEC. 31➢ **New Year's Eve** is celebrated with fireworks over Fremont Street in downtown Las Vegas, televised nationally. ☎ 702/382–6397.

MAR.➢ The **LPGA Invitational golf tournament** draws top women golfers who compete for a money prize. ☎ 702/382–6616.

SPRING

APR.➢ The **Clark County Fair** takes place 60 miles north of Las Vegas in Logandale. ☎ 702/398–3247.

APR.–MAY➢ The **World Series of Poker** draws crowds to the Binion's Horseshoe casino to watch the poker faces of players from around the world. This monthlong tournament culminates in a four-day final round, in which nearly 300 players each invest $10,000 in hopes of winning first prize: $1 million. ☎ 702/366–7397.

EARLY MAY➢ Over-50s gather at the Desert Inn for the four-day **Senior Classic golf tournament,** started in 1985. ☎ 702/382–6616.

MAY OR JUNE➢ **Helldorado Days and Rodeo** celebrates the Old West with parades, contests, western costumes, and a championship rodeo at the Thomas and Mack Center. ☎ 702/870–1221.

AUTUMN

MID-SEPT.➢ **Football season** begins at the University of Nevada, Las Vegas. ☎ 702/895–3900.

MID-OCT.➢ The **Las Vegas Invitational golf tournament,** a five-day event, is played on three courses, with television coverage. ☎ 702/382–6616.

MID-OCT.➢ The **U.S. Triathlon Series national championships and world invitational** draws top competitors from around the globe. ☎ 702/731–2115.

2 Playing the Games

OVER THE PAST 50 YEARS, the name Las Vegas has become synonymous with gambling. Nine out of 10 visitors gamble while they're in town. It would be practically perverse to visit Las Vegas and *not* gamble. But while unreasonable expectations can lead to disappointment—or worse, as in the loss of a lot of money—the key to having a good time is to approach the casinos with the idea that, contrary to popular opinion, you *can* win or, at the very least, get much more than your money's worth of playing time. Your success depends less on luck and more on being familiar with the rules of the games, being aware of the concepts *behind* the games, and being conversant with the strategies that enable you to play not only with confidence but also with a fair shot at winning.

CASINO STRATEGY

The House Advantage

The first important concept to understand about gambling in Las Vegas is that the odds for all the games provide an advantage for the casino ("house"), generally known, appropriately enough, as the "house advantage" (or "edge" or "vigorish"). The casino is a business, and wagering is its product. Since the house establishes the rules, procedures, and payoffs on every game, it builds an automatic commission into every bet to ensure a profit margin.

Here's how it works. Let's pretend that I'm the house and you're the customer and we're betting on a series of coin flips. The deal that I make with you is that every time the coin lands heads up, I win and you pay me a dollar. Every time the coin lands tails up, you win—but I only pay you 90¢. The law of averages maintains that out of every hundred coin tosses, heads will win 50 times and tails will win the other 50. If I take a dime out of every one of your winning payoffs, the longer you play, the more dimes will wind up in my pocket. If you started with a $50 bankroll, after 1,000 tosses, *even if you win half of them,* you'd be busted out. (Since it requires two trials—win one, lose one—to get dinged for the 10¢ "commission," your "negative expectation," or house edge, in this example is 5%.)

The second important gambling concept is known as "fluctuation" (or "variance"). In plain English, we're talking about "luck." Looking at our coin-toss game through the lens of averages, if you and I flip a coin 1,000 times, it's reasonable to expect that the coin will land heads up and tails up close to 500 times each. However, if we flip the coin only 10 times, it's conceivable that the coin could land heads up only twice or as many as eight times. Now let's say that we made the same betting deal as above but we limited the number of tosses to 10. This would largely eliminate your 5% disadvantage and leave it up to "the luck of the toss" or, in other words, the fluctuation. Thus, a short-term fluctuation in the law of averages eliminates the long-term threat of the negative expectation.

How do these concepts—the house advantage and negative expectation, as well as short-term fluctuation—apply to the choices that you make as a casino customer? Your decisions, based on these concepts, will determine not only what you play, but also how you play, how long you play, and, ultimately, how well you play.

Luck Versus the Edge

The average "bankroll" (cash carried for the sole purpose of gambling) of a Las Vegas visitor who plans to spend some time in the casino is roughly $500. This is a crucial statistic. The amount of your bankroll and your preferred style of "action" (how you risk your bankroll) define your relationship to luck and the house edge.

Basically, the parameters of gambling action are fast and slow. Some people, though they're in the minority, like their action fast and loose and high risk; these are true "gamblers," in the old-fashioned sense of the word. The extreme version of this type of action is to take the whole $500 bankroll and lay it down on a single play—say, red or black on the roulette table. The odds are not quite even. The green 0 and 00 on the roulette table give the house an advantage of 5.26% (*see* Roulette, *below*). Still, even though the odds are less than fair, the immediate result will be the same: double or nothing.

Making one play eliminates both the law of averages and the long-term threat of the house advantage; here you rely solely on the luck of the draw. If you want to go on a roller-coaster ride of luck, with a minute or so of adrenaline-pumping, heart-pounding excitement, lay it all down at once. In a matter of moments, you'll either be rich or broke.

A less extreme version of this wild ride is to break your bankroll into two units, and make two bets. Here you can either double your money, lose it all, or break even. Similarly, if you separate your $500 bankroll into five units and make five bets, or 10 units and make 10 bets, your ride lasts a little longer and your outcome is a little less black and white: You can double, bust out, break even, or come out somewhat ahead or behind. Still, the cumulative danger of the house advantage barely comes into play.

Luck can supersede the house advantage, but only in the short run. And though luck accounts for winners big and small, such as the California nurse who lines up four Megabucks symbols on the $3 pay line for $9 million or the $2 dice shooter who parlays a hot hand into a couple of hundred bucks, the lack of luck can obliterate a bankroll faster than a crooked S&L.

Besides, most people who come to Las Vegas like to gamble for as long as they can without running out of money. These people take their $500 bankrolls and split them into 100 units to make $5 bets, 250 units for $2 bets, 500 units for $1 bets, or even 2,000 units for 25¢ bets. This guarantees plenty of time for the law of averages to even out the fluctuations. On the other hand, it puts the house advantage and the long-term negative expectation right back into the game.

So how do you play as long as you like without the certainty of the house advantage grinding your bankroll into dust?

The Good Bets

The first part of any viable casino strategy is to risk the most money on wagers that present the lowest edge for the house. Blackjack, craps, video poker, and baccarat are the most advantageous to the bettor in this regard (all the games are described in detail below). The two types of bets at baccarat have a house advantage of a little more than 1%. The basic line bets at craps, if backed up with full odds, can be as low as ½%. Blackjack and video poker, at times, can not only put you even with the house (a true 50-50 proposition), but actually give you a slight long-term advantage.

How can a casino possibly provide you with a 50-50 or even a positive expectation at some of its games? First, because a vast number of suckers make the bad bets (those with a house advantage of 5%–35%, such as roulette, keno, and slots) day in and day out. Second, because the casino knows that very few people are aware of the opportunities to beat the odds. Third, because it takes skill—requiring study and practice—to be in a position to exploit these opportunities the casino presents. However, a mere hour or two spent learning strategies for the beatable games will put you light years ahead of the vast majority of visitors who give the gambling industry an average 12%–15% profit margin.

Comps, Clubs, and Coupons

Not only can you even out the odds to a certain extent, but you can also take advantage of the various attractive incentives casinos offer so that the suckers will stay and play—and, in the long run, lose, whether because of the house advantage or basic ignorance. These available, profitable, and somewhat prestigious incentives are known as "comps" (short for complimentaries) or freebies. The most common comps are free parking in downtown parking structures (all you have to do is walk into the casino and validate your ticket at the cashier window) and free cocktails (all you have to do is play at any table or machine). Other comps range from a "line pass" (the right to proceed directly into a showroom or restaurant without having to wait in line) all the way to a penthouse suite complete with private swimming pool, butler and chef, and round-trip airfare from anywhere in the world. It all depends on how much you're willing to risk: Comps are calculated by multiplying your average bet by the amount of time you play by the house advantage.

Say, for example, you play at a $25-a-hand blackjack table for eight hours. The casino expects you to participate in 60 hands an hour and lose at a rate of 2% (what the casino calculates as its average advantage). Sixty hands an hour times $25 a hand times eight hours times 2% equals $240. Of that anticipated profit, the house is prepared to return 30%–40% to you in complimentaries in order to "reward" you for your action. Thus, under the described circumstances, you'll qualify for $72–$96 worth of comps, whether you win, lose, or break even.

To be eligible for comps, you have to get "rated" as a player. When you sit down to play, have the dealer call over the pit boss—the person who supervises the action on the gaming tables—and tell him that you'd like to have your play rated. The pit boss will fill out a rating card with your name, average bet, and length of play. These data are input into the marketing department computer; based on your "comp equivalency" (for example, the $72–$96 you've qualified for), you'll be provided with your free food or room or perks. The kings of comps are the "high rollers," those willing to risk a lot of money at high-stakes games.

Slot clubs are another good way to reconcile the house advantage with playing for as long as you like. These clubs, introduced in the late 1980s to give slot players some high-roller status, are similar to frequent-flier programs offered by the airlines. It costs nothing to sign up for slot clubs and the benefits can be substantial. When you become a member, you're given a plastic credit card that you insert into the slot machine you're using; the card tracks your play and you receive points based on the amount of money you risk. Slot-club points can be redeemed for free gifts, food, rooms, invitations to special parties and slot tournaments, VIP status, and even cash. You can join slot clubs at as many casinos as you like, then play at the places that offer the best perks.

Finally, the best bet in any casino is one that is accompanied by a gambling coupon. These are most often found in hotel "funbooks," small coupon booklets given out free for the asking at casino "welcome centers"; generally all you need is a hotel room key and an out-of-state ID (this prevents locals from taking advantage of the valuable promotions). Most funbooks contain coupons that return 7 to 5, 3 to 2, even 2 to 1 on even-money wagers.

Playing with coupons gives you a decided advantage over the house. In our coin-toss example, you'd wager a dollar of your own and a coupon for another dollar. If you won, I'd pay you $2 (for a return of $3). That extra dollar, though it might not seem like much, would pay my commission on 10 additional coin tosses. Furthermore, since most of the major hotel-casinos distribute funbooks free, you and a partner can collect a dozen of them and then go on a "coupon run." You make even-money bets backed up by coupons, touring a number of casinos while you're at it. Done properly, you could conceivably fill up an entire Las Vegas visit making positive plays with casino coupons.

THE GAMES

The following sections explain the rules, the plays, the odds, and the strategies for the most popular games in Las Vegas, Reno, and Lake Tahoe casinos. When you've decided on the kind of action you wish to pursue, you can choose a game that best suits your style. Then, if you take the time to learn the basics and fine points thoroughly, you'll be adequately prepared to play with as much of an edge as the game, combined with comps and coupons if possible, provides. In the meantime, good short-term fluctuation!

Blackjack

Blackjack is the most popular table game in the casino. It's easy to learn and fun to play. It involves skill, and therefore presents varying levels of challenge, from beginner to post-graduate. Blackjack also boasts one of the lowest house advantages. Furthermore, it's the game of choice when it comes to qualifying for comps: You can play for as long as you like, stand a real chance of breaking even or winning, *and* be treated like visiting royalty while you're at it.

Because blackjack is the only table game in the casino in which players can gain a long-term advantage over the house, it is the only table game in the casino (other than poker) that can be played professionally. And because blackjack can be played professionally, it is the most written-about and discussed casino game. Dozens of how-to books, trade journals, magazines, newsletters, computer programs, videos, theses, and novels are available on every aspect of blackjack, from how to add to 21 to how to play against a variety of shuffles, from when to stand or hit to the Level-Two Zen Count. Blackjack pros can spend hours debating whether the two-deck game at the Las Vegas Hilton has a starting house edge of .03 or .0275 due to the doubling-down-after-splitting option, or if the Hi-Opt II count system's 88% betting efficiency correlation makes it stronger than the unbalanced count's perfect insurance indicator. Of course, training someone to play black-

Blackjack Table

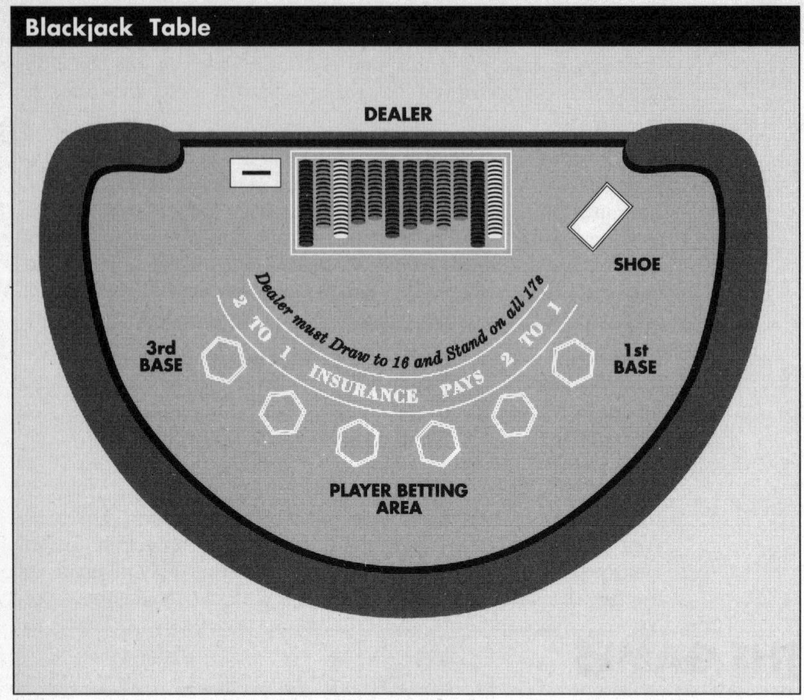

jack professionally is beyond the scope of this guide. Contact the Gambler's Book Club (☎ 702/382-7555) for a catalogue of gambling books, software, and videotape, including the largest selection on blackjack around.

The Rules

Basically, here's how it works: You play blackjack against a dealer, and whichever of you comes closest to a card total of 21 is the winner. Number cards are worth their face value, picture cards are worth 10, and aces are worth either 1 or 11. (Hands with aces in them are known as "soft" hands. Always count the ace first as an 11; if you also have a 10, your total will be 21, not 11.) If the dealer has a 17 and you have a 16, you lose. If you have an 18 against a dealer's 17, you win (even money). If both you and the dealer have a 17, it's a tie (or "push") and no money changes hands. If you go over a total of 21 (or "bust"), you lose immediately, even if the dealer also busts later in the hand. If your first two cards add up to 21 (a "natural"), you're paid 3 to 2. However, if the dealer also has a natural, it's a push. A natural beats a total of 21 achieved with more than two cards.

You're dealt two cards, either face down or face up, depending on the custom of the particular casino. The dealer also gives herself two cards, one face down and one face up (except in double-exposure blackjack, where both the dealer's cards are visible). Depending on your first two cards and the dealer's up card, you can:

stand, or refuse to take another card.

hit, or take as many cards as you need until you stand or bust.

double down, or double your bet and take one card.

split a like pair; if you're dealt two 8s, for example, you can double your bet and play the 8s as if they're two hands.

buy insurance if the dealer is showing an ace. Here you're wagering half your initial bet that the dealer does have a natural; if so, you lose your initial bet, but are paid 2 to 1 on the insurance (which means the whole thing is a push).

surrender half your initial bet if you're holding a bad hand (known as a "stiff") such as a 15 or 16 against a high-up card like a 9 or 10.

Buying In and Playing 21

First you must select a table to play at. A small sign in the left-hand corner of the "layout" (the diagram printed on the felt tabletop; *see* the Blackjack Table illustration) indicates the table minimum and maximum, and often displays the house rules. You can be sure that the $2-minimum tables will be packed, the $5-minimum tables will be crowded, and the $25 tables will have some empty seats. Look carefully before you sit, so as to avoid the embarrassment of parking yourself at a $25 table with $1 chips.

There are generally six or seven betting circles (or squares) on a blackjack layout. When you find an empty space at a table with your chosen minimum, you can join a game in progress between hands. Sometimes you'll have to squeeze in and the other players might not be too anxious to make room for you for one reason or another (almost every one of them superstitious). The dealer should help make room for you. If everybody is particularly unfriendly, feel free to leave at any time, but it's to your advantage to spend as much time as possible playing at a crowded table, especially if your intention is to be rated for comps. The more crowded the table, the fewer hands will be played every hour, which reduces your risk. If everybody makes plenty of room for you to be comfortable and the dealer is friendly, you've got it made for hours.

Once you're settled, it's time to "buy in" (convert your cash to casino chips). Place your money on the layout between the betting circles or in the insurance space. If you lay cash *inside* the betting area, the dealer will say something like, "Money plays," and you might wind up betting your whole buy-in amount on the next hand! The dealer should exchange your cash for chips and deposit the bills in the drop slot, using a small plastic "pusher."

Now you can place your wager in the betting circle. You're dealt your two cards. If they're face down, you can pick them up, with one hand, and hold them. If they're face up, don't touch them. If you have a natural, turn them over and the dealer will pay you immediately and take your cards. Otherwise, everyone plays out his or her hand one at a time, from the right side of the table ("first base") to the left ("third base"). If you opt to stand, slide your two cards under your chips, then sit back and relax. If you want to hit, scratch the cards on the layout (seeing this done once will show you how). When you're ready to stand, slide the cards under the chips; if you bust, turn the cards over and the dealer will collect them and your bet. When everyone else has played, the dealer will turn over her down (or "hole") card and play out her hand, then pay off all the players according to whether they won, lost, or pushed. Then the whole process will start all over again.

Playing blackjack is not only knowing the rules and etiquette. It's also knowing *how* to play. Many people devote a great deal of time to learning strategies, two of which are discussed in the sections that follow. However, if you don't have the time, energy, or inclination to get seriously involved, the following basic rules, which cover more than half the situations you'll face, should allow you to play the game with a modicum of skill and a paucity of humiliation:

1) When your hand is a stiff (a total of 12, 13, 14, 15, or 16) and the dealer shows a 2, 3, 4, 5, or 6, always stand.

2) When your hand is a stiff and the dealer shows a 7, 8, 9, 10, or ace, always hit.

3) When you hold 17, 18, 19, or 20, always stand.

4) When you hold a 10 or 11 and the dealer shows a 2, 3, 4, 5, 6, 7, 8, or 9, always double down.

5) When you hold a pair of aces or a pair of 8s, always split.

6) Never buy insurance.

Basic Strategy

Available to anyone with an interest in the game, a system called "basic strategy" consists of a large set of exact decisions for optimum play at blackjack based on a player's hand versus the dealer's up card. These decisions have been developed via computer simulations of hundreds of millions of blackjack hands; they're not open to debate. You must spend several hours memorizing the basic-strategy chart and then spend another several hours practicing basic strategy with playing cards. And then you must make the correct play on every hand, regardless of your "hunches" or what the person sitting next to you might recommend.

The accompanying Basic Strategy Chart lists all the possible combinations of blackjack hands against the dealer's up card. Here's how to read it. Say you're dealt a 7 and a 5 and the dealer is showing a 9. First look at the left-hand column, under YOUR HAND for the total, 12. Then follow the line across to the column under the number 9. The "H" stands for hit. So you would hit this hand. Now, suppose you're then dealt a 4. Look back at the left-hand column for the new total, 16. Then follow it across to the number-9 column again. Again you have to hit. (Pray for a 5 or less, your only way out of this worst-case blackjack scenario. Most of the time you'll bust.)

Say you're dealt, on the next hand, an ace and a 4 against the dealer's 3; counting the ace as 11, you have a total of 15. Find the A,4 listing in the YOUR HAND column and follow it across to the dealer's 3. According to basic strategy, you should hit. If you get a 6, you've got 21, not 12. If you get a 5, you've got 20; of course you should stand. (If you're in doubt, look up the A,9 listing.) If you get a 9, however, you'll have to count the ace as a 1, for a total of 14; otherwise you'd bust with 23. Now you look up the proper play for 14 against a dealer's 3; you'd stand.

Finally, suppose you're dealt a pair of 7s against a dealer's 7. The chart tells you to split the pair. Here you place both cards face up near your initial bet (don't worry about the exact position; no matter how close you place them, the dealer will *always* rearrange them slightly) and then place a second bet equivalent to the first. Then you play each 7 as its own hand. What if you're dealt a 4 on your first 7 for a total of 11? Some casinos will let you double down after splitting. Ask the dealer if she doesn't volunteer this information. What if you're dealt another 7? Again, some casinos will let you split the new pair and play out three hands.

H = Hit
S = Stand
D = Double
SP = Split

Blackjack Basic Strategy Chart

Your Hand	Dealer's up card 2	3	4	5	6	7	8	9	10	A
5	H	H	H	H	H	H	H	H	H	H
6	H	H	H	H	H	H	H	H	H	H
7	H	H	H	H	H	H	H	H	H	H
8	H	H	H	H	H	H	H	H	H	H
9	D	D	D	D	D	H	H	H	H	H
10	D	D	D	D	D	D	D	D	H	H
11	D	D	D	D	D	D	D	D	D	D
12	H	H	S	S	S	H	H	H	H	H
13	S	S	S	S	S	H	H	H	H	H
14	S	S	S	S	S	H	H	H	H	H
15	S	S	S	S	S	H	H	H	H	H
16	S	S	S	S	S	H	H	H	H	H
17	S	S	S	S	S	S	S	S	S	S
18	S	S	S	S	S	S	S	S	S	S
19	S	S	S	S	S	S	S	S	S	S
20	S	S	S	S	S	S	S	S	S	S
21	S	S	S	S	S	S	S	S	S	S
A,2	H	H	D	D	D	H	H	H	H	H
A,3	H	H	D	D	D	H	H	H	H	H
A,4	H	H	D	D	D	H	H	H	H	H
A,5	H	H	D	D	D	H	H	H	H	H
A,6	D	D	D	D	D	H	H	H	H	H
A,7	S	D	D	D	D	S	S	H	H	H
A,8	S	S	S	S	S	S	S	S	S	S
A,9	S	S	S	S	S	S	S	S	S	S
A,A	SP	SP	SP	SP	SP	SP	SP	SP	SP	SP
2,2	H	SP	SP	SP	SP	SP	H	H	H	H
3,3	H	H	SP	SP	SP	SP	H	H	H	H
4,4	H	H	H	D	D	H	H	H	H	H
5,5	D	D	D	D	D	D	D	D	D	H
6,6	SP	SP	SP	SP	SP	H	H	H	H	H
7,7	SP	SP	SP	SP	SP	SP	H	H	H	H
8,8	SP	SP	SP	SP	SP	SP	SP	SP	SP	SP
9,9	SP	SP	SP	SP	SP	S	SP	SP	S	S
10,10	S	S	S	S	S	S	S	S	S	S

Rules vary from house to house and city to city. The chart printed here holds for common Las Vegas rules. In Reno, you can only double down on a 10 or 11. In Las Vegas, some places allow you to surrender; some don't. At some places, dealers stand on soft 17; some places they don't. Basic strategy can get fairly advanced, and there are times when certain variations apply. The best place to play high-level basic-strategy blackjack is at the Las Vegas Club downtown. Here you can double down on any 2, 3, or 4 cards; surrender; and split and resplit pairs, including aces. If you're dealt a six-card "charlie," you win automatically. You might alter your strategy for certain low-card plays and double-down or surrender situations at the Las Vegas Club, but even without the fine tuning, this is the best multideck game in town.

Card Counting

Card counting is an exacting technique for tracking the cards that have been played during a blackjack round and thereby determining whether the cards remaining to be played are favorable or unfavorable to the player. Card counters designate different plus or minus values for cards that are removed from the deck in play; based on the count, players can make better-informed decisions about playing and betting strategies. *Blackjack Count Analyzer,* a computer program written by the inimitable blackjack guru Stanford Wong, provides a hands-on and interactive training course in card counting for use on IBM or compatible computers. It's available from Huntington Press (5280 S. Valley View Blvd., Suite B-3F, Las Vegas, NV 89118, ☎ 702/597–1884).

Roulette

Roulette is a casino game that utilizes a perfectly balanced wheel with 38 numbers (0, 00, and 1 through 36), a small white ball, a large layout with 11 different betting options (*see* the Roulette Table illustration), and special "wheel chips." The layout organizes 11 different bets into six "inside bets" (the single numbers, or those closest to the dealer) and five "outside bets" (the grouped bets, or those closest to the players).

The dealer stands between the layout and the roulette wheel, and chairs for five or six players are set around the roulette table. At crowded times, players also stand among and behind those seated, reaching over and around to place their bets. *Always* keep a close eye on your chips at these times to guard against "rack thieves," clever sleight-of-hand artists who can steal from your pile of chips right in front of your nose.

To buy in, place your cash on the layout near the wheel. Inform the dealer of the denomination of the individual unit you intend to play (usually 25¢ or $1, but it can go up as high as $500). Know the table limits (displayed on a sign in the dealer area); don't ask for a 25¢ denomination if the minimum is $1. The dealer gives you a stack of wheel chips of a different color from those of all the other players, and places a chip marker atop one of your wheel chips on the rim of the wheel to identify its denomination. Note that you must cash in your wheel chips at the roulette table before you leave the game. Only the dealer can verify how much they're worth.

The dealer spins the wheel clockwise and the ball counterclockwise. When the ball slows, the dealer announces, "No more bets." The ball drops from the "back track" to the "bottom track," caroming off built-in brass barriers and bouncing in and out of the different cups in the wheel before settling into the cup of the winning number. Then the dealer,

Roulette Table

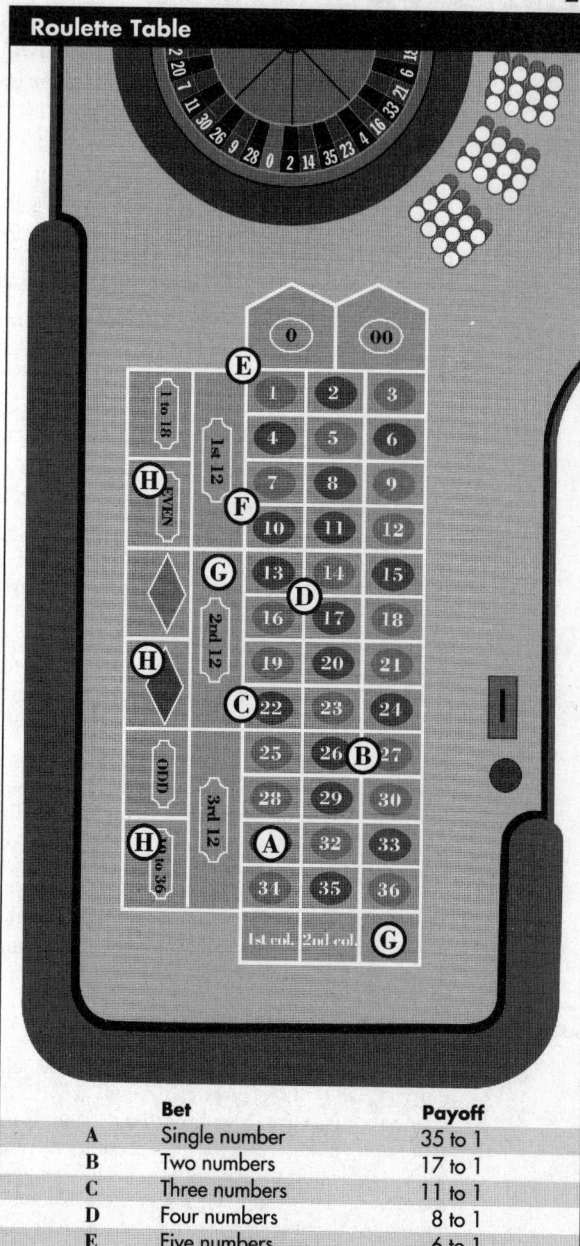

	Bet	Payoff
A	Single number	35 to 1
B	Two numbers	17 to 1
C	Three numbers	11 to 1
D	Four numbers	8 to 1
E	Five numbers	6 to 1
F	Six numbers	5 to 1
G	12 numbers (column)	2 to 1
G	1st 12, 2nd 12, 3rd 12	2 to 1
H	1-18 or 19-36	1 to 1
H	Odd or Even	1 to 1
H	Red or black	1 to 1

who knows the winning bettors by the color of their wheel chips, places a marker on the number and scoops all the losing chips into her corner. Depending on how crowded the game is, the casino can count on roughly 50 spins of the wheel per hour.

How to Place Inside Bets

You can lay any number of chips (depending on the table limits) on a single number, 1 through 36 or 0 or 00. If the number hits, your payoff is 35 to 1, for a return of $36. You could, conceivably, place a $1 chip on all 38 numbers, but the return of $36 would leave you $2 short, which divides out to 5.26%, the house advantage.

If you place a chip on the line between two numbers and one of those numbers hits, you're paid 17 to 1 for a return of $18 (again, $2 short of the true odds).

Betting on three numbers returns 11 to 1, four numbers returns 8 to 1, five numbers pays 6 to 1 (this is the worst bet at roulette, with a 7.89% disadvantage), and six numbers pays 5 to 1.

How to Place Outside Bets

Lay a chip on one of three "columns" at the lower end of the layout next to numbers 34, 35, and 36; this pays 2 to 1. A bet placed in the first 12, second 12, or third 12 boxes also pays 2 to 1. A bet on red or black, odd or even, and 1 through 18 or 19 through 36 pays off at even money, 1 to 1. If you think you can bet on red *and* black, or odd *and* even, in order to play roulette and drink for free all night, think again. The green 0 or 00, which fall outside these two basic categories, will come up on average once every 19 spins of the wheel.

The house advantage of 5.26% on every roulette bet (except, as noted, the five-number bet) is five times as much as the best bets at craps and five times less than the average bet at keno. Only one roulette game in Las Vegas features the European-style wheel, which has a single green 0. This slashes the house edge in half to 2.7%. The only permanent roulette wheel in Las Vegas with a single 0 is found in the high-roller Monte Carlo pit at the MGM Grand (high minimum bets). Occasionally, places like the Mirage and Caesars will offer single-0 roulette to high rollers who want to play, usually with a $25 minimum.

Craps

Craps is a dice game played at a large rectangular table with rounded corners. Up to 12 players can crowd around the table, all standing. The layout (*see* the Crap Table illustration) is mounted at the bottom of a surrounding "rail," which prevents the dice from being thrown off the table and provides an opposite wall against which to bounce the dice. It's important, when you're the "shooter," to roll the dice hard enough so that they bounce off the end wall of the table; this ensures a random bounce and shows that you're not trying to control the dice with a "soft roll." The layout grid is duplicated on the right and left side of the table, so players on either end will see exactly the same design. The top of the railing is grooved to hold the bettors' chips; as always, keep a close eye on your stash to prevent victimization by rail thieves.

It can require up to four pit personnel to run an action-packed, fast-paced game of craps. Two dealers handle the bets made on either side of the layout. A "stickman" wields the long wooden "stick," curved at one end, which is used to move the dice around the table; the stickman also calls the number that's rolled and books the proposition bets

Crap Table

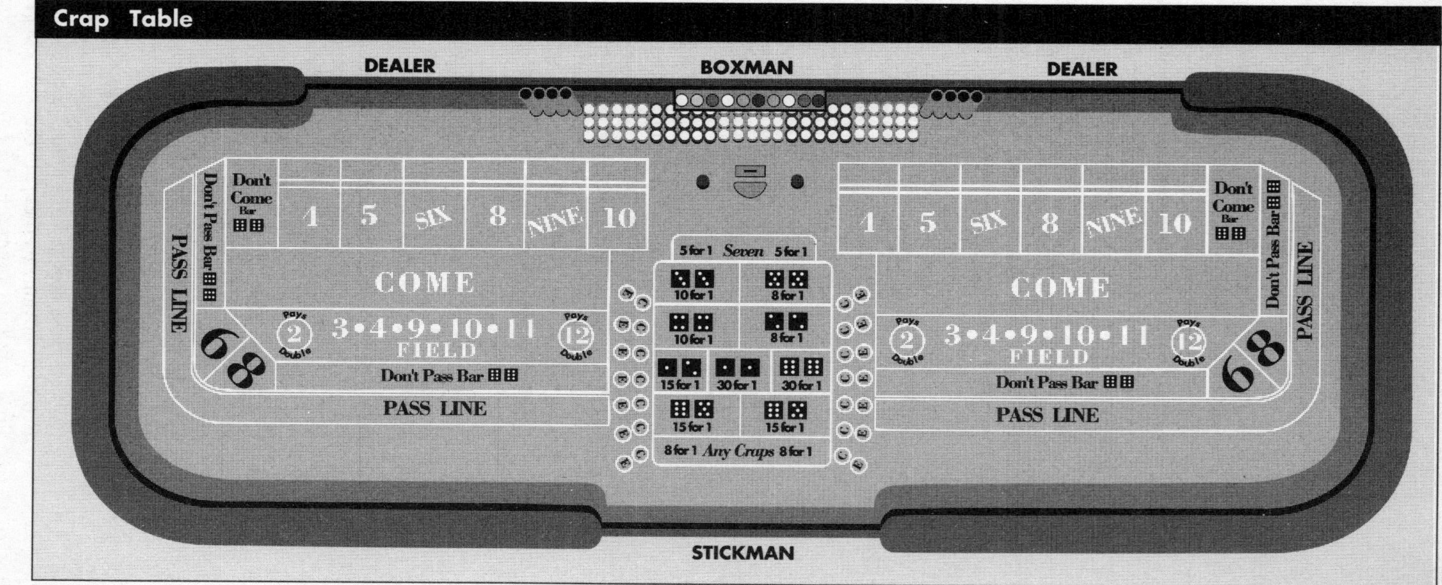
DEALER
BOXMAN
DEALER
PASS LINE
Don't Pass Bar
Don't Come Bar
4
5
SIX
8
NINE
10
COME
Pays 2 Double
3•4•9•10•11
FIELD
Pays 12 Double
6 8
Don't Pass Bar
PASS LINE
5 for 1 Seven 5 for 1
10 for 1
8 for 1
10 for 1
8 for 1
15 for 1
30 for 1
30 for 1
15 for 1
15 for 1
8 for 1 Any Craps 8 for 1
STICKMAN

(*see below*) made in the middle of the layout. The "boxman" sits between the two dealers and oversees the game; he settles any disputes about rules, payoffs, mistakes, etc. A slow crap game is often handled by a single employee, who performs stick, box, and dealer functions. A portable end wall can be placed near the middle of the table so that only one side is functional.

To play, just join in, standing at the table wherever you can find an open space. You can start betting casino chips immediately, but you have to wait your turn to be the shooter. The dice move around the table in a clockwise fashion: The person to your right shoots before you, the one to the left after (the stickman will give you the dice at the appropriate time).

Playing craps is fairly straightforward; it's betting on it that's complicated. The basic concepts are as follows: If, the first time the shooter rolls the dice, he or she turns up a 7 or 11, that's called a "natural"—an automatic win. If a 2, 3, or 12 come up on the first throw (called the "come-out roll"), that's termed "craps"—an automatic lose. Each of the numbers 4, 5, 6, 8, 9, or 10 on a first roll is known as a "point": The shooter has to keep rolling the dice until that number comes up again. If a 7 turns up before the number does, that's another loser. Then, when either the point (the original number thrown) or a 7 is rolled, this is known as a "decision"; one is made on average every 3.3 rolls.

But "winning" and "losing" rolls of the dice are entirely relative in this game, because there are two ways you can bet at craps: "for" the shooter or "against" the shooter. Betting for means that the shooter will "make his point" (win). Betting against means that the shooter will "seven out" (lose). (Either way, you're actually betting against the house, which books all wagers.) If you're betting "for" on the come-out, you'd place your chips on the layout's "pass line." If a 7 or 11 is rolled, you win even money. If a 2, 3, or 12 (craps) is rolled, you lose your bet. If you're betting "against" on the come-out, you place your chips in the "don't pass bar." A 7 or 11 loses, a 2, 3, or 12 wins. A shooter can bet for or against himself or herself, as well as for or against the other players.

At the same time, you can make roughly two dozen wagers on any single roll of the dice. Besides the "for" and "against" (pass and don't pass) bets, you can also make the following wagers at craps:

Come/Don't Come: After a pass-line point is established, the come bet renders every subsequent roll of the dice a come-out roll. When you place your chips in the come box, it's the same as a pass line bet. If a 7 or 11 is rolled, you win even money. If a 2, 3, or 12 is rolled, you've crapped out. If a 4, 5, 6, 8, 9, or 10 is rolled, it becomes another point, and the dealer moves your chips into the corresponding box on the layout. Now if that number comes up before the 7, you win the come bet. The opposite is true for the don't come box: 7 and 11 lose, 2, 3, and 12 win, and if the 7 is rolled before the point, you win.

Odds: The house allows you to take odds on whether or not the shooter will make his or her point, once it's established. Since the house pays off these bets at "true odds," rather than withholding a unit or two to its advantage, these are the best bets in a crap game. Odds on the 6 and 8 pay off at 6 to 5, on the 5 and 9 at 3 to 2, and on the 4 and 10 at 2 to 1. "Back up" your pass line bets with single, double, triple, or up to 10 times odds (depending on the house rules) by placing your chips behind your line bet. For example, if the point is a 10 and your bet is $5, backing up your bet with single odds ($5) returns

$25 ($5 + $5 on the line and $5 + $10 single odds); taking triple odds returns $55 ($5 + $5 on the line and $15 + $30). To take the odds on a come bet, toss your chips onto the layout and tell the dealer, "Odds on the come."

Place: Instead of waiting for a point to be rolled on the come, you can simply lay your bet on the point of your choice. Drop your chips on the layout in front of you and tell the dealer to "place" your number. The dealer puts your chips on the point; when it's rolled you win. The 6 and 8 pay 7 to 6, the 5 and 9 pay 7 to 5, and the 4 and 10 pay 9 to 5. In other words, if you place $6 on the 8 and it hits, you win $7. Place bets don't pay off at true odds, which is how the house maintains its edge (1.51% on the 6 and 8, 4% on the 5 and 9, and 6.66% on the 4 and 10). You can "call your place bet down" (take it back) at any time; otherwise the place bet will "stay up" until a 7 is rolled.

Buy: Buy bets are the same as place bets, except that the house pays off at true odds and takes a 5% commission if they win. Since buy bets have an edge of 4.7%, you should only buy the 4 and 10 (rather than place them at a 6.6% disadvantage).

Big 6 and 8: Place your own chips in these boxes; you win if the 6 or 8 comes up, and lose on the 7. Since they pay off at even money, rather than true odds, the house edge is large—9.09%.

Field: This is a "one-roll" bet (a bet that's decided with each roll). Numbers 3, 4, 9, 10, and 11 pay even money, while 2 and 12 pay 2 to 1 (the 12 or "boxcars" pays 3 to 1 in Reno). The house edge on the field is 5.5%.

Proposition Bets: All the proposition bets are booked in the grid in the middle of the layout by the stickman. "Hardways" means a pair of numbers on the dice (two 3s for a hardways 6, two 4s for a hardways 8, etc.). A hardways 4 or 10 pays 7 to 1 (11.1% edge), and 6 or 8 pays 9 to 1 (9.09%). If a 7 or the 4, 6, 8, or 10 is rolled the "easy way," hardways bets lose. "Any seven" is a one-roll wager on the 7, paying 4 to 1 with a whopping 16.6% edge. "Yo'leven" is also a one-roll wonder paying 14 to 1 with a 16.6% edge. "Any craps" is a one-roll bet on the 2, 3, or 12, paying 7 to 1 (11.1%). Other bad proposition bets include the "horn" (one-roll bet on 2, 3, 11, or 12 separately; 16.6%), and "c and e" (craps or 11; 11.1%).

Note: The players place their own pass line, field, Big 6 and 8, and come line bets. Players must drop their chips on the table in front of the dealers and instruct them to make their place and buy bets, and to take or lay the odds on their come bets. Chips are tossed to the stickman, who makes the hardways, any craps, any seven, and c and e bets in the middle of the layout.

Baccarat

The most "glamorous" game in the casino, American baccarat (pronounced *bah*-kuh-rah) is a version of *chemin de fer,* popular in European gambling halls. The Italian word *baccara* means "zero"; this refers to the point value of 10s and picture cards. Most Las Vegas casinos like to surround baccarat with an aura of mystique: the game is played in a separate pit, supervised by personnel in tuxedos (including a "ladderman" who sits high up over the table); the game's ritual is somewhat esoteric; and the minimum bet is usually $20 to $25. Mini-baccarat is the same game but played in the main blackjack pit, sans tuxedos, ritual, and $20 minimums.

Up to 15 players can be seated around a baccarat table (six or seven at minibaccarat). The game is run by four pit personnel. Two dealers sit side by side in the middle of the table; they handle the winning and losing bets and keep track of each player's "commission" (explained below). The "caller" stands in the middle of the other side of the table and dictates the action. The ladderman supervises the game and acts as final judge if any disputes arise.

Baccarat is played with eight decks of cards dealt from a large "shoe" (or card holder). Each player is offered a turn at handling the shoe and dealing the cards. Two two-card hands are dealt, the "player" and the "bank" hands. The player who deals the cards is called the banker, though the house, of course, banks both hands. The players bet on which hand, player or banker, will come closest to adding up to 9 (a "natural"). The cards are totaled as follows: ace through 9 retain face value, while 10s and picture cards are worth zero. If you have a hand adding up to more than 10, the number 10 is subtracted from the total. For example, if one hand contains a 10 and a 4, the hand adds up to 4. If the other holds an ace and 6, it adds up to 7. If a hand has a 7 and 9, it adds up to 6.

Depending on the two hands, the caller either declares a winner and loser (if either hand actually adds up to 8 or 9), or calls for another card for the player hand (if it totals 1, 2, 3, 4, 5, or 10). The bank hand then either stands pat or draws a card, determined by a complex series of rules depending on what the player's total is and dictated by the caller. When one or the other hand is declared a winner, the dealers go into action to pay off the winning wagers, collect the losing wagers, and add up the commission (usually 5%) that the house collects on the bank hand. Both bets have a house advantage of slightly more than 1%.

The player-dealer (or banker) continues to hold the shoe as long as the bank hand wins. As soon as the player hand wins, the shoe moves counterclockwise around the table. Players are not required to deal; they can refuse the shoe and pass it to the next player. Most players bet on the bank hand when they deal, since they "represent" the bank, and to do otherwise would seem as if they were betting "against" themselves. This isn't really true, but it seems that way.

Making a bet at baccarat is very simple. All you have to do is place your money in either the bank, player, or tie box on the layout (*see* the Baccarat Table illustration), which appears directly in front of where you sit at the table. If you're betting that the bank hand will win, you put your chips in the bank box; bets for the player hand go in the player box. (Only real suckers bet on the tie.)

Because the caller dictates the action, the player responsibilities are minimal. It's not necessary to know any of the card-drawing rules, even if you're the banker. Playing baccarat is a simple matter of guessing whether the player or banker hand will come closest to 9, and deciding how much to bet on the outcome.

Keno

Craps, blackjack, baccarat, and roulette arrived in Nevada casinos from Europe, but an early version of keno was brought over in the mid-1800s from China, where this bingo-type game was popular. It was rapidly Americanized in Reno casinos as soon as gambling was legalized in the 1930s.

Baccarat Table

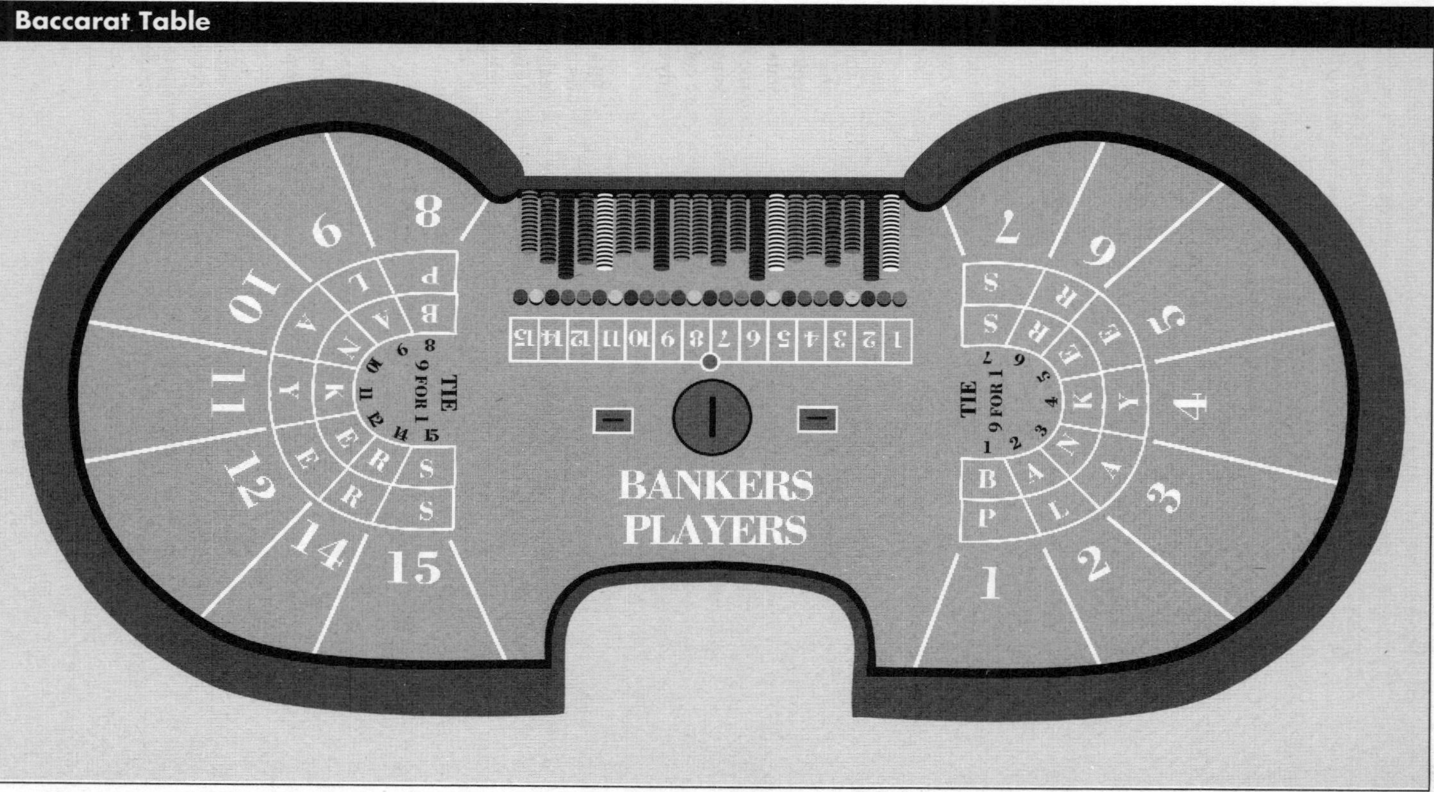

Keno games are played once every seven or eight minutes. You participate by using a black crayon (provided) to mark a "ticket," imprinted with 80 boxes numbered 1 through 80, with one to 15 "spots" or numbers of your choice. You decide how many spots you want to mark based on how much money you're willing to bet. Eighty numbered Ping-Pong balls lying in a round plastic or wire bowl (the "goose") are mixed by an electric fan; the forced air blows the balls into two elongated tubes that hold 10 balls each. The numbers on the balls are announced over a public address system to the players in the keno "lounge," and are displayed on keno "boards" that hang all around the casino—in the coffee shop, restaurants, and bars. If enough of your numbers match the board's numbers, you win an amount enumerated in the keno payoff booklet (*see* the Keno Payoffs chart).

You can bring your ticket to the central keno "counter," where a "writer" gives you a duplicate ticket and books your wager, or you can fill out a ticket at one of the casino's bars and restaurants, which are served by keno "runners," who collect tickets and bets and run them to the central counter where they are processed. The runners then deliver the duplicate tickets to the far-flung customers. After the game has been played and the winning numbers are displayed, the runner returns to check if there are any winners. If there are, the runner redeems the winning tickets for her customers—at which point it's customary to tip her.

There are six different types of keno tickets, the most common of which are the "straight," "replay," and "split" tickets. On a straight ticket, you mark off your chosen numbers—say, eight of them (remember, you're allowed to mark as many as 15). Looking at the payout chart, you can see that if four or fewer of your numbers match the called numbers, you lose. If five out of the eight match, you win $9 (on the $1 bet). If all eight match, you're an $18,000 winner. If you mark 15 spots and all 15 match (fat chance!), you win the big jackpot, usually $50,000.

A replay ticket uses the same numbers that you bet on with a previous ticket. Simply hand your bet (which doesn't have to be for the same amount) and the duplicate ticket from a prior game to the writer. A split ticket means that you're making two straight bets on a single ticket. Mark your numbers for the first straight bet and draw a line to separate them from the numbers for the second straight bet. Be sure to tell the writer that this is a split ticket.

Like the split ticket, "way" and "combination" wagers use one ticket to make what are often large and complex numbers of bets—a method of reducing paperwork. But these bets are really just a fancier and faster way to lose money at keno. If you want to try them out, most keno lounges have a booklet explaining the way and combination bets.

Keno has the highest house advantage in the casino, but this doesn't seem to have much of an effect on its popularity. Even though you can expect to lose 25¢ to 40¢ on every dollar you wager, many people like keno. Why? It's easy to play and slow-paced; you can sit in the lounge, drink, and visit with your fellow suckers. You can also maintain a level of action while eating or drinking in a restaurant or bar. But mostly it's a long-shot game, at which you can win $25,000, $50,000, and, at some places, even $100,000 by risking only a buck.

Video keno is played similarly to "live" keno. You drop your nickel or quarter into the machine, then use the attached "pen" to touch your numbers of choice. When you press the button that says "play" or "start," the machine illuminates the winning numbers, usually ac-

Keno Payoffs *(for a bet of $1)*

Numbers Marked	Winning Numbers	Pays $
1	1 number	3
2	2 numbers	12
3	2 numbers	1
	3 numbers	42
4	2 numbers	1
	3 numbers	4
	4 numbers	112
5	3 numbers	2
	4 numbers	20
	5 numbers	480
6	3 numbers	1
	4 numbers	4
	5 numbers	88
	6 numbers	1,480
7	4 numbers	2
	5 numbers	24
	6 numbers	360
	7 numbers	5,000
8	5 numbers	9
	6 numbers	92
	7 numbers	1,480
	8 numbers	18,000
9	5 numbers	4
	6 numbers	44
	7 numbers	300
	8 numbers	4,000
	9 numbers	20,000
10	5 numbers	2
	6 numbers	20
	7 numbers	132
	8 numbers	960
	9 numbers	3,800
	10 numbers	25,000

Numbers Marked	Winning Numbers	Pays $
11	5 numbers	1
	6 numbers	8
	7 numbers	72
	8 numbers	360
	9 numbers	1,800
	10 numbers	12,000
	11 numbers	28,000
12	6 numbers	5
	7 numbers	32
	8 numbers	240
	9 numbers	600
	10 numbers	1,480
	11 numbers	8,000
	12 numbers	36,000
13	6 numbers	1
	7 numbers	16
	8 numbers	80
	9 numbers	720
	10 numbers	4,000
	11 numbers	8,000
	12 numbers	20,000
	13 numbers	40,000
14	6 numbers	1
	7 numbers	10
	8 numbers	40
	9 numbers	300
	10 numbers	1,000
	11 numbers	3,200
	12 numbers	16,000
	13 numbers	24,000
	14 numbers	50,000
15	7 numbers	8
	8 numbers	28
	9 numbers	132
	10 numbers	300
	11 numbers	2,600
	12 numbers	8,000
	13 numbers	20,000
	14 numbers	32,000
	15 numbers	50,000

companied by a beep. If enough of your numbers match the machine's, you're paid off either in coins or credits.

Wheel of Fortune (Big Six)

Prize wheels are some of the oldest games of chance and some of the easiest to play and lose. Nevada-style big six is modeled after the old carnival wheels that attracted suckers on the midway. The standard wheel, usually 6 feet across, is divided into nine sections and 54 individual slots or stops. Fifty-two of the stops are marked by dollar denominations: 23 $1, 15 $2, eight $5, four $10, and two $20 stops. The other two stops are marked by a joker or the casino logo. A leather "flapper" mounted at the top of the wheel clicks as it hits the wood or metal pegs that separate each slot. When the wheel stops, the flapper falls between two pegs and indicates the winning number.

You lay your bet on a glass-covered table in front of the wheel. The layout display consists of the actual currency, which matches the numbers on the wheel (a Washington, Lincoln, Hamilton, Jackson, etc.). To play, you simply place a chip or cash atop the bill you think the flapper will stop at. The payoff is a multiple of the denomination: A $1 bet on the $1 bill pays a buck; a $1 bet on the $2 bill pays $2; a $5 bet on the $20 pays $100. The joker, casino logo, or other nonnumerical symbol on the wheel, however, pays 40 to 1: a successful $1 bet on one of these will get you back $40.

The house advantage starts at 11.1% on the $5 bet and rockets to 22.2% on the $20 bet and 24% on the joker. This isn't a game you'll want to play all night, or for more than a few spins. But the big six often draws a crowd. Even hardened gamblers like to stop and watch and listen to the wheel spin, with its hypnotic clicking of flapper against pegs, to see where it stops. They'd probably even lay down a buck or two, but they'd be too embarrassed in front of the dealer!

Slot Machines

Of all the games in the casino, slot machines are the most American: Around the turn of the century, Charlie Fey built the first mechanical slot in his San Francisco basement. Today, slot machines occupy more casino floor space and account for more gross casino winnings than all the table games combined. In fact, 1992 was the first year in history that machine profits surpassed those of table games on the tony Las Vegas Strip, and there's been no looking back since. Slots (along with video poker, keno, and blackjack machines) are the state of Nevada's number-one export product.

Slot-machine technology has exploded in the past 20 years, and now there are hundreds of different models, which accept everything from pennies to specially minted $500 tokens. The old "mechanical" or "electromechanical" slots—all more than 25 years old—can be found at some casinos. They feature small skinny reels with fruit symbols; usually accept only one coin; don't have any lighting or sound effects; have a single pay line; and pay back minor amounts. "Multipliers" are machines that accept more than one coin (usually three to five, maximum) and are mostly electronically operated—with flashing lights, bells, and whistles, and spin, credit, and cash-out buttons. Multipliers frequently have a variety of pay lines: three horizontal for example, or five horizontal and diagonal.

The major advance in the game, however, is the progressive jackpot. Banks of slots within a particular casino are connected by computer, and the jackpot total is displayed on a digital meter above the machines. Generally, the total increases by 5% of the wager. If you're playing a dollar machine, each time you pull the handle (or press the spin button), a nickel is added to the jackpot. Progressive slots in many casinos are also connected by modem throughout the state, and these jackpots often reach into the millions of dollars. The largest slot jackpot ever paid—roughly $9.3 million, won by a California nurse at Harrah's Reno in 1992—was on a Megabucks progressive, which is competitive with surrounding state lotteries. (One form of gambling that is specifically illegal in Nevada is the lottery.) Nevada Nickels and Quartermania are the lower-denomination versions of the statewide progressive.

To play, insert your penny, nickel, quarter, silver dollar, or dollar token into the slot at the far right edge of the machine. Pull the handle or press the spin button, then wait for the reels to spin and stop one by one, and for the machine to determine whether you're a winner (occasionally) or a loser (the rest of the time). It's pretty simple—but because there are so many different types of machines nowadays, be sure you know exactly how the one you're playing operates. If it's a progressive machine, you must play the maximum number of coins to qualify for the jackpot. For example, the maximum bet at Megabucks is $3. You can play $1; this limits the action to the first-coin pay line (usually the middle line across the reels). The same goes for $2 and the second-coin pay line (the top line). But to win the progressive total, the four Megabucks symbols must be lined up on the third-coin pay line (not surprisingly, the bottom line). Can you imagine lining up four Megabucks symbols on the third pay line with only a dollar or two played? Instead of winning $3 to $4 million, you wind up with bupkus!

The house advantage on slots varies widely from machine to machine, between 3% and 25%. Casinos that advertise a 97% payback are telling you that at least one of their slot machines has a house advantage of 3%. Which one? There's really no way of knowing. Generally, $1 machines pay back at a higher percentage than quarter or nickel machines. On the other hand, machines with smaller jackpots pay back more money more frequently, meaning that you'll be playing with more of your winnings. One good thing to keep in mind is this: In a recent nationwide study of slot-machine paybacks, a major gambling publication determined that downtown Las Vegas has the "loosest" slots.

One of the all-time great myths about slot machines is that they're "due" for a jackpot. Slots, like roulette, craps, keno, and the big six, are subject to the Law of Independent Trials, which means the odds are permanently and unalterably fixed. If the odds of lining up three sevens on a 25¢ slot machine have been set by the casino at 1 in 10,000, then those odds remain 1 in 10,000 whether the three 7s have been hit three times in a row or not hit for 90,000 plays. Don't waste a lot of time playing a machine that you suspect is "ready," and don't think if someone hits a jackpot on a particular machine only minutes after you've finished playing on it that it was "yours."

If you have the hots for slots, remember to join as many slot clubs as you can. You're paying a pretty hefty commission for your romance with cherries, lemons, and 7s, so it's more than worth it to be rewarded with comps and perks.

Video Poker

Like blackjack, video poker is a game of strategy and skill, and at select times on select machines, the player actually holds the advantage,

9/6 Video Poker Payout Schedule					
Royal Flush	250	500	750	1000	4000
Straight Flush	50	100	150	200	250
Four of a Kind	25	50	75	100	125
Full House	9	18	27	36	45
Flush	6	12	18	24	30
Three of a Kind	3	6	9	12	15
Two Pair	2	4	6	8	10
Jacks or Better	1	2	3	4	5

however slight, over the house. Unlike slot machines, you can determine the exact edge of video poker machines (in gambler's lingo, "handicap" the machine). Like slots, however, video poker machines are often tied into a progressive meter; when the jackpot total reaches high enough, you can beat the casino at its own game.

The variety of video poker machines is already large, and it's growing steadily larger. All of the different machines are played in similar fashion, but the strategies are different. This section deals only with straight-draw video poker.

You must first ascertain what denomination of coin a straight-draw video poker machine accepts. The only penny video poker machines in Nevada are at the Gold Spike Casino in downtown Las Vegas. Thousands of nickel, quarter, and dollar machines occupy casinos in Las Vegas, Reno, and Tahoe. Five-dollar machines are becoming more popular around the state, and $25 and $100 machines can be played at places like the Mirage, Golden Nugget, and Caesars Palace.

The schedule for the payback on winning hands is posted on the machine, usually above the screen. It lists the returns for a high pair (generally jacks or better), two pair, three of a kind, a flush, full house, straight flush, four of a kind, and royal flush, depending on the number of coins played—usually 1, 2, 3, 4, or 5. (The machine assumes you're familiar with poker and its terminology.) Look for machines that pay with a single coin played: one coin for "jacks or better" (meaning a pair of jacks, queens, kings, or aces; any other pair is a stiff), two coins for two pairs, three for three of a kind, six for a flush, nine for a full house, 50 for a straight flush, 100 for four of a kind, and 250 for a royal flush. This is known as a 9/6 machine: one that gives a nine-coin payback for the full house and a six-coin payback for the flush with one coin played (*see* the 9/6 Video Poker Payout Schedule chart). Some machines pay a unit for a pair of 10s, but get you back by returning only one unit for two pair. Other machines are known as 8/5 (8 for the full house, 5 for the flush), 7/5, and 6/5.

The return from a standard 9/6 straight-draw machine (with a 4,000-coin "flattop" or royal-flush jackpot) is 99.5%; you give up a half percent to the house. An 8/5 machine with a 4,000 flattop returns 97.3%. On 6/5 machines (such as you find in supermarkets, 7-Elevens, and Laundromats around the city), the figure drops to 95.1%, slightly better than roulette. The return from a 25¢, 8/5 progressive machine doesn't reach 100% until the meter hits $2,200—a rare sight. (You can figure nickel, $1, and $5 progressives by the $2,200 figure. A 100% payback on nickels is $440, on $1 is $8,800, and on $5 is $44,000.) Machines with varying paybacks are scattered throughout the casinos. In some you'll see an 8/5 machine right next to a 9/6, and someone will be blithely playing the 8/5 machine!

As with slot machines, it's always optimum to play the maximum number of coins in order to qualify for the jackpot. You insert five coins into the slot and press the "deal" button. Five cards appear on the screen—say, 5, J, Q, 5, 9. To hold the pair of 5s, you press the hold buttons under the first and fourth cards. The word "hold" appears underneath the two 5s. You then press the "draw" button (often the same button as "deal") and three new cards appear on the screen—say, 10, J, 5. You have three 5s; with five coins bet, the machine will give you 15 credits. Now you can press the "max bet" button: five units will be removed from your number of credits, and five new cards will appear on the screen. You repeat the hold and draw process; if you hit a winning hand, the proper payback will be added to your credits. Those who want coins rather than credit can hit the "cash out" button at any time. Some older machines don't have credit counters and automatically dispense coins for a winning hand.

Like blackjack, video poker has a basic strategy that's been formulated by the computer simulation of hundreds of millions of hands. The most effective way to learn it is with a video poker computer program that deals the cards on your screen, then tutors you in how to play each hand properly. The best program is *Stanford Wong's Video Poker,* available from Huntington Press (5280 S. Valley View Blvd., Suite B-3F, Las Vegas, NV 89118, ☎ 702/597–1884).

If you don't want to devote that much time to the study of video poker, memorizing these six rules will help you make the right decision for more than half the hands you'll be dealt:

If you're dealt a completely "stiff" hand (no like cards and no picture cards), draw five new cards.

2) If you're dealt a hand with no like cards but with one jack, queen, king, or ace, always hold on to the picture card; if you're dealt two different picture cards, hold both. But if you're dealt three different picture cards, only hold two (the two of the same suit, if that's an option).

3) If you're dealt a pair, always hold it, no matter what the face value.

4) Never hold a picture card with a pair of 2s through 10s.

5) Never draw two cards to try for a straight or flush.

6) Never draw one card to try for an inside straight.

Bingo

Bingo is one of the world's best known and best loved games. In the United States alone, more than 35,000 bingo halls serve an estimated 30 million players, 20 million of whom are women. Bingo is also responsible for raising more money for charities, service organizations, religious institutions, and Native American tribes than any other fundraising activity.

One of the least profitable games for casinos, bingo was originally included in the roster of casino games for the same reason that extravaganzas were introduced to the showrooms, cheap steaks and breakfasts appeared in the restaurants, and coupons for free souvenirs are distributed via funbooks: to attract people into the casino. Simply by offering bingo, casinos can fill large halls full of players, who have to pass by the pit and slots on the way in and out, where they'll drop a few bucks on a roulette wheel or in a slot machine.

Bingo is derived from the Italian game lotto, but is similar to the original Chinese game of keno. Both use numbered cards, numbered Ping-Pong balls blown from a cage, a caller, and a master board. There, however, the similarities pretty much dissolve. Bingo is played on paper cards marked with a "dauber" or on two-ply cardboard "boards" marked with little round plastic tabs. The bingo cards contain 25 squares. Five horizontal columns are topped with the letters B-I-N-G-O. Under the B are five boxes, with a number in each box from 1 to 15; under the I five boxes with numbers 16 to 30; under the N four numbered boxes (31 to 45) and a "free" box in the center of the card; under the G numbers 46 to 60; and under the O 61 to 75.

The caller announces the letter and number of each ejected Ping-Pong ball and illuminates them on the master board. For example, if the caller announces "G-58" or "Number 58, under G," the players check their cards under the column topped by the G for the number 58. If it appears, they mark the number with the ink dauber or the plastic tabs. A winning card will have five numbers lined up in a row, either horizontally, vertically, or diagonally. The "free" square is always considered marked, so frequently you'll only need to match four numbers to win a game.

When a player lines up a card with the proper configuration of markings, she yells out "Bingo!" A floor person picks up the card and verifies the player's numbers by those on the big board, then declares her the winner. The caller gives the other players a few moments to determine whether they, too, have won; if there's another winner, the two split the total prize money. Most of the time, however, there's only one winner per game, because great pains are taken to ensure that each card is unique. Prize money can range from $10 on a regular bingo game up to $50,000 for a progressive jackpot.

The variety of patterns for bingo games is vast, from the "no-number" card, where not a single number on the card has been called, to the "coverall" or "black-out," where every number on the card is marked. Configurations such as "inside corner," "outside corner," and shapes such as "diamond," "square," "picture frame" or the letters "L," "X," "T," "H," and "U" are announced by the caller at the start of each game, and the patterns illuminated on secondary boards around the room.

There are almost as many different buy-ins as there are patterns. Cards start at 25¢ and can go up to $500 and higher for special promotions and tournaments. Different-color cards have different buy-in denominations (for example, blue costs $3, green $6, orange $9, etc.); the prize money is determined by the card's worth. "Game packs" or "booklets" consist of a given number of paper cards stapled together and used up in a "session." A quick call to the bingo room can tell you which sessions are played when.

Each game moves fairly quickly. The numbers are called one right after the other, leaving the players just enough time to look for them on their cards. Old bingo hands can play scores of cards simultaneously, but beginners should limit themselves to a dozen at the most. When you buy in, if it's a paper session (i.e., one played on paper cards), make sure you have a dauber on hand when the game starts; they're for sale at the bingo cashier for $1 or so. After the first few games of a session, by watching, asking your neighbors or a floor person a quick question about something you don't quite understand, and playing, you'll be right into the swing of things.

Though the pace of bingo can often be blistering, the games start out fairly relaxed, when the cards are empty and the players are gearing up for the pattern. The tension mounts as more numbers are called, the cards fill up, and the players await the magic number or two that will make them winners. Finally, someone yells, "Binnnnnngooooo!" and for a brief moment the tension remains while the other players catch up on the last number or two. Then, as people realize they're not co-winners, the room deflates like a popped balloon. Quickly, the winner is verified and a new game starts the process all over again.

Sports Betting

In Las Vegas, the word "book" rarely denotes a work of literature. More often than not, book isn't even used as a noun, but when it is, book almost always refers to the large room, generally an annex of a casino, where sports wagers are made and paid, the odds on sporting events are displayed, and sports bettors (often called "wise guys") watch the main events on large TV screens. Bookmakers (or bookies) are people in the business of taking wagers. Book as a verb is the action of accepting and recording a wager, primarily on sporting events, but also on casino games; the house books your blackjack, crap, and slot machine action.

The first sports book in a casino opened in 1975. Today, nearly every major casino books sports bets. A sports book can be as small as a table with a clerk who quotes the odds and handwrites your receipt for a bet, or as large as the Las Vegas Hilton's "super book," which boasts 46 video screens and 500 seats.

In Nevada, you can bet on professional football, baseball, basketball, and hockey; college football and basketball; boxing matches; horse racing; and special events. But of all the sports, pro football draws the most action by far.

Football Betting

A wager laid on a football game is one of the best gambling (and entertainment) bargains in the business. It costs you all of $1 in commission to the house to place a $10 bet on a team; the return is several hours of heightened excitement while the game is played. As anyone who's made a casual bet with a friend or group of coworkers knows, having a little money riding on a game introduces a whole new level of energy and interest to it.

There are four ways to bet a football game: point spread, money line, parlay, and teaser. A wager based on the "point spread" (or a "straight bet") means that you're not only betting that one team will beat the other, but that it will win by a predetermined number of points. The point spreads are calculated for all pro football games by an outside "handicapper" (or oddsmaker) based on the relative strengths or weaknesses of the teams playing. For example, when a strong team, such as the San Francisco 49ers, plays a weak team, such as the Cincinnati Bengals, the spread will favor the 49ers by, say, 17 points. This means that the 49ers have to beat the Bengals by 18 points in order for a wager placed on San Francisco to win. If the 49ers beat the Bengals by 10 points, they didn't "cover" the spread, so a bet on the Bengals would win. If the 49ers win by 17 points exactly, it's a "push" or a tie, and the original bet (minus the commission) is returned.

Parlay Betting Odds

Number of Teams	Payout Odds	True Odds
2	13–5	3–1
3	6–1	7–1
4	10–1	15–1
5	20–1	31–1
6	35–1	63–1
7	50–1	127–1
8	100–1	225–1
9	200–1	511–1
10	400–1	1023–1

Teaser Betting Odds

Number of Teams	6 points	6½ points	7 points
2	even	10–11	1–12
3	9–5	8–5	3–2
4	3–1	5–2	2–1
5	9–2	4–1	7–2
6	7–1	6–1	5–1

The "money line" bet on a pro football game uses odds instead of points, and is determined simply by who wins and who loses. The money line for the San Francisco–Cincinnati game might be a "minus 240 plus 180." This means you have to bet $24 to win $10 (for a total of $34) on the heavily favored 49ers; conversely, a bet of $10 on the underdog Bengals will win you $18 (for a total of $28).

A "parlay" is a bet on two, three, or four teams (sometimes more), all of which have to cover the point spread for you to win. (*See* the Parlay Betting Odds chart.) If two out of the three teams cover and the third team wins but doesn't cover, you lose the whole bet. The payout on a two-team parlay is generally 13 to 5, on a three-team parlay 6 to 1, and on a four-team parlay 10 to 1.

A "teaser" is similar to a parlay, except that the point spreads are more variable than for a straight or parlay bet. (*See* the Teaser Betting Odds chart.) If you win a three-team teaser after taking an additional 6 points on the spread, you're paid at 9 to 5; with 6½ additional points it's 8 to 5 and with 7 points, 3 to 2.

Football bets are usually made in denominations of $11, which includes the house's $1 commission for booking the bet. Winning bets pay off in denominations of $10. So, for example, you might bet $33 on the 49ers to cover the point spread. If the 49ers cover, you win $30 (for a total payback of $63).

To make a football bet (or a bet on any sporting event), go to the sports book and step up to the counter. Study the board that lists all the games, and pick out the one(s) you want to put your money on. The teams are numbered. Give the team number, amount of the bet, and type of bet (points or money line) to the "writer," who inputs your bet into a computer, and prints out your "ticket" or receipt. (Parlay and teaser cards are filled out and presented to the writer.) Check your ticket carefully to make sure the writer has given you the exact bet that you intended to make.

Then sit back and root for your team. If you lose, wallpaper your bathroom with the ticket. If you win, return to the casino where you made the bet, present the ticket to the sports book cashier, and receive your due.

3 Casinos

POPULAR WISDOM NOTWITHSTANDING, you *can* win in the casinos and many people do. But, as discussed in the previous chapter, almost all of the odds are riding against you. And that's just for starters. The dazzling lights, the free beer and cocktails, the play money, the lack of windows and clocks, even the oxygen—and, lately, seductive aromas—pumped into the air are all calculated to overwhelm you with a sense of holiday impetuousness that keeps you reaching into your pocket or purse for the green.

Tens of millions of people who *don't* know the odds of, or the strategies for, casino games come to Las Vegas every year, and some of them even win now and then. But let's face it. Kirk Kerkorian didn't invest $1 billion to build his new MGM Grand on the Strip because he expected to make a lot of money on hotel rooms and bacon-and-egg breakfasts. He knew that millions of people would come to gawk at his new showplace—and he made sure plenty of dealers were on hand to take their money while they were at it.

Las Vegas casinos make a fortune, nearly $6 billion a year, by taking a big bite out of millions of bankrolls. With table games they keep on average 15% of the money; with the slot machines—the number-one game in Nevada—they hold around 25%.

If you want to beat the odds, take the time to read up on the games before you go to Nevada. Then, when you have some idea of the basics, plan on attending the free gambling lessons provided at most casinos. Even if you think you know the rules, these lessons will give you an opportunity to play the game at an actual session and learn the etiquette using practice chips instead of your own cash.

Casino Etiquette

Casinos can be confusing places for the first-time visitor. They tend to be large, open rooms full of people who seem to know exactly what they're doing, while you wander around lost. Cameras hung from the ceiling watch your movements, and all the security guards, pit bosses, and dealers seem to be doing the same. Worst of all, there are no signs, announcements, or tour guides to inform newcomers of the rules of behavior. So we'll do that right here.

All players must be 21 years of age. No exceptions. A pit boss or security guard is likely to ask to see your ID if you look underage. If you're 19 or 20 and can pass for 21, you might get away with gambling—until you hit a jackpot. Any slot or video poker winnings of more than $1,200, or keno winnings of more than $1,500, require the casino to fill out IRS form W-2G. When the casino boss asks to see your identification, if you're under 21, not only will you not be paid, you'll also be summarily evicted. Many court cases over the years have challenged this procedure, every one to no avail. If you're playing a slot with a kid by your side, a security guard will quickly appear (dispatched by casino surveillance) and ask you to leave. But you can walk through the casino with your youngster in tow; as long as you're on the move, you're okay.

No photographs may be taken in most of the casinos: Management fears that players may feel uncomfortable if captured on film and will get up and leave. (You can take pictures in the Four Queens, Excalibur, California, and Harrah's casinos if you like.)

Always take a few moments to orient yourself to a casino when you first arrive. Allow your senses to become accustomed to the surplus of stimuli. You can check out the slot machines without any problem. But be careful when walking around the pit (main table-game area). Never cut between the tables to get to the other side; the inner sanctum of the tables is an employees-only area.

Before you sit down or step up to a table, be sure to look at the little placard that announces the betting minimum and maximum. For example, blackjack tables have minimums of $1, $2, $3, $5, $10, $25, or $100 and maximums of $500 to $2,000. Minimums in casinos on the Strip are generally higher than those of downtown casinos.

If you're with a friend who chooses not to gamble, he or she will have to stand and watch; the chairs are for players only. (To watch roulette and craps, primarily standing games, your friend should stand behind the row of players.) An old wives' tale holds that dealers aren't allowed to talk to players. Not true. The trend among dealers is to be friendlier and more helpful, but there will always be those stony-faced dealers who grumble when spoken to. Don't hesitate to ask any question you like. If a dealer doesn't answer, or is rude, walk away to another table—or another casino.

At some of the smaller and less crowded gambling houses, dealers will take time with new players to point out the right ways and wrong ways of the game. If you're a newcomer to the tables, avoid the larger houses, especially at peak hours, because much of the time the personnel will be too busy to give you effective help should you need it.

Consider also the timing of your casino visit. If you arrive at a busy hour, it may be hard to find a table with room for two or with the minimum bet that's right for you. Your best move is to arrive early—the earlier the better. The activity of Las Vegas starts to get under way around 11 AM, builds to 5 PM, remains steady until 8 PM, and then grows busier and peaks between 11 PM and midnight. If you like your action rammin' and jammin', you won't mind playing during prime time. If not, the hours between 4 AM and 11 AM are probably more to your liking. At those hours the dealers are usually more amicable, and less smoke will be blown in your face. Most casinos now have tables or entire pits and whole slot sections for nonsmokers.

How Not to Go Broke

Remember, the goal of the casino is to keep you playing as long as possible. Set your own limits in terms of the size of your bankroll, the hours you intend to play, the size of your betting unit, and how much money you're willing to lose, then stick to them religiously. Avoid the cash machines, which will hit you with hefty service charges. Try not to let the alcohol and adrenaline go to your head, or your wallet. If you wind up a winner, take it in stride. Don't start thinking that you can't lose; put the winnings aside to add to your bankroll the next time you play. Try to adopt a similarly sober outlook if you end up losing. As long as you've stuck to your limits, it shouldn't be too much of a disaster.

Tipping

Dealers are paid minimum wage at the casinos, and they expect to be tipped when you are winning. It's neither mandatory nor necessary, however, only up to your own discretion. Slipping a dealer or change person a chip is like any other tip: a small gratuity for services rendered. You can also place a bet for the dealer, and not only at blackjack, but at any table. Simply lay down an extra chip or two and announce, "This one's for you." (At craps, the expression is "a two-way bet.") This small generosity usually relaxes the dealer, and thus the game, considerably. At most casinos, dealers pool their tips and then split them evenly. So be aware that no matter how much you toke a good dealer, he or she will receive only a percentage.

Las Vegas Lingo

Before you enter the neon jungle of Las Vegas, you'll want to learn some key words in the local language.

Buy-in. The amount of cash with which a player enters a game.

Cage. The casino cashier station where you can exchange your chips back to cash.

Comp. A gift from the casino of a complimentary drink, room, dinner, or show; a freebie (*see* Chapter 2, Playing the Games, for details).

George. A good tipper. If a dealer refers to you as "George," you've been paid a compliment.

Grind joint. A gambling house that promotes low table minimums and slot denominations. You won't find too many high rollers at one.

High roller. A casino customer who plays with a bankroll of $5,000 or more. Some grind joints consider a $1,000 bankroll to be high-roller action; some premium joints require a $10,000 bankroll.

Juice. Influence, the ultimate Vegas intoxication. Politicians use juice daily to get what they want. "You scratch my back, and I'll scratch yours" is another way of putting it.

Marker. A casino IOU. Players sign markers and get chips at the tables; they then pay off the markers with chips or cash.

Pit boss. The person who supervises the action on the gaming tables. The pit boss's domain, the pit, is an area surrounded by tables that is off-limits to the general public.

RFB. The cream of comps—room, food, and beverage, courtesy of the casino. All you have to do is play (depending on the casino) $75–$250 a hand for four hours a day.

Shill. A person employed by the casino to sit at the tables and play games during the less busy hours—with the casino's money. Casino bosses believe that gamblers are more comfortable playing at a table with other people rather than at an empty table.

Stiff. Cheapskate. When you fail to tip your dealer or a cab driver, you might hear him mutter that you're a stiff. Not to worry; a contract has not been put out on you.

Toke. A tip (short for token, or token of your esteem). This may be the word you'll hear most often; many of the folks you encounter will be expecting a toke.

THE CASINOS

Our review of the casinos begins at Hacienda Road, the southern end of the Strip, and proceeds north on Las Vegas Boulevard to the Stratosphere Hotel and Tower at the northern end. Then we cover the downtown casinos on and near Fremont Street. The descriptions that follow are intended to help you find the casinos that will most appeal to you. If you'd like to save time by sleeping where you gamble, *see* Chapter

9, Lodging, for details of the hotels in which most of these casinos are found.

The Strip

Twenty-seven casinos line the Strip, 22 major and five minor—more than 2 million square feet of gambling fever. Strip casinos run the gamut of size and style, from the overwhelming spectacle of the MGM Grand to the small pit at Slots A Fun, and from low-roller heaven at Circus Circus to high-roller tension at the Mirage. In general, however, Strip casinos are big and ritzy, with high playing minimums. Keep in mind, though, that Las Vegas casinos, whether premium or shabby, welcome all comers, no matter what they're wearing. When it comes right down to it, the casinos really care about only one aspect of your attire: that it include a wallet or purse from which you can easily remove your cash.

Hacienda Hotel and Casino (3950 Las Vegas Blvd. S, ☎ 702/739–8911). The large building outstretched parallel to the bottom end of the Strip is a good place to begin a casino tour. The blackjack minimums are affordable and there's almost always a seat. What's more, the poker room isn't filled with sharks, and there are often parking spaces directly in front of the hotel. Cascading water greets you when you pass through the swinging doors, and slots jangle in the background. The recent purchase of the Hacienda by Circus Circus has focused a lot of attention on this casino, but for now it remains low-key and friendly.

Luxor (3900 Las Vegas Blvd. S, ☎ 702/262–4000). This magnificent bronze-tinted pyramid, owned by Circus Circus, opened in October 1993. It's arguably the most unusual casino in the world, inside and out. Standing right at the base of one of the exterior walls and looking up, you'll get a glimpse of infinity—and have a direct experience of Egyptian geometry. The Egyptian theme is continued inside—from the King Tut Museum to the Nile River ride. The high-tech entertainment is on the second floor, where you also get the full impact of the 29 million cubic feet of open space soaring to the apex. Luxor has the only round casino in town: plenty of elbow room, surprisingly fresh air, a muted noise level, and enough slot machines and table games for every gambler in ancient Thebes.

Tropicana Resort and Casino (3801 Las Vegas Blvd. S, ☎ 702/739–2222). To hear them tell it, the Tropicana is not a hotel-casino, but the "Island of Las Vegas." The Trop's 5-acre water park, set off by the two hotel towers, features the only swim-up blackjack in Las Vegas: Yes, you can actually sit in the pool and play 21. Stuff some cash in your swimsuit pocket and when you reach the table, put it into the Trop's money dryer. If you wind up blowing your soggy bankroll, just return to your breaststroke. Indoors, the casino continues the tropical theme, with palms, parrots, and Polynesiana. An exquisite stained-glass dome extends the length of the main pit. The casino offers excellent perks for points accumulated by members of its Island Winners slot club. There are no-smoking crap tables and slots, and at noon on weekdays, penny roulette is offered as a learning session. Crap and blackjack lessons are also offered, though the upscale Tropicana has few $2 blackjack tables.

Excalibur (3850 Las Vegas Blvd. S, ☎ 702/597–7777). This medieval-theme 4,032-room resort, opened by Circus Circus in 1990, has a giant, 100,000-square-foot casino. The Bavarian castle, which has been called "the greatest hole in God's own miniature golf course," offers inexpensive and plentiful meals, a Renaissance midway, 2,630 slot machines, a poker room, and race and sports book. The King's Pavilion is a beau-

Aladdin Hotel and Casino, **7**
Bally's Casino Resort, **10**
Barbary Coast Hotel and Casino, **12**
Bourbon Street Hotel and Casino, **9**
Caesars Palace, **11**
Circus Circus, **28**
Excalibur, **4**
The Flamingo Hilton and Tower, **13**
Frontier Hotel and Gambling Hall, **21**
Gold Coast Hotel and Casino, **33**
Hacienda Hotel and Casino, **1**
Harrah's Hotel and Casino, **16**
Imperial Palace Hotel and Casino, **15**
ITT Sheraton Desert Inn Hotel and Casino, **20**
Las Vegas Hilton, **25**
Little Caesar's Gambling Casino, **6**
Luxor, **2**
Maxim Hotel and Casino, **8**
MGM Grand Hotel and Theme Park, **5**
The Mirage, **17**
O'Sheas Casino, **14**
Palace Station Hotel and Casino, **29**
Rio Suites Hotel and Casino, **32**
Riviera Hotel, **26**
Sahara Las Vegas Hotel, **30**
Sands Hotel and Casino, **19**
Silver City, **24**
Slots-A-Fun, **27**
Stardust Hotel and Casino, **22**
Treasure Island, **18**
Tropicana Resort and Casino, **3**
Vegas World Hotel and Casino, **31**
Westward Ho Motel and Casino, **23**

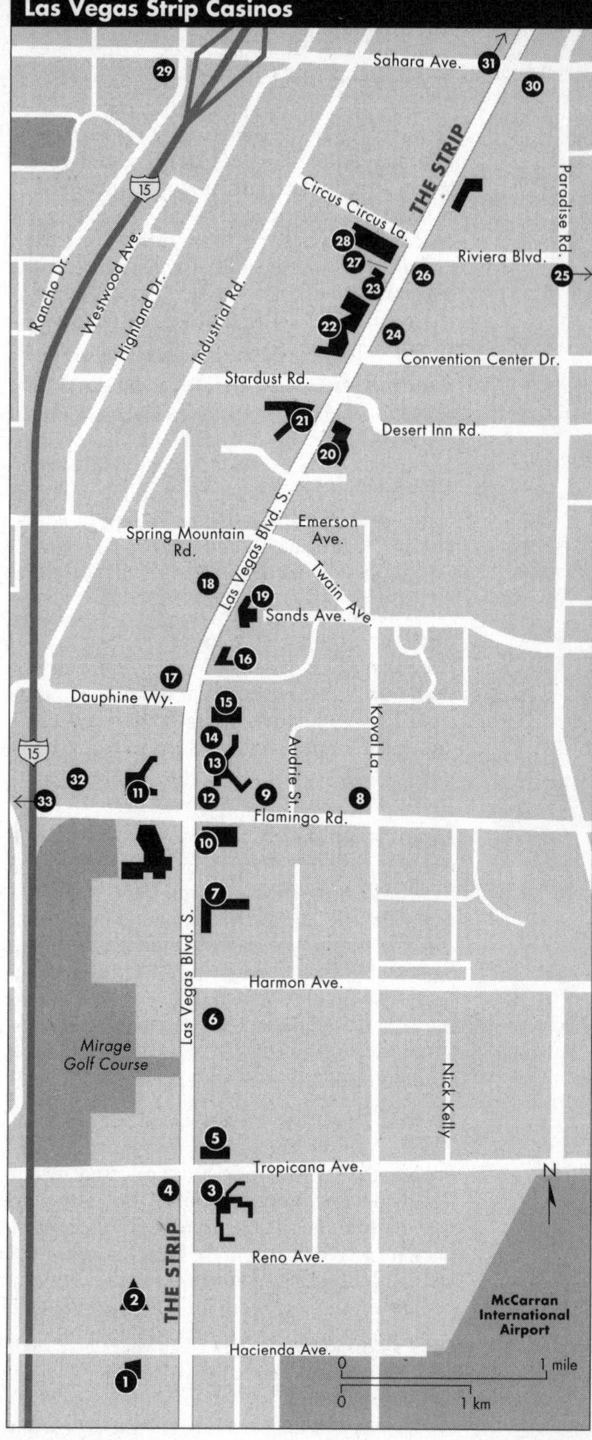

tiful circular bar in the middle of the casino, with a grand fake oak and bar-top video.

MGM Grand Hotel and Theme Park (3805 Las Vegas Blvd. S, ☎ 702/891–1111). This gargantuan gambler gobbler is the largest hotel-casino-entertainment complex in the world. The Hollywood, Emerald City, and Monte Carlo sections of the casino combine for 171,000 square feet of casino space (50,000 more square feet than any other casino), with 3,500 slot machines (some "cashless"), 165 table games, a fancy baccarat pit, a big race and sports book, a truly grand main entrance, and a mind-blowing wall of synchronized video monitors behind the registration desk. A half mile of restaurants, arcades, and shops inside leads up to a 33-acre amusement park behind the hotel. (Plan on spending at least six hours to go from one end of the joint to the other.)

New York–New York Hotel and Casino (3790 Las Vegas Blvd. S, ☎ 800/693–6763; opening in December 1996). A joint venture between the MGM Grand and the Primadonna group (which owns three casinos at the California state line, 45 miles southwest of Las Vegas), this $300 million, 2,150-room hotel will reproduce the Manhattan skyline, complete with a 48-story Empire State Building and a 150-foot Statue of Liberty. A Coney Island–style roller coaster will encircle the property. Inside, the Big Apple theme will also run rampant.

Aladdin Hotel and Casino (3667 Las Vegas Blvd. S, ☎ 702/736–0111). Here's another great Las Vegas image: atop a hotel roof, a neon genie's lamp that glows all night long. If only you could rub it, maybe your wish—and what else would it be but to make a killing?—would come true! The Aladdin has an *Arabian Nights* theme, with Islamic arches and the decor of a harem. Gamblers will find low- to upper-range minimums: plenty of $3 tables and 25¢ slots, plenty of $25 tables and $1 slots. Tables for nonsmokers are available.

Maxim Hotel and Casino (160 E. Flamingo Rd., ☎ 702/731–4300). The slightly off-Strip location of the Maxim makes it a nice alternative to the Strip's busier casinos and a favorite with blackjack pros, comp hustlers, coupon runners, and slot players. The dark-green casino sports a sunken pit, plenty of low-limit gambling opportunities, and high-profile dealers and bosses. The Maxim maintains an old-time comp policy: If you play here, they'll feed you; just ask a floor manager for the criteria. In addition, card counters swear by the Maxim, not only for its laissez-faire blackjack policy, but also for its consistent deep penetration (dealing the entire deck out).

Bourbon Street Hotel and Casino (120 E. Flamingo Rd., ☎ 702/737–7200). New Orleans is the theme here, with Dixieland bands and French Quarter decor. In order to compete with its larger neighbors, Bourbon Street keeps food prices and table-game minimums low, and runs frequent gambling promotions for low rollers. The $1.99 breakfasts are served all day in the French Market Restaurant, and there are plenty of $2 tables. When the crowds at the Flamingo and Bally's get you down, the neighboring Bourbon Street will bring you back up.

Bally's Casino Resort (3645 Las Vegas Blvd. S, ☎ 702/739–4111). At 100,000 square feet, Bally's is certainly one of the largest casinos in Las Vegas, though MGM's is almost twice as big and the Riviera, Circus Circus, and Excalibur are at least as big. What makes Bally's seem so monumental is that, unlike the others, it's a single expanse, front to back and side to side. Also, Bally's is usually packed. It owns a huge chunk of one of the most popular intersections in the world—it's across the street from the Flamingo and Caesars Palace—and it accommodates a perpetually large convention trade. Yet the casino is so roomy that when the crowds become at all oppressive, you can almost always find a more open part of the floor. Bally's tends to attract high rollers, so its table minimums are rarely less than $5. Craps, baccarat, blackjack, and roulette lessons are given daily. Bally's has recently announced plans to build an as-yet-unnamed 2,500-room, all-suite resort on the vacant lot to the east of the existing property.

Bellagio Hotel and Casino. The details of the Mirage group's new $900 million, 3,000-room hyper-resort, scheduled to open in late 1997, are as yet sketchy. One thing is clear, however: Bellagio, which will occupy a large chunk of the old Dunes property on the southwest corner of Flamingo and the Strip, will be the most opulent (and probably the most expensive to build) new property to open in Las Vegas in this decade.

Caesars Palace (3570 Las Vegas Blvd. S, ☎ 702/731–7110). Caesars is home to the never-ending casino, two sprawling wings in a gentle horseshoe shape that extends from one end of the huge property to the other. The old wing—low ceiling, many pits, high stakes—is home to *serious* gamblers, people who are probably comped in Caesars's exclusive suites and restaurants, and are eligible for unlimited room service, too. The newer Olympic Casino wing, with its high ceiling, soaring marble columns, graceful rooftop arches, and lower limits, accommodates the low-stakes gamblers. Since the Mirage opened next door, Caesars has embraced the middle market with a slot club, food court, and 5¢ slots. The huge, plush race and sports book with its megadisplay must be seen to be believed.

Barbary Coast Hotel and Casino (3595 Las Vegas Blvd. S, ☎ 702/737–7111). The Barbary Coast casino is modeled after late-19th-century San Francisco saloons, with Victorian chandeliers and lamps, tasteful stained-glass signs (including the largest stained-glass mural in the world), and Klondike Annie cocktail waitresses who wear garters on their thighs. Want to send a message from the Coast? A Western Union office here will wire it. The casino is usually pretty crowded, though not on the same scale as its neighbors—Bally's, the Flamingo Hilton, and Caesars. A pleasant brick plaza with wooden benches fronts the casino.

Flamingo Hilton and Tower (3555 Las Vegas Blvd. S, ☎ 702/733–3111). History lovers: This is where modern Las Vegas began. Prior to 1946, when Benjamin (Bugsy) Siegel imported Miami luxury to the desert, Las Vegas was still trying to keep alive the last little sliver of the Wild West. But Bugsy was intent on introducing a class joint to the new casino town, a place where his Hollywood buddies and Manhattan partners could gamble legally, where the lure of big-time entertainment would bring the beautiful people to play, and where the ordinary Joe would show up because he wanted to feel like a big shot. Bugsy, of course, wasn't able to hang around long enough to enjoy the fruits of his labor or to observe the impact of his vision, but the Fabulous Flamingo has had one hell of a 50-year run. The Flamingo hasn't officially been "Fabulous" since the Hilton organization took over in 1970, but the most massive expansion project in town has rendered it unofficially fantastic. There are now a magnificent casino, a casino annex—the two-story **O'Sheas,** with an Irish theme, opened in a portion of what had been the parking lot—a poker parlor and sports book, and some of the most intense action in town. Table minimums at the Flamingo are on the high side. The Flamingo recently completed the final phase of its 20-year expansion—a sixth tower and a 15-acre pool park, including a wild-animal park and a wedding chapel—but it had to tear down the last remnant of Bugsy's Flamingo to do it.

Imperial Palace Hotel and Casino (3535 Las Vegas Blvd. S, ☎ 702/731–3311). A blue pagoda-style building with an Oriental theme, this house of dragons does a booming business with tour groups. The casino is large, crowded, and confusing; of all the hotel-casino mazes in Las Vegas, the Imperial Palace is probably the most intricate. Plan on spending a few minutes confronting the splendid Zen challenge of finding your way around (the fact that there are no signs adds to the sport). Escalators behind the hotel's front desk carry you up to the third floor (showroom and sports book) and beyond to the fifth floor (five restaurants); escalators in the middle of the casino go to the coffee shop and buffet. The gaming school, one of the first and best in town, offers free blackjack and crap lessons Monday through Friday. The table minimums are more in the $5 than the $3 range.

Harrah's Hotel and Casino (3475 Las Vegas Blvd. S, ☎ 702/369–5000). You can't miss Harrah's, the 450-foot-long "Ship on the Strip," with its 80-foot neon paddle wheel and 85-foot-tall smokestacks; it even toots at intervals—perhaps so those who can no longer see straight after staring at slots for hours can hear their way back here. Strips of red neon hang above the slots, red wallpaper covers the walls, and the dealers adorn their white shirts with red string ties and garters. Harrah's is a good place for beginning gamblers and players on a budget. In keeping with the "good old days" theme, dealers here tend to be friendly and table limits are low. In fact, Harrah's was the first to introduce the "party pit," with $2 tables and dealers who perform a specialized schtick. The bingo parlor was transformed in 1995 into **An Evening at the Improv** (*see* Chapter 10, Nightlife, for details).

The Mirage (3400 Las Vegas Blvd. S, ☎ 702/791–7111). When the Mirage opened in November 1989, it was the first new Strip hotel to be built for 16 years, and it triggered the current boom in Boomtown, U.S.A. The ultimate carpet joint, the Mirage has high minimums (such as $500 slots and a plush private pit where the minimum bet is $1,000), ionospheric maximums, and intense security. The decor is rain-forest rustic: Pits are distinguished by separate thatched roofs. Other eccentric attractions include a 20,000-gallon aquarium, white tiger habitat, dolphin pools, and the Siegfried and Roy illusion extravaganza in the showroom (tickets cost $80 apiece).

Treasure Island (3300 Las Vegas Blvd. S, ☎ 702/894–7111). A Steve Wynn–Mirage Resorts production, Treasure Island is a smaller, cheaper version of the Mirage. The seven-minute pyrotechnic pirate show in Buccaneer Bay on the Strip side of the hotel is the best free show in town. The crowds, however, ferocious any time of the night and day, are especially troublesome when one of the five pirate performances ends. At those times the casino population reaches critical mass, and it's best to try and grab a seat at one of the bars, buy a roll of quarters for the video poker machines, and sip on a drink until the throngs disperse. You can also escape into the retail shops, the Circus Circus–like game room, or on the monorail that connects Treasure Island to the Mirage.

Sands Hotel and Casino (3355 Las Vegas Blvd. S, ☎ 702/733–5000). You can still live the 1950s and 1960s Sands experience in the hotel's gardens and pool area, which haven't changed much since the day the Las Vegas News Bureau (now defunct) shot a classic publicity photo of a "floating" crap game in the Sands pool. You can also relive the heady days of the late '50s and early '60s in the original Copa Showroom, where Frank and Dino and Sammy and Lena held court as the Rat Pack. One other Sands tradition still remains: the famous free coffee mug, of which millions have been given away. Indoors, however, the casino has changed a lot. The latest renovation has added slots, expanded the race and sports book, opened the casino up to the Strip sidewalk, and tacked on the fine Xanadu restaurant.

Sheraton Desert Inn Hotel and Casino (3145 Las Vegas Blvd. S, ☏ 702/733–4444). The Desert Inn is one of the few hotels in Las Vegas that has not undergone a series of expansions in recent years. Opened in 1950 as Wilbur Clark's Desert Inn and once owned by Howard Hughes, the hotel has just 800 rooms—small compared to the other Las Vegas monoliths. The DI has always gone for an upscale clientele that likes to golf (the hotel has a large golf course right in its backyard) and gamble; the casino is more refined, smaller, and less noisy than most others on the Strip. ITT Sheraton took over the DI in 1992, and recently renovated the hotel and golf course.

Frontier Hotel and Gambling Hall (3120 Las Vegas Blvd. S, ☏ 702/794–8200). Though the Frontier was the second hotel to open on the seminal Strip in 1943 (the first Strip hotel, the El Rancho Vegas, burned in 1960), it has been torn down and rebuilt three times since then. The Elardi family bought it in 1988 and took it drastically downscale. Rather than glitzy shows, the star is now single-deck blackjack. The $3 and $5 tables are always crowded with a youngish clientele. There's a bingo room, walled off from the casino with glass, and a seafood restaurant, the Grotto, with a rock creek running through it. Beginning poker lessons are given every day but Sunday.

Stardust Hotel and Casino (3000 Las Vegas Blvd. S, ☏ 702/732–6111). The Stardust has one of the best neon shows on the Strip: Pink and blue neon tubing runs down the front of the hotel, leading to a 183-foot multiprogrammed sign that erupts in bursts of neon stars; on its debut in 1958, the sign was the largest and brightest in Las Vegas, its glow visible for miles. Of all the hotels built in the 1950s, the Stardust has best kept up with the Las Vegas times. Because of its size and sprawling layout, the Stardust never feels overly crowded or claustrophobic. The poker room is popular, the slot club offers excellent perks (especially the constant free-room offers), and blackjack, crap, and roulette lessons are given daily.

Westward Ho Motel and Casino (2900 Las Vegas Blvd. S, ☏ 702/731–2900). The Ho has something few Strip casinos can offer: parking close to the casino! It also has plenty of low-limit blackjack tables, and the progressive video poker machines are the best in town. Like the Stardust next door, the slot-club perks are exceptional. In addition, the casino snack bar has good cheap sandwiches and the biggest strawberry shortcake you'll ever eat. The 27-ounce margaritas at the casino bar won't disappoint, either.

Las Vegas Hilton (3000 W. Paradise Rd., ☏ 702/732–5111). What began in 1969 as Kirk Kerkorian's International Hotel became, just a few years later, the Hilton organization's first foray into gambling. Today the Hilton hotel-casinos in Las Vegas, Laughlin, and Reno account for 75% of the corporation's annual profits. The Hilton's main pit runs down the middle of the casino, surrounded by slots, keno, a separate baccarat room, a hopping new lounge, and the giant race and sports "super book"—Las Vegas's largest and most elegant (with 46 video screens). The clientele tend to be high rollers; in the movie *Indecent Proposal,*

Robert Redford played his $100,000 chips here. Because the Hilton is next door to the Las Vegas Convention Center, many delegates stay here, and they pack the casino at all hours. Crap, blackjack, and roulette lessons are given daily.

Silver City (3001 Las Vegas Blvd. S, ☎ 702/732–4152). Another gambling house in the style of the Wild West, with free popcorn, 50¢ hot dogs, $1 blackjack, and pictures of cowboys on the walls, Silver City has a much more relaxed atmosphere than that of its next-door neighbor, the large Riviera. You can park in the lot directly in front of the casino.

Riviera Hotel (2901 Las Vegas Blvd. S, ☎ 702/734–5110). When the Riviera was built in 1955, it was the tallest hotel in town, a nine-story, T-shape structure. It's gone through a lot of changes in the last 40 years, and now boasts an enormous casino—125,000 square feet, the largest in the world until the 171,000-square-foot MGM Grand (*see above*) opened. The Riviera appealed primarily to the nabobs and high rollers until it changed its image in the 1980s and lured a less extravagant clientele. The casino has a new race and sports book, two new keno parlors, and a convenient fast-food court. With nearly 90 table games, the casino has betting minimums ranging from $3 to $5; there are more than 1,500 slot and video poker machines.

Circus Circus (2880 Las Vegas Blvd. S, ☎ 702/734–0410). Only in Las Vegas would you find a 125-foot neon sign of a clown sucking a lollipop next to a statue of a nude dancer. And only in Las Vegas could you find Circus Circus, the tent-shape casino with live circus acts performing over the gamblers' heads. Under the Circus Circus tent, the clowns, trapeze stars, high-wire artists, unicyclists, and aerial dancers perform daily every 20 minutes from 11 AM to midnight. In addition to the circus acts, a midway features such games as dime toss, milk can, bushel basket, and Fascination, along with clown-face painting, a video arcade, fun-house mirrors, corn dogs, and pizza. Many parents park their kids on the midway while they go off to pull handles and press buttons downstairs. On the casino floor, almost always packed solid, you'll walk and walk and walk, passing dealers in pink shirts and cocktail waitresses wearing yellow toga outfits that look like rejects from Caesars Palace. The two must-see attractions here are the slot merry-go-round—20 slots sit on a revolving stage, and players ride in circles as they operate the machines—and the merry-go-round bar on the midway, with actual carousel horses. Don't look for $100 blackjack games here; bets of more than $10 will raise eyebrows. Because the slots pay the bills, you'll see lots more slot machines than table games. Blackjack, crap, and roulette lessons are given every morning.

As you leave Circus Circus, you'll be handed a sheet of coupons for free popcorn, 50¢ hot dogs, 99¢ shrimp cocktails, free pulls of a slot machine, and a free gift (usually a key chain) at **Slots A Fun,** a noisy, smoky casino next door with lots of slots and $1 and $2 blackjack tables.

Sahara Las Vegas Hotel (2535 Las Vegas Blvd. S, ☎ 702/737–2111). Another Las Vegas hotel built in the early 1950s, the Sahara retains the oasis theme it established when it opened, with statues of camels in the parking lot. A middle-market hotel, the Sahara appeals to weekend slot and table game players, and minimums are in the middle range, with a few $2 tables. The slot club and frequent gambling promotions make the Sahara a popular place to play. Baccarat lessons are offered daily, and the baccarat commission is only 4%. The strains emanating from the open Casbar lounge, which hosted Shecky Green, Keely

Smith, and Don Rickles in the 1950s, create a musical presence that surpasses the sounds of coins dropping from slots and shouts emanating from the crap tables.

Stratosphere (2000 Las Vegas Blvd. S, ☎ 702/382–4446; opening spring 1996). The legendary, flamboyant Bob Stupak of Las Vegas was, until 1994, the sole proprietor of Vegas World Hotel and Casino, and the sole investor of the Stratosphere Tower being built next door. Financial setbacks forced Stupak to sell 75% of his interest in the hotel and tower to his old poker buddy Lyle Berman, president of the hugely successful Grand Casinos (of Minnesota and Mississippi). Vegas World closed in February 1995 so that the entire hotel could be expanded and renovated in anticipation of an April 1996 opening. When it opens, Stratosphere Tower could be point zero in Las Vegas: the spot from which all distances are measured. With a 1,149-foot tower, a revolving restaurant and bar, high-roller suites, wedding chapels, and two thrill rides (a roller coaster and a zero-gravity simulator), not to mention the plain old spectacular view, Stratosphere Tower should prove to be the most successful, if not most profitable, attraction in Las Vegas.

Beyond the Strip

Palace Station Hotel and Casino (2411 W. Sahara Ave., ☎ 702/367–2411). Palace Station was originally the Bingo Palace, and it still has one of the most popular bingo rooms in town, but the theme has been updated (or backdated): railroads. Palace Station looks and feels like a big, smoky railroad station, with Pullman cars for restaurants and a depot for the lobby. This is a friendly, low-minimum casino with great food deals whose only fault is that it's so popular with locals that it can become too crowded for comfort's sake.

Rio Suite Hotel and Casino (3200 W. Flamingo Rd., ☎ 702/252–7777). Rio Rita symbolizes the Brazilian theme of this popular off-Strip hotel, which opened in 1990 and has tripled in size since. Known for its vibrant Latin atmosphere and its remarkable buffet, the Rio is a favorite place for locals, as well as knowledgeable visitors, to gamble, eat, and party. The big neon sign out front wins the Best Sign honors annually. The table minimums are affordable and the dealers are friendly. An interesting feature is TV monitors above video poker screens—if you get tired of dealing and drawing, simply look up to see *America's Funniest Home Videos* or *Mr. Ed.*

Gold Coast Hotel and Casino (4000 W. Flamingo Rd., ☎ 702/367–7111). Whenever you're at the airport and you see people losing money in the slots, think of the Gold Coast: This casino west of the Strip and west of Interstate 15 was built on airport slot losses. Popular with local gamblers, the Gold Coast shows up regularly in the *Las Vegas Review-Journal*'s reader polls for having some of the loosest slots in town. There's also a poker room, bingo parlor, race and sports book, 72-lane bowling center, and a movie theater. Like Palace Station (*see above*), the Gold Coast has low minimums, a friendly atmosphere, and considerable local crowds at times.

Downtown

Fremont Street is the place to come for low table minimums, food bargains, a motley street life, and the brightest and most colorful concentration of neon lights in the world. The downtown casinos have enough 25¢ craps, 50¢ roulette, $1 blackjack, and even 1¢ video poker to accommodate Las Vegas's hordes of beginning and low-stakes play-

Binion's Horseshoe Hotel and Casino, **4**

California Hotel and Casino, **2**

El Cortez Hotel, **11**

Fitzgeralds Hotel and Casino, **8**

Four Queens Hotel and Casino, **6**

Fremont Hotel and Casino, **7**

Gold Spike Hotel and Casino, **10**

Golden Nugget Hotel and Casino, **5**

Lady Luck Casino and Hotel, **9**

Las Vegas Club Hotel and Casino, **3**

Plaza Hotel and Casino, **1**

Sam's Town Hotel and Casino, **12**

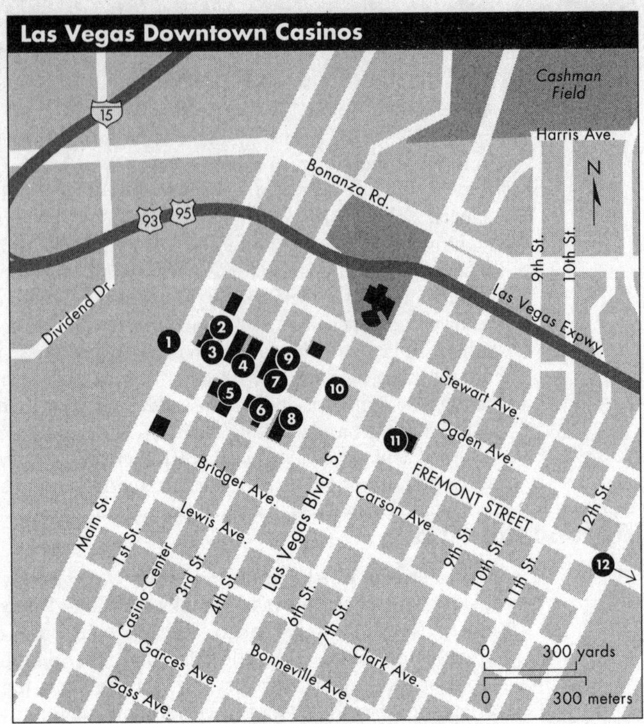

ers, tinhorns, slummers, and, of course, locals. However, what happens to downtown now that the $65 million Fremont Street Experience is up and running remains to be seen. The 100-foot-high awning that encloses Glitter Gulch (the core four blocks between Main and 4th on Fremont) has made a beautiful pedestrian mall of the main street downtown, unifying all the hotels under one roof, so to speak, and providing spectacular entertainment in the form of a 2-million-bulb light show every night. Two signs that downtown will not entirely abandon its Old West motif, which prevailed from Las Vegas's founding in 1905 through the early 1960s, are the pair of neon cowpokes, Vegas Vic and Vegas Vicky, which still preside over Glitter Gulch.

Plaza Hotel and Casino (1 Main St., ☎ 702/386–2110). Back in the 1920s, when cowboys rode their horses on Fremont Street and miners came to town to gamble and buy grub, the corner of Main and Fremont was anchored by the railroad depot. It still is, but today that station has a 1,000-room hotel and giant casino around it. As a result, Amtrak passengers have it over those who fly into Las Vegas: The airport has only 25¢ to $1 slots, but the Plaza has low-minimum ($1 and $2) tables as well as a bank of eight 1¢ slots where the jackpots can reach $30,000.

California Hotel and Casino (12 E. Ogden Ave., ☎ 702/385–1222). The California is a hotel that doesn't quite have its geography together. Given the name, you might expect a Gold Rush or sunny southern California theme, but instead you'll find that the motif is Hawaiian: All the dealers wear Hawaiian shirts, the carpet features tropical flowers, the snack bars serve Hawaiian dishes, and the customers are distinctly islanders. Aggressive marketing on the part of tour operators in the 50th state brings many Hawaiian tourists to this hotel. The casino has lots of $2 tables, 5¢ slots, and room in which to move around.

Las Vegas Club Hotel and Casino (18 E. Fremont St., ☎ 702/385–1664). A lobby wall devoted to hall-of-fame memorabilia and dealers wearing baseball shirts announces the sports theme of the Las Vegas Club. The house rules for 21 are the most liberal in town. You can double down on two, three, or four cards at any time; you can split and resplit aces and split and resplit any pair as often as you want; six cards totaling 21 or less wins automatically; and you may surrender your original hand (first two cards) for half the amount of your bet. All the blackjack games are four-deckers, making the Las Vegas Club the best multideck game in town. You'll need to be proficient in basic strategy, however, to take advantage of all these good rules. (*See* Chapter 2, Playing the Games.)

Binion's Horseshoe Hotel and Casino (128 E. Fremont St., ☎ 702/382–1600). The Horseshoe is where serious gamblers come to play, the only house in town where you'll see a line of people waiting to get to a 21 table; it's also the only place with a single pit that holds eight crap tables, all crowded. Behind the hotel, by the parking garage, is a 15-foot statue of Horseshoe founder Benny Binion, wearing a Stetson and sitting on a horse. A former bootlegger, Binion came to Vegas from Texas in the 1950s, set up a respectable shop (though he served time on a tax-evasion charge in the 1950s), and built a joint boasting the highest table limits in the world. No entertainment, no fancy hotel rooms—just good cheap food and gambling. Benny never did come around to calling it "gaming," as most everybody else now does: "That's like calling a whorehouse a brothel." Binion died in 1989, and the Horseshoe is run by his son, Jack, and his daughter, Becky. In 1988 they bought their neighbor, the Mint, knocked a wall down, and the Horseshoe became an entire city block long and wide. It's still like two different establishments. On one side is the rustic, smoky, Wild West atmosphere of the original Horseshoe; on the other side, now the West Horseshoe, is a modern red casino. This is the home of the annual World Series of Poker in April and May; the final event has a $10,000 buy-in and a $1 million first prize. The Horseshoe is also the only place in Las Vegas where you can have your picture taken with $1 million in cash—a hundred gorgeous $10,000 bills. The Horseshoe will provide a complimentary photograph of you standing in front of all that money.

Golden Nugget Hotel and Casino (129 E. Fremont St., ☎ 702/385–7111). This is the only downtown casino that can truly be called elegant. The enormous Golden Nugget sign, a common subject of Las Vegas postcards and photographs for 30 years, was torn down as part of the upgrading done by Steve Wynn, who acquired the hotel in the 1970s. But there's enough glitter inside to compensate: gold-plated elevators, pay phones, slot machines—and the world's largest gold nugget. Weighing 63 pounds and valued at $1 million, it was discovered in Australia and now resides behind plate glass in the lobby. On the other hand, the Nugget, in a nod to its location, has become a luxurious grind joint: You'll find 5¢ slots and $1 blackjack tables, and the high-roller blackjack tables in the baccarat pit have a minimum of a mere $10, even on a busy weekend night.

Four Queens Hotel and Casino (202 E. Fremont St., ☎ 702/385–4011). You'll know you've found this casino when you walk along Fremont Street and come upon four painted playing cards in the pavement—four queens, in fact. The Queens Machine has been certified by Guinness as the world's largest slot: It's the size of a motor home, 18 feet long and 7 feet high, and six people can play at one time. The players sit in chairs and invest $1 tokens from their consoles; then a slot attendant pulls the machine's handle. The goal is to get at least three of the eight reels (queen faces, cherries, lemons, etc.) to line up consecutively either from the right or left on the three pay lines. If all 24 symbols come up queens, it's a $300,000 jackpot. Free poker and slot classes are given daily.

Fremont Hotel and Casino (200 E. Fremont St., ☎ 702/385–3232). Located in the heart of Glitter Gulch and adding immeasurably to the light show with its block-long neon facade, the Fremont has been a popular landmark since it opened in 1956. Now owned by the Boyd Group, the resort has undergone an extensive modernization over the past five years. The hotel also has one of the oldest and most respected race and sports books, which attracts a lot of gamblers, especially during football season. Wayne Newton made his debut in the lounge of this casino.

Fitzgeralds Hotel and Casino (301 E. Fremont St., ☎ 702/388–2400). This was the Sundance Hotel & Casino until a group of Reno businessmen who run a Fitzgerald up north bought it, painted it green, and renamed it. The Fitz calls itself the Luck Capital of Las Vegas: Its theme is the luck of the Irish, and leprechauns and four-leaf clovers are rampant. The Fitzgeralds funbook always features a good free souvenir and $3 to $4 worth of gambling coupons. And the Fitz has an entire area of the second floor reserved for nonsmoking slot and video poker players. Twenty-one, crap, roulette, and Red Dog instruction is available daily.

Lady Luck Casino and Hotel (206 N. 3rd St., ☎ 702/477–3000). The Lady Luck, at 3rd and Ogden streets across from the Gold Spike (*see below*), is a bit off the beaten track, but folks are drawn here by good $1 video poker machines: 9/6 with a 4,700-coin royal jackpot. Many professional tournament players come to the Lady's popular mini-tournaments—with $25 entry fees and $500 first prizes—to hone their skills for the major tournaments at places like the Riviera, Stardust, and Imperial Palace. The casino is lined with big picture windows, making it the lightest and airiest downtown. The casino funbook is famous for its free foot-long frankfurter.

Gold Spike Hotel and Casino (400 E. Ogden Ave., ☎ 702/384–8444). This small gambling hall, one block north of Fremont Street, is the sort of place you'd imagine might have lurked in the room behind a cigar or candy store in the old days. The blackjack table limits are the opposite of usual—$1 and $2 mostly, with a $5 here and there. The Spike features 5¢ video keno and poker machines, live 40¢ keno, and 10¢ roulette. But the casino's unique feature, in terms of both the game and the gamers, is the bank of 1¢ video poker machines, jammed day and night with the hard core, the desperate, the addicted—in short, the downtown fringe. For a fistful of penny rolls you can join Las Vegas's looniest subculture.

El Cortez Hotel (600 E. Fremont St., ☎ 702/385–5200). The oldest standing casino in Las Vegas, the El Cortez opened for business on Fremont Street in 1941, when cowboys still rode up and down the street on horses. While the venerable sign out front proclaims GAMBLING/COFFEE SHOP/FLOOR SHOW, there are no more floor shows at El Cortez. (The last bona fide floor show in Las Vegas is believed to have been Donn Arden's dancers, at the Desert Inn in 1951.) The casino makes up in history what it lacks in charm. A newer wing (built in the mid-1980s) provides a grand contrast. The gambling-table minimums are low; food is as inexpensive as the portions are large.

Beyond Downtown

Sam's Town Hotel and Casino (5111 W. Boulder Hwy., ☎ 702/456–7777). About 5 miles from downtown, on the route to the Hoover Dam, is Sam's Town, a Boyd Group property (along with the Stardust, Fremont, and California). For 15 years Sam's Town was a small 200-room hotel with a country-western motif, popular with locals. But in June 1994 Sam's Town unveiled its 450-room expansion and instantly transformed itself into an off-Strip must-see. From the outside the new wing looks like a gymnasium, but inside it's a nine-story establishment with a turn-of-the-century western flavor, built around a 25,000-square-foot indoor park. (*see* Chapter 9, Lodging, for more details). The two-story casino is now a larger version of its old self, with row after row of 25¢ video poker machines, a hardwood floor under the pit, a country band working up a sweat in the lounge, a dance hall, and a country store that sells everything from Tony Lama's to jelly beans. If you're driving to Hoover Dam (Boulder Highway is much more picturesque than the freeway), you might stop in on your way; just head out East Fremont Street, which turns into Boulder Highway; you'll be at Sam's Town, on the left-hand side of the road, in 10 minutes.

4 Las Vegas for Children

IN THE OLD DAYS you left your kids at home when you came to Vegas. Too young to gamble, too young for the shows, too young to stay up all night, children found Vegas a bore. That was the old days; this is now. As you fly into 1990s Las Vegas you'll notice how much it resembles a huge theme park, a mammoth amusement arena; a pyramid here, a castle there, not to mention pirate ships, giant totem poles, and the famous sea of neon. Las Vegas is focusing more and more on family entertainment. Amusement parks, dramatic spectacles, and G-rated theme hotels are sprouting up on the Strip faster than you can say, "Lookout, Disney!" Grand Slam Canyon, Luxor, Treasure Island, MGM Grand, the Stratosphere Tower—for the first time ever in Las Vegas, all the new projects are targeting the growing family market. More and more production shows are offering performances suitable for youngsters. Bowling, midways, even ice-skating are growing in popularity. Arcades are expanding and feature the latest in video technology. And new museums now provide both educational and entertaining diversions for children. With this new look, kiddie-friendly Vegas is sending a clear message that it intends to inherit the title of America's number-one family vacation destination.

Sightseeing

Museums

Guinness World of Records Museum (*see* Museums and Galleries *in* Chapter 5, Exploring Las Vegas). This hall of fame for the biggest and the best from all corners of the globe holds special appeal for children, who always seem to delight in the weird exhibits.

Imperial Palace Automobile Museum (*see* Tour 1 *in* Chapter 5, Exploring Las Vegas).

Las Vegas Museum of Natural History. The museum is home to displays of mammals from Alaska to Africa and has rooms full of sharks (including a 300-gallon aquarium), birds, dinosaur fossils, and hands-on exhibits. It also houses a big gift shop full of games, puzzles, books, clothes, and animals. *900 Las Vegas Blvd. N,* ☎ *702/384–3466.* ☛ *$5 adults; $4 senior citizens, military personnel, and students; $2.50 children 4–12.* ⏲ *Daily 9–4.*

Lied Discovery Children's Museum. One of the largest children's museums in the nation, the Lied (pronounced "leed") contains more than 100 hands-on exhibits geared toward kids in the sciences, arts, and humanities. Children can pilot a space shuttle, perform on stage, or stand in a giant bubble. *833 Las Vegas Blvd. N,* ☎ *702/382–5437.* ☛ *$5 adults, $4 senior citizens and children 12–17, $3 children 3–11.* ⏲ *Tues. and Thurs.–Sat. 10–5, Wed. 10–7, Sun. noon–5.*

Parks and Playgrounds

Funtazmic. This family fun center just off the Strip (on West Tropicana) has go-carts and bumper boats (big ones for big kids, little ones for toddlers), trampolines, and a large arcade. *4975 Polaris Ave.,* ☎ *702/795–4386.* ☛ *$2–$3.49 per ride, with different ride packages available.*

Grand Slam Canyon Adventuredome. This 5-acre indoor amusement park behind Circus Circus is covered by a pink dome. Inside are the world's largest indoor roller coaster, a flume ride, a laser-tag room, bumper cars, four kiddie rides, a carnival midway, an arcade, and a snack bar. The roller coaster has two 360-degree loops and a corkscrew;

it's a rough 90-second ride, but quite a thrill. The flume has a giant splashdown where you can get soaked. Grand Slam Canyon is perfect for kids 8–16. *2800 Las Vegas Blvd. S, ☎ 702/794–3939. ☛ $3, includes 1 ride, individual rides $1–$3, all-day wristbands $13.95 adults, $9.95 children. ⏲ Sun.-Thurs. 10–6, Fri.-Sat. 10–midnight.*

MGM Grand Adventures Theme Park. This is a tame little amusement park, excellent for children in the 7- to 12-year-old range. There are seven main rides: a 60-second ho-hum roller coaster, a five-minute relaxing back-lot river tour, a wet Grand Canyon rapids ride, a flume ride with a 60-foot drop (the only real thrill in the park), an interesting motion simulator, bumper cars, and a fairly lame haunted mine. There are also four theater presentations, of which the Dueling Pirates is the best—the sets and staging are excellent, the acting and stunts thrilling, and the energy level high. A number of fast-food outlets will keep you going if you plan on killing the whole day. Otherwise you can do everything there is to do once, and the best stuff twice, in three or four hours. *MGM Grand Hotel, 3805 Las Vegas Blvd. S, ☎ 702/891–1111. ☛ Free, rides $1–$3, shows $3, all-day wristband $15 adults, $10 children. ⏲ Winter, daily 10–6; summer, daily 11–7.*

Mountasia Family Fun Center. This amusement park in Green Valley, a fast-growing suburb in southeastern Las Vegas, features miniature golf, a roller-skating rink, go-carts, bumper boats, a Ferris wheel, and an arcade. *2050 Olympic Ave., Henderson, ☎ 702/454–4386. ☛ $2–$5.50 per ride. ⏲ Mon.-Thurs. 2–10, Fri. 2–midnight, Sat. 10 AM–midnight, Sun. 10–10.*

Scandia Family Fun Center. The center has three 18-hole miniature-golf courses, a video arcade, baseball batting, and the Li'l Indy Raceway for miniature-car racing. *2900 Sirius Ave., ☎ 702/364–0070. ☛ Free; fee to play each game. ⏲ Sun.-Thurs. 10 AM–10:30 PM, Fri.-Sat. 10 AM–midnight.*

Wet 'N Wild water park (*see* Tour 1 *in* Chapter 5, Exploring Las Vegas). The 500,000-gallon wave pool is the main attraction at this splash-and-soak theme park.

Zoos and the Outdoors

Bonnie Springs Ranch (Old Nevada, ☎ 702/875–4191) is terrific for children (*see* Excursions *in* Chapter 5, Exploring Las Vegas).

Red Rock Canyon Discovery Trail. Seven miles past the Red Rock Canyon Visitor Center on the one-way scenic loop road is a turnoff for Willow Springs/Lost Creek. A half-mile easy loop trail has been designated a children's discovery trail. It starts in the valley, then climbs up into a wooded area, with rest stops and benches by Lost Creek. The visitor center also makes available a "Junior Rangers" booklet in a question-and-answer format about the local ecology; when children hand in the completed booklet, they get a badge and certificate. *Red Rock Canyon Visitor Center, 1000 Scenic Dr., ☎ 702/363–1921. ☛ Free. ⏲ 8–4:30, loop road: 8–7.*

Southern Nevada Zoological Park. Five minutes from downtown, the hot desert air helps keep a Bengal tiger, an Asian spotted leopard, and African green monkeys happy at the zoo. Among other attractions are a large collection of exotic birds, a rare- and endangered-species breeding program, and a petting zoo with smaller animals. *1775 N. Rancho Dr., ☎ 702/648–5955. ☛ $5 adults, $3 children 2–12. ⏲ Daily 9–4:30.*

Entertainment

Spectaculars

Circus Circus's performances, midway, and video game room (*see* Tour 1 *in* Chapter 5, Exploring Las Vegas).

Dolphins at the Mirage. Seven Atlantic bottlenose dolphins live in a 2.5-million-gallon saltwater habitat behind the Mirage, the largest saltwater pool in the world. The 15-minute tour, which leaves from the pool area, passes through an underwater observation area and winds up in a video room where you can watch tapes of two dolphin births at the habitat. A gift shop sells dolphin souvenirs, and there's a snack bar next door. This is possibly the best place to forget you're in Las Vegas. *The Mirage, 3400 Las Vegas Blvd. S, ☎ 702/791–7111. ☛ $3 adults, children under 10 free. ⌚ Weekdays 11–7, weekends 9–7.*

Excalibur Hotel/Casino. Excalibur's Medieval Village has shops; an open stage where jugglers, puppeteers, and magicians perform; and themed restaurants. Fantasy Faire is a carnival of games, Magic Motion Machine rides, and international gifts. Families enjoy the extravaganza in the showroom, "King Arthur's Tournament." *Excalibur Hotel and Casino, 3850 Las Vegas Blvd. S, ☎ 702/597–7777 or 800/937–7777.*

Production Shows. A handful of Las Vegas shows welcome children. Both "Siegfried and Roy" (at the Mirage) and "Mystere" (at Treasure Island) are suitable for the entire family; "Mystere," a Cirque du Soleil production, is probably the best show in Las Vegas for children four or older. "Country Tonite" (at the Aladdin) and "Legends in Concert" (at the Imperial Palace) are kid-suitable. "Spellbound" (at Harrah's) and "Folies Bergere" (at the Tropicana) welcome children seven and older. And the early show of "Melinda—First Lady of Magic" (at the Lady Luck) is the family performance.

Treasure Island Pirate Show. It's free, it's performed seven times a day (weather cooperating), and it's amazing. In short, it's a must-see, one of the top attractions in Las Vegas. The British Navy frigate H.M.S. *Britannia* sails around the corner from its parking place on Spring Mountain Road across from the Fashion Show Mall to Buccaneer Bay on the Strip. There it encounters the pirate schooner *Hispaniola,* orders the crew to surrender, and then fires on them when they don't. The ensuing battle rages with spectacular pyrotechnics, an impressive sound system, and major stunts (in which all 20 actors wind up in the drink). The pirates score the knockout blow and the frigate sinks, water covering the entire deck. The captain goes down with the ship, but be sure to linger to see him come back up with the ship, a full three minutes later! You'll want to see this show at least twice, once in the daylight (to get the details) and once after dark (to get the full effect of the explosions). *Treasure Island Hotel and Casino, 3300 Las Vegas Blvd. S, ☎ 702/894–7111. ☛ Free. Performances: 1:30, 3, 4:30, 6, 7:30, 9, and 10:30* PM.

Movies

Luxor Hotel/Casino. Three high-tech theaters on the Attractions Level present state-of-the-art media and motion: Theater 1 has sophisticated motion simulation; Theater 2 an ultra-high-resolution big-screen video and a sensational 3-D segment; and Theater 3 the big-screen IMAX format. All three shows are held together by a plot involving the discovery of a lost temple directly below Luxor. Very small children will especially enjoy the 15-minute Nile barge ride around the perimeter of the casino level. *3900 Las Vegas Blvd. S, ☎ 702/262–4000. Theater*

1: ☛ $5, ⏲ 9 AM–11 PM; Theater 2: ☛ $4, ⏲ 10 AM-11 PM; Theater 3: ☛ $5, ⏲ 10 AM–11 PM; Nile barge ride: ☛ $4, ⏲ 9 AM–12:30 AM.

Omnimax Theater. The large-screen, 70mm movies shown in the round at the Caesars Palace cinema are the kind you'll see at major expositions and at the Smithsonian in Washington, D.C. Their subjects include such topics as rafting the Grand Canyon, surfing in Hawaii, and space exploration. *Caesars Palace, 3570 Las Vegas Blvd. S, ☎ 702/731–7900. ☛ $6 adults, $4 children under 13. Shows daily, on the hr, Sun.–Thurs. 2–10 PM, Fri. and Sat. 1–11 PM.*

Sports

Biking. All the rental outlets have bikes for children (*see* Participant Sports and Fitness *in* Chapter 7, Sports and the Outdoors), but the intense Nevada heat may make it unsuitable for kids to ride in summer.

Bowling (*see* Participant Sports and Fitness *in* Chapter 7, Sports and the Outdoors).

Ice-skating at Santa Fe. This is the only ice-skating rink in southern Nevada. The 200-by-85-foot hockey-size rink is open to the public year-round. You might even see Olympic stars Viktor Petrenko (who lives in Las Vegas) and Oksana Baiul (who visits him frequently) there. *Santa Fe Hotel and Casino, 4949 N. Rancho Dr., ☎ 702/658–4900. ☛ $5 adults, $4 children under 13, skate rentals $1.50. ⏲ Weekdays noon–2 and 3–5, weekends 2–4 and 8–10.*

Video Arcades

The best video arcades are found at Bally's, Circus Circus, Luxor, the Riviera, and downstairs at the Forum Shops at Caesars Palace (*see* The Strip *in* Chapter 5, Exploring Las Vegas).

Child Care

Baby-Sitting

Nanny's and Granny's (3790 Redwood Dr., ☎ 702/362–9255) charges $4 an hour per child (five weeks to 12 years). Nanny's and Granny's will also send a baby-sitter to your hotel room (four-hour minimum at $8 an hour, $6 an hour after that). **Vegas Valley Babysitters** (3111 S. Valley View, ☎ 702/871–5161) provides a similar in-room service.

Casino Day Care

Four casinos provide free child-care facilities for children: **Gold Coast** (4000 W. Flamingo Rd., ☎ 702/367–7111), **Sam's Town** (5111 Boulder Hwy., ☎ 702/456–7777), **Showboat** (2800 Fremont St., ☎ 702/385–9123), and **Santa Fe** (4949 N. Rancho Dr., ☎ 702/658–4900). The facilities at Showboat, Sam's Town, and Gold Coast are free for casino patrons, two-hour maximum; you must stay in the building. The Santa Fe's is more for locals; there's an annual registration fee and an hourly rate. At the Gold Coast and Sam's Town, children must be potty-trained.

Children in Casinos

Only those over 21 can gamble in casinos and you can't even play with a kid by your side. But you can walk through the casino with your children, so long as you keep moving and don't gamble (*see* Casino Etiquette *in* Chapter 3, Casinos).

5 Exploring Las Vegas

THE HEART OF LAS VEGAS is the Strip, the 3½-mile stretch of Las Vegas Boulevard South between Hacienda and Sahara avenues. The soul of Las Vegas is the downtown area north of the Strip, whose core is Fremont Street. By exploring these two areas, you'll experience both the commercial lifeblood and pioneer spirit of this most flamboyant of American cities.

Tour 1 proceeds the length of the Strip, starting just south of Hacienda Avenue and taking in all the major hotels and casinos, two shopping malls, a museum, a water park, and other attractions. You can start from the beginning of this tour, or jump in at any point, at any hour of the day. But the earlier you set out, the fewer crowds and the less heat you'll have to contend with. The best time would be around 10 AM, after morning rush hour.

Tour 2 takes you to Fremont Street and newly reurbanized downtown Las Vegas, now a four-block pedestrian mall: palm trees, outdoor cafés, a 100-foot-high vaulted canopy with a "sky parade" light show forming an umbrella over the famous neon icon of Glitter Gulch. The best time to see the Fremont Street Experience is after dark; a few of the nearby attractions are better experienced in the daytime, perhaps in the afternoon.

It's easy to get around Las Vegas by car, even for those who are terrible with directions. Las Vegas Boulevard is the main thoroughfare. Most of the major east–west streets that cross the Strip portion of it are named for major hotels: Tropicana Avenue, Flamingo Road, Desert Inn Road, Sahara Avenue.

Although the 3½ miles from one end of the Strip to the other may not seem such a great stretch, when you add walking from the street to and around the hotels, especially the large ones, you can easily double that distance. Even a stroll "next door" from one enormous property to another may take 15 minutes. And if you're from a place with high humidity, you might not realize just how hot Las Vegas is and get dehydrated rather quickly. The Strip Trolley, which runs every 30 minutes, is the most convenient means of hotel-hopping, since it picks up and drops off passengers at the hotel front door. The local buses are more frequent, though less handy.

Driving the length of the Strip might take only five minutes on a Tuesday morning, but it could take 35 minutes on a Friday or a Saturday night. The best way to use a car on these tours is to park and see the sights in sections. Caesars's garage is also accessible to the Mirage, Barbary Coast, Treasure Island, Flamingo, Imperial Palace, Harrah's, and Sands. You can leave your car in the Frontier parking lot to tour the Desert Inn, Stardust, Silver City, Riviera, Circus Circus, Slots A Fun, and Westward Ho. Park at Excalibur to tour the Tropicana, Luxor, and MGM Grand. Parking downtown is a snap in the lots or structures; it's also free if you validate your ticket at the casino cashier.

Tour 1: The Strip

Numbers in the margin correspond to points of interest on the Las Vegas Strip map. More details on the casinos and hotels noted below are provided in Chapters 3 and 9, respectively.

At the southern end of Las Vegas Boulevard, two blocks south of Ha-
1 cienda Avenue, the **WELCOME TO LAS VEGAS** sign, a familiar part of the land-

scape since the early 1950s, makes a fitting start for a Las Vegas tour and a great photo backdrop, especially at the beginning of a home-video record of your trip. Wait for an ebb in traffic: The sign is on an island in the middle of the street.

Across the street are the big blue gates of the **Las Vegas Air Charter Terminal** at the southwest corner of McCarran International Airport. The traffic here is that of charter flights and fixed base operators, those who fly their own planes into town.

Heading north on the boulevard, you'll see the Las Vegas **Tourist Bureau** on your right. This is a good place to pick up brochures, casino coupon promotions, and funbooks (good for free souvenirs and shrimp cocktails, lucky bucks, 3-for-2 coupons, etc.); you can also book hotel rooms here. Be aware, however, that if you stop in, you're likely to be pressured to sign up for a tour, and that a hefty service charge is added to any show tickets you buy here; you're better off dealing directly with the hotel that offers the entertainment. *5191 Las Vegas Blvd. S,* ☎ *702/739–1482.* ⏲ *Daily 7 AM–midnight.*

If you continue up the Strip about a mile to Reno Avenue, you'll see the **Luxor Hotel,** a perfect pyramid with 2,500 rooms and the largest atrium in the world. Next door is Luxor's sister hotel—both are owned by the Circus Circus corporation—the pink-and-blue, turreted-and-towered, 4,032-room **Excalibur,** the world's largest hotel for three whole years, until it was deposed of its title when the MGM Grand (*see below*) opened.

Across the Strip from Excalibur, sprawling at the southeast corner of Tropicana Avenue and Las Vegas Boulevard, is the **Tropicana Resort and Casino,** featuring the "Island of Las Vegas," an oversize swimming pool within a simulated lagoon that has rock waterfalls and exotic fish, birds, and vegetation. Across Tropicana Avenue from the Trop is **MGM Grand**—with 5,005 rooms, a 171,000-square-foot casino, and a 33-acre amusement park. Now that the Grand and Luxor are in service, this Four Corners area may well be the most magnetic tourist intersection in the country.

A photo that frequently accompanied magazine articles on Las Vegas
2 in the 1950s showed a Strip gas station with a **FREE ASPIRIN AND TENDER SYMPATHY** sign. The sign still stands today, with an invitation on the other side: ASK US ANYTHING. You'll find the sign on the west side of the Strip, one block north of Tropicana Avenue, at the front of the Kenneth L. Lehman Strip Union 76 gas station.

About a block farther up the boulevard, on the east side, the large gold hotel with a magic lamp shining atop is—what else?—the **Aladdin Hotel and Casino.** A short side trip east of the Aladdin on Harmon Avenue is the new **Hard Rock Hotel;** it opened in March 1995 and is billed as the "world's only rock 'n roll casino." Rock memorabilia abound, slot-machine handles are in the shape of guitar necks, rock music blares over a million speakers, and the crap tables feature Grateful Dead lyrics. The crowd, dealers, and other employees are young, friendly, and hip.

Back on the Strip, north of the Aladdin, is the old Four Corners area of the Strip, named for the four large casino hotels that once ruled over the intersection of Las Vegas Boulevard and Flamingo Road. The southwest corner was once dominated by the **Dunes Hotel and Country Club,** which was leveled in two spectacular implosions; one tower was demolished to coincide with the opening of Treasure Island, while the other tower sustained a more workmanlike and less public implo-

Bonanza, **12**
Caesars Palace, **3**
Candlelight Wedding Chapel, **9**
Circus Circus, **8**
FREE ASPIRIN AND TENDER SYMPATHY sign, **2**
Guardian Angel Cathedral, **6**
Guinness World of Records Museum, **10**
Imperial Palace Automobile Museum, **4**
Las Vegas Convention Center, **7**
The Mirage, **5**
WELCOME TO LAS VEGAS sign, **1**
Wet N Wild water park, **11**

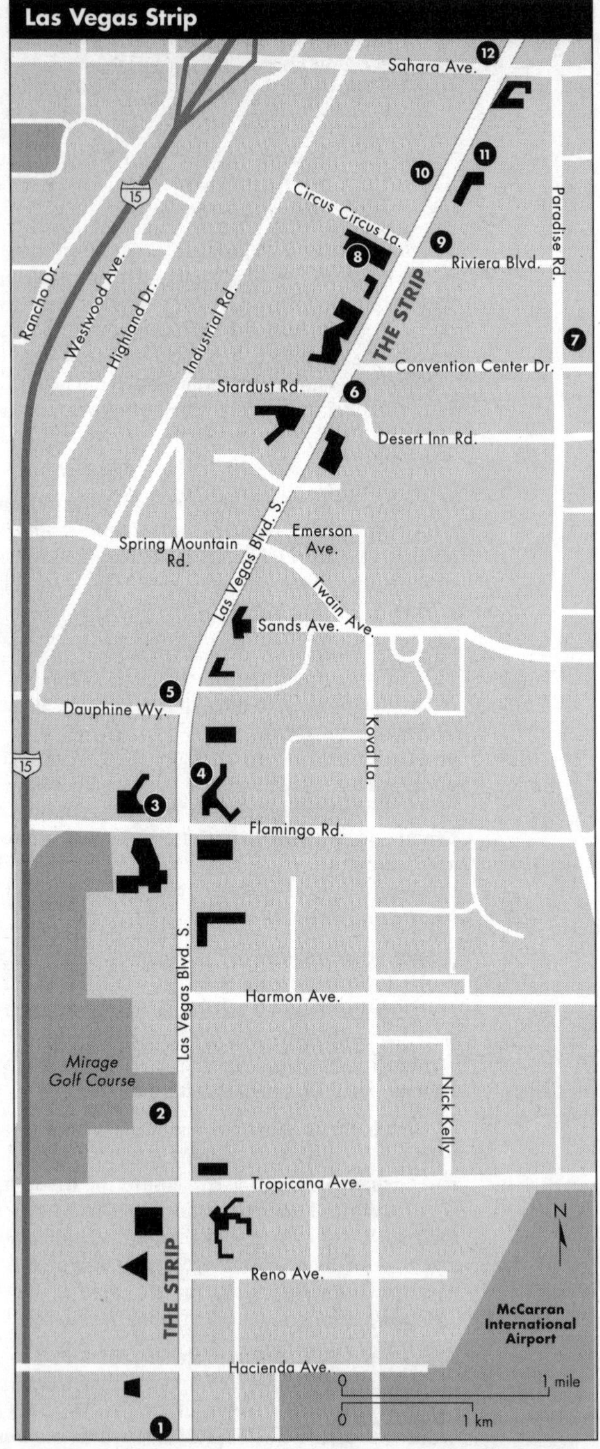

sion to make way for two huge new megaresorts, **Bellagio** and **Victoria,** that are being built on the Dunes property. **Caesars Palace** occupies the northwest corner (plus more than half of the long block); **Bally's Casino Resort** stretches from the southeast corner of Las Vegas Boulevard and Flamingo Road; and the **Flamingo Hilton and Tower** had the northeast corner covered until the small **Barbary Coast Hotel and Casino** interposed itself between the Flamingo Hilton and Flamingo Road.

★ 3 **Caesars Palace** (3570 Las Vegas Blvd. S, ☎ 702/731–7110) is a must-see casino. Until all the new theme resorts went up, Caesars's designers could lay claim to having done the best job of transforming Bugsy Siegel's vision of Las Vegas into a reality: Walking into Caesars is like entering another world. The best way to approach the hotel is via the middle people mover, where a muscular centurion bearing a shield and wearing ancient garb invites you into the $2.5 million domed World of Caesar. The moving sidewalk carries you into a darkened rotunda with a miniature re-creation of ancient Rome that employs holography, fiber optics, and laser-powered audio effects; it then proceeds into the monumental Olympic Casino. Now you're on your own. If you go right, you enter the Forum Shops, one of the most imaginative and upmarket malls in the country (*see* Chapter 6, Shopping, for details). Head to the left and you'll pass the old high-roller casino, the sumptuous buffet, the huge race and sports book, and the shopping area, overseen by a giant replica of Michelangelo's *David.* Continue in this general direction and you'll run into Cleopatra, smiling down at you from the bow of her vessel, *Cleopatra's Barge,* where lounge musicians—and the dancing they inspire—get the boat rocking, literally.

East of the corner of Flamingo and the Strip, beyond the Barbary Coast, are two off-Strip casinos popular with local residents. **Bourbon Street Hotel and Casino** and **Maxim Hotel and Casino** offer lower table minimums, smaller crowds, and better gambling promotions than you'll find in the Strip casinos. The Flamingo Hilton's solution to the crowd-control problem in 1989 was to build another casino next door—**O'Sheas Casino,** with a Luck of the Irish theme.

The next stop north on the Strip, the Oriental-style **Imperial Palace Hotel**
4 **and Casino** hosts the **Imperial Palace Automobile Museum,** a collection of more than 200 antique, classic, and special-interest vehicles displayed on an upper level of the hotel's parking garage. Among the cars, trucks, and motorcycles on view is a 1939 Mercedes touring sedan once owned by Adolf Hitler, said to be worth more than $600,000. In 1992, the museum opened the world's largest Deusenberg collection, comprising 25 vehicles built between 1925 and 1937. *3535 Las Vegas Blvd. S,* ☎ *702/731–3311.* ☛ *$6.95 adults, $3 senior citizens and children under 12 (note: coupons for free admission are usually handed out in front of the hotel).* ⏲ *Daily 9:30 AM–11:30 PM.*

Harrah's showboat, adjoined by a small outdoor shopping arcade, is north of the Imperial Palace. One of Las Vegas's most popular spec-
★ 5 tacles, the gleaming, golden **Mirage** stands opposite the showboat on the west side of the boulevard. A towering, man-made waterfall, cascading over several levels into a giant pool, marks your entrance. Crowning the waterfall and stopping nighttime traffic along the Strip, a computer-driven volcano erupts every 30 minutes in a tower of flames. The rare white tigers used in the Siegfried and Roy show guard the south entrance behind a Plexiglas enclosure.

Back on the east side of the Strip, beyond Harrah's Casino, the **Sands Hotel and Casino** was the locale in 1960 for the film *Ocean's 11,* with Frank Sinatra, Dean Martin, Sammy Davis Jr., Peter Lawford, and Joey Bishop.

The large building at the northwest corner of Spring Mountain Road and Las Vegas Boulevard is the **Fashion Show Mall,** a Strip shopping attraction that has more than 140 specialty shops and boutiques (*see* Chapter 6, Shopping, for details). The **Frontier Hotel and Gambling Hall,** north of the mall, was the second resort to open on the Strip (as the Last Frontier); these days, its lures are a young crowd, minisuites, and bargain food. Opposite the Frontier, on the east side of the boulevard, the **Desert Inn Hotel and Casino** is where the reclusive billionaire Howard Hughes ran his $300 million Las Vegas business for four years; popular mythology has it that from Thanksgiving 1966 until December 1970 Hughes never left his room.

6 The busiest church in town, **Guardian Angel Cathedral** (336 E. Desert Inn Rd., ☎ 702/735–5241), just east of the Strip, has standing room only on Saturday, as visitors pray for luck and drop casino chips in the collection cups during a special tourist mass. Once a week a priest takes the chips to Caesars Palace to cash them in. The 4 PM mass on Saturday is so crowded, usually with 300 standees, that visitors are asked to attend the 5:15 mass or one of the five Sunday masses instead.

Back on the west side of Las Vegas Boulevard, the **Stardust Hotel and Casino,** with one of the most impressive neon signs in Las Vegas, and, to the north, the **Westward Ho Motel and Casino,** a large motel with a small casino, are separated by the only McDonald's in America with a flashing neon sign. The window seats inside the restaurant provide a good view of the lights and the traffic on the Strip.

Opposite the Stardust, Convention Center Drive leads east from Las Vegas Boulevard to Paradise Road. On the way is **Debbie Reynolds Hollywood Hotel and Casino,** a 200-room miniresort owned and run hands-on by the unsinkable woman herself. Debbie performs in the showroom most nights; a small part of her vast collection of Hollywood memorabilia is on display in the Hollywood Museum. Just to the north of the Las Vegas Convention Center, on the east side of Paradise Road, stands what was for many years the country's largest hotel, the **Las Vegas Hilton,** with 3,147 rooms. The big news at the Hilton is its partnership with Paramount; together, the two huge corporations plan to build a Star Trek virtual-reality attraction, scheduled to open in late 1996.

One of the most important aspects of Las Vegas's commercial life is its conventions, which account for about 15% of the visitor volume. More than 700 conventions of varying sizes are held here every year,
7 most of them in the **Las Vegas Convention Center** (3150 Paradise Rd., ☎ 702/892–0711). One of the most attractive aspects of the convention center is its proximity to all of the hotels and the airport.

If you head back to the Strip on Convention Center Drive and con-
8 tinue north on Las Vegas Boulevard, you'll come to **Circus Circus,** the busiest casino in town. It's almost always a madhouse beneath this pink-and-white big top, and it may require an effort to deal with the traffic in getting here, but if you have kids, you will probably want to visit. On the main floor are a mammoth casino, gift shops, a buffet, and a wedding chapel. The mezzanine boasts a midway with carnival games, fun-house mirrors, and free circus acts daily, 11 AM–midnight. Out back is Grand Slam Canyon, a 5-acre amusement park enclosed by a bright

pink space frame, complete with the largest indoor roller coaster in the world. Little wonder that kids seem to prefer Circus Circus to any other Las Vegas casino experience. The smaller casino out front, **Slots A Fun,** has the least-expensive snack-bar food on the Strip, some of the lowest minimums, and—what else?—lotsa slots.

Across the Strip you'll find **Silver City,** a Circus Circus enterprise with lower minimum betting and smaller crowds than the parent casino (bets here run a little higher than at sister casino, Slots A Fun). Beyond it, the Riviera Hotel has an indoor fast-food court, along with three production shows and a comedy club, and the world's second-largest casino.

9 Just north of the Riviera, the **Candlelight Wedding Chapel** (2855 Las Vegas Blvd. S, ☎ 702/735–4179) is the busiest place to get married in town. Especially on Saturday, you'll see couples lined up here, waiting to tie the knot. This is a convenient place to watch a Las Vegas wedding ceremony; just walk in and take a seat. Some ceremonies take place in the gazebo outside the chapel.

Adjacent to the chapel are another shopping minimall and Trader Ann's Trading Post, a good spot to buy tacky Las Vegas souvenirs at night; it's open until 1 AM.

Back on the west side of Las Vegas Boulevard and a short distance to
10 the north, you'll find the **Guinness World of Records Museum,** with colorful displays, video footage, and computer data banks of the best, biggest, and most bizarre in sports, science, nature, entertainment, and more. *2780 Las Vegas Blvd. S,* ☎ *702/792–3766.* ☛ *$4.95 adults, $3.95 senior citizens and military, $2.95 children under 12.* ⏲ *9 AM–6 PM.*

If you cross the Strip again, you'll come to the entrance of the 26-acre
11 **Wet 'N Wild water park,** which provides family-oriented recreation in a 500,000-gallon wave pool, three water flumes, a water roller coaster, slides, cascading fountains, and lagoons. Showers, changing rooms, and lockers are available, and inner tubes and rafts are for rent. Shops and concession stands sell souvenirs and food. *2601 Las Vegas Blvd. S,* ☎ *702/737–3819.* ☛ *$18.95 adults, $14.95 children 3–12.* ⏲ *May–Oct., daily 10–8.*

Just to the north is the Sahara Hotel, where most people think the Strip ends; however, the Stratosphere complex (*see below*) is the final casino you'll encounter along Las Vegas Boulevard.

Those who are determined to visit only one gift shop in Las Vegas will
12 want to make it **Bonanza,** World's Largest Gift Shop, on the west side of the Strip opposite the Sahara. If it's not really the world's largest, it is the biggest and best in town, with an impressive collection of Las Vegas knickknacks, gimcracks, and gewgaws (this is where you'll find your life-size Wayne Newton blow-up doll), the most extensive selection of Las Vegas T-shirts and postcards, along with jewelry, gambling supplies, western memorabilia, film, fudge, and aspirin. *2460 Las Vegas Blvd. S,* ☎ *702/385–7359.* ⏲ *Daily 8 AM–midnight.*

At Sahara Avenue, you've come to the end of the Strip proper, but not the last casino you'll want to see. A half mile north on the west side of Las Vegas Boulevard is the **Stratosphere Hotel and Tower,** which used to be Bob Stupak's Vegas World. Vegas World closed in early 1995, was renovated and expanded, and is reopening in spring 1996, along with the 1,149-foot Stratosphere Tower, the tallest observation tower in the country, and the tallest building west of the Mississippi.

Tour 2: Downtown

Numbers in the margin correspond to points of interest on the Las Vegas Downtown map. More details on the casinos and hotels described below are provided in Chapters 3 and 9, respectively.

Two miles from the northern end of the Strip at Sahara Avenue, Las Vegas Boulevard meets Fremont Street in downtown Las Vegas. One of the world's great collections of neon signs is here, along with a spectacular light show under a four-block-long canopy, but it can only be appreciated after the sun has gone down. Because the downtown hotels are almost on top of each other, you're hit with a blast of bright lights when you first glimpse Fremont Street at night, especially from Las Vegas Boulevard. Las Vegas gambling began on Fremont in the 1930s, and the original honky-tonk atmosphere remained up until recently, when the Fremont Street Experience transformed Glitter Gulch into a mall. However, the 50-foot-tall neon cowboy (Vegas Vic) and cowgirl (Vegas Vicky), the street barkers, and the crowds of wide-eyed international tourists all lend a carnival atmosphere to the scene.

To enter fully into the swing of downtown, don't be afraid to get sucked in by the aggressive sidewalk solicitors. The come-ons vary (spin the wheel, crack the safe, take the tokens), but the object is always the same: to hustle you inside and get you to feed the hungry slots. As long as you don't succumb to the hard sell, start pulling out big bills, and making sucker bets, you can enjoy whatever outrageousness is going on in the vicinity, take as much advantage as you can of the free or extremely inexpensive food and drink, and bring home a special memory of the wacky world of downtown Las Vegas.

Fremont Street runs east from Main Street, which is five blocks west of, and runs parallel to, Las Vegas Boulevard. At the corner of Main and Fremont, the **Plaza Hotel** houses the Amtrak station and a casino. The heart of downtown Las Vegas, called Glitter Gulch, is the four-block stretch of Fremont Street that begins at the Plaza. Across Main Street from the Plaza is the **Las Vegas Club Hotel and Casino,** with its sports theme and, like many downtown casinos, relatively low table minimums; unlike most other Fremont Street joints, it has a nice high
1 ceiling. Across the street, atop the venerable Pioneer Club, is **Vegas Vic,** who's been waving to and welcoming visitors to downtown Las Vegas since 1951. Be sure to check out the **Nevada Gold Museum** inside the Pioneer, full of rare casino chips from around the state and black-and-white historical photos of Las Vegas.

At 1st Street, you might walk a block north to Ogden Avenue to inspect the **California Hotel and Casino** (that's the one with the Hawaiian decor). The 100 block on Fremont Street finds the block-long **Binion's Horseshoe Hotel and Casino** on the north facing the **Golden Nugget Hotel and Casino** on the south. Binion's hosts the annual World Series of Poker, and people often wait in line for a place at a blackjack table; its old-time ambience—hardwood walls and dealers wearing string ties—is so convincing that you get the feeling Binion's has been here forever. You may have your picture taken in front of a cool million dollars—it's not only the best souvenir of Las Vegas, it's also free; show up between 4 PM and midnight at Binion's display of a hundred rare $10,000 bills to get your picture snapped. The white-marble walls, gold-plated slots, and display of the world's largest gold nuggets of the upscale Golden Nugget put this casino in a radically different class from that of all the other downtown gambling halls.

Cashman Field, **2**
Las Vegas Academy of International Studies, Visual and Performing Arts, **3**
Vegas Vic, **1**

Las Vegas Downtown

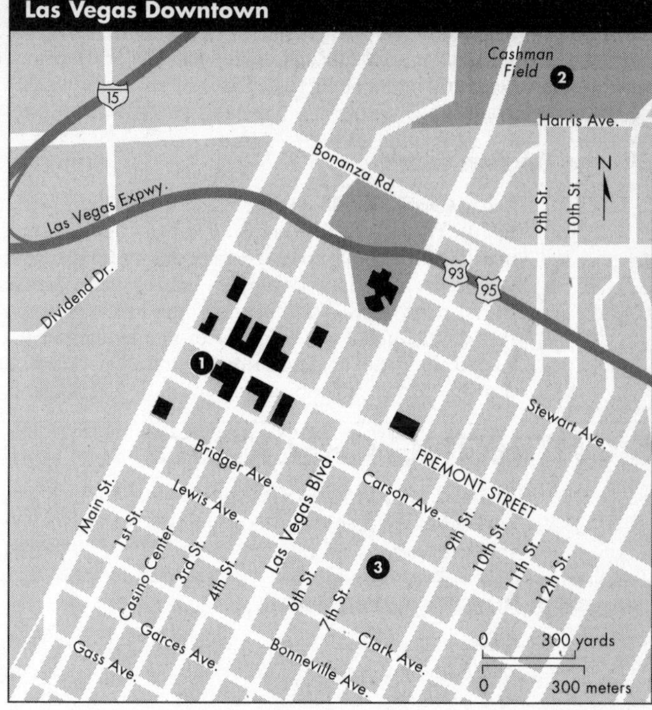

In the next block east on Fremont Street, the **Fremont Hotel and Casino** on the north, with a photogenic neon sign outside and a bingo room inside, faces the **Four Queens Hotel and Casino** on the south; stop into the Queens to see the largest slot machine in the world.

A turn to the north on 3rd Street and a one-block walk to Ogden Avenue will take you to the crowded **Lady Luck Casino and Hotel,** which, with its big picture windows, is the brightest and airiest casino downtown. In the next block east on Ogden Avenue, the **Gold Spike Hotel and Casino** offers Las Vegas's lowest limits on everything—blackjack, keno, craps, and video poker.

In the 300 block of Fremont Street, across 3rd Street from the Four Queens, the 34-story **Fitzgerald's Hotel and Casino**—formerly the Sundance—is the second tallest building in Nevada.

For a look at the other convention center in Las Vegas, which doubles as a sports facility, drive 1 mile north from Fremont Street on Las Vegas
2 Boulevard. **Cashman Field** (850 Las Vegas Blvd. N, ☎ 702/386–7100) has a 100,000-square-foot exhibit hall, 17,000 square feet of meeting space, and the 2,000-seat auditorium that was used as the courtroom for the trial of Wayne Newton's libel suit against NBC News.

Our last casino stop on Fremont Street, one block east of Las Vegas Boulevard between 6th and 7th streets, is the city's oldest standing casino, **El Cortez Hotel,** which opened for business in 1941; Bugsy Siegel started out his short but illustrious Vegas career here.

A two-block stroll south on 7th Street to Bridger Avenue will take you miles from the honky-tonk of downtown and bring you to the every-
3 day life of the **Las Vegas Academy of International Studies, Visual and Performing Arts** (315 S. 7th St., ☎ 702/799–7800). Until 1993, this

was the venerable Las Vegas High School, but it remains the oldest permanent school building in Las Vegas. Built in 1930 for $350,000, the structure is a state historical landmark, the only example of 1930s Art Deco architecture in the city. Many Nevada officials are Las Vegas High graduates.

Off the Beaten Track

Young Electric Sign Company (YESCO; 5119 Cameron St., ☎ 702/876–8080). The headquarters of the company that has been taking advantage of Nevada's liberal sign regulations for 60 years is less than 2 miles west of the Strip. Its backyard is a bizarre yet picturesque "graveyard" of old neon signs. You probably won't get permission to rummage through them, but you can drive by and around the parking lot to get a good glimpse of a unique neon history. YESCO is on Cameron Street, near the corner of Tropicana Avenue.

SIGHTSEEING CHECKLISTS

These lists of Las Vegas's principal attractions include those that were covered in the preceding tours and others that are described here for the first time.

Historical Buildings and Sites

Golden Gate Hotel. Stripped of a facade that was installed over the original adobe in the mid-1950s, this building at the corner of Fremont and Main streets was restored to its appearance in the early days of Las Vegas. The **Victory Hotel,** a block south on Main Street, was built in 1910 and retains the original balcony and veranda.

El Cortez casino wing (Tour 2).

Las Vegas Academy of International Arts (Tour 2).

Old Las Vegas Mormon Fort. Southern Nevada's oldest historical site was built by the Mormons in 1855 as an agricultural mission to give refuge to travelers along the Salt Lake–Los Angeles trail, many of whom were bound for the California goldfields. Left to the Native Americans after the gold rush, the adobe fort was later revitalized by a miner and his partners. In 1895 it was turned into a resort, and the city's first swimming pool was constructed by damming Las Vegas Creek. Today the restored fort contains more than half the original bricks; antiques and relics help re-create a turn-of-the-century Mormon living room. *Corner of Washington Ave. and Las Vegas Blvd. N, at Cashman Field (enter through parking lot B), ☎ 702/486–3511. ☛ Free. ⏲ Daily 8–4.*

Wedding Chapels

At the same time that "wide-open" gambling was legalized in 1931, Nevada also adopted liberal divorce and marriage laws as part of the strategy to attract tourists. A divorce could be obtained after six weeks of residency. A wedding could be arranged without a blood test or a waiting period; once you had a license, a justice of the peace could unite you in marital bliss in five minutes. The rules haven't changed for more than 60 years, and today weddings are big business in Las Vegas, to the tune of more than $3 million in marriage licenses alone. New Year's Eve and Valentine's Day are the most popular wedding dates.

Celebrities (Bruce Willis, Bette Midler, Joan Collins, Michael Jordan, Richard Gere) have found it handy to pop into a chapel and have a quick ceremony. It's also a popular formula for nearly 85,000 couples a year from around the country. Critics complain that the 15-minute weddings have all the charm of an assembly line; proponents argue that, at a time when families can drive a couple crazy with expensive preparations and guilt-producing obligations, the bride- and groom-to-be can hop in a car and enjoy the experience by themselves.

Candlelight Wedding Chapel (2855 Las Vegas Blvd. S, ☎ 702/735–4179), **Little Church of the West** (3960 Las Vegas Blvd. S, ☎ 702/739–7971), and **Little White Chapel** (1301 Las Vegas Blvd. S, ☎ 702/382–5943 or 800/545–8111) are the three most popular wedding chapels. All operate in basically the same way: You make an appointment, show up, pay a fee for the ceremony (usually $50), and everything else (photos, music, flowers, videos) is extra. So is the suggested "donation" of $35 for the minister. Most chapels accept credit cards but ask that the donation be paid in cash. Wedding ceremonies can also be performed in your hotel room, your car at the drive-up wedding window of Little White Chapel, in a hot-air balloon, or wherever your heart, your wallet, and your fiancé desire.

Marriage Licenses

Clark County Marriage License Bureau is the place to obtain a marriage license, which costs $35. Both applicants must apply in person; those ages 16 to 18 need the consent of their parents or legal guardians. Blood tests are not required, and there is no waiting period. *200 S. 3rd St., ☎ 702/455–3156 or 702/455–4415 (after 5 PM, weekends, and holidays). ⏲ Mon.–Thurs. 8 AM–midnight and from Fri. at 8 AM to Sun. at midnight.*

Throughout Vegas you'll see signs offering "free wedding information" services; what you'll get from them is what you've just read here—plus a sales pitch for whatever chapel is paying that service a commission. If you have questions about Las Vegas weddings, call the chapels.

Museums and Galleries

Clark County Heritage Museum. Exhibits on settler life, early gambling, and nuclear testing are displayed in a chronological history of southern Nevada. Other attractions include a fully restored bungalow home from the 1920s, built by a pioneer Las Vegas merchant; a replica of a 19th-century frontier print shop; and buildings, structures, and machinery dating from the turn of the century. The gift shop sells Native American artifacts. *1830 S. Boulder Hwy., Henderson, ☎ 702/455–7955. ☛ $1.50 adults, $1 ages 3–18 and senior citizens. ⏲ 9–4:30.*

Guinness World of Records Museum. Various Guinness world records (the most married man, the smallest woman, the largest snowplow, etc.) are brought to life in graphic exhibits, video and audio, and computer data banks. The Las Vegas display alone is worth the price of admission. *2780 Las Vegas Blvd. S, ☎ 702/792–3766. ☛ $4.95 adults; $3.95 senior citizens, students, and military personnel. ⏲ Daily 9 AM–6 PM.*

Imperial Palace Automobile Museum (Tour 1).

James R. Dickinson Library. The special-collections department of this library of the University of Nevada, Las Vegas, has the best gathering of materials about Las Vegas and gambling that you'll find anywhere. *4505 Maryland Pkwy., ☎ 702/739–3285. ☛ Free. ⏲ Mon.–Thurs. 8 AM–midnight, Fri.–Sat. 9–6, Sun. 9–7.*

Las Vegas Art Museum. Constructed in 1935 from railroad ties, the art museum has both a permanent collection and changing exhibitions of the work of local and national artists. *3333 W. Washington Blvd.,* ☎ *702/647–4300.* ☛ *Free.* ⏲ *Mon.–Sat. 10–3, Sun. noon–3.*

Las Vegas Museum of Natural History (*see* Chapter 4, Las Vegas for Children).

★ **Liberace Museum.** Costumes, cars, photographs, even mannequins of the late entertainer make this museum the kitschiest place in town. In addition to Lee's collection of pianos (one of them was played by Chopin; another, a concert grand, was owned by George Gershwin), you can see his Czar Nicholas uniform and a blue-velvet cape styled after the coronation robes of King George V. Be sure to check out the gift shop—where else can you find Liberace soap, ashtrays, and other novelties? *1775 E. Tropicana Ave.,* ☎ *702/798–5595.* ☛ *$6.50 adults, $4.50 senior citizens, $2 children under 12.* ⏲ *Mon.–Sat. 10–5, Sun. 1–5.*

Nevada State Museum and Historical Society. Regional history from the time of the Spanish exploration and the building of Las Vegas after World War II are the big subjects in this museum of the history, archaeology, and anthropology of southern Nevada. Outdoors, the park and ponds that surround the lakeside museum in Lorenzi Park show plants and animals native to the region. *700 E. Twin Lakes Dr.,* ☎ *702/486–5205.* ☛ *$2 adults, under 18 free.* ⏲ *Daily 9–5.*

EXCURSIONS

If the city of Las Vegas lacks in variety, the number of man-made and natural scenic wonders a short drive away more than makes up for it. The price categories of hotels and restaurants mentioned in the excursion tours are those used in the Reno section of Chapter 11, Reno and Lake Tahoe.

Hoover Dam and Lake Mead

Numbers in the margin correspond to points of interest on the Excursions from Las Vegas map.

Boulder City, the enormous Hoover Dam, and Lake Mead to the north of it are where most day-trippers head first.

On leaving Las Vegas, follow Boulder Highway (U.S. 93/95) through the Las Vegas suburbs, city of Henderson, and desert terrain for 23
❶ miles to reach **Boulder City.** In the early 1930s, this town was built by the federal government to house 5,000 construction workers on the Hoover Dam project. A strict moral code was enforced, and to this day, the 65-year-old model city is the only community in Nevada where gambling is illegal. After the dam was completed, the town shrunk by more than half, kept alive by the management and maintenance crews of the dam and Lake Mead. But Boulder City slowly recovered, and is now a vibrant little Southwest town with a movie theater, numerous gift shops, and a historic hotel. The **Boulder City Chamber of Commerce** (☎ 702/293–2034) is a good source of information.

❷ Continue east on U.S. 93 about 11 miles to reach the site of **Hoover Dam.** Congress authorized the funding of the $175 million dam in 1928 for two purposes: flood control and the generation of electricity. One of the seven man-made wonders of the world, the dam is 727 feet high (the equivalent of a 70-story building) and 660 feet thick. Construction of the dam required 4.4 million cubic yards of concrete—enough to build a two-lane highway from San Francisco to New York. Orig-

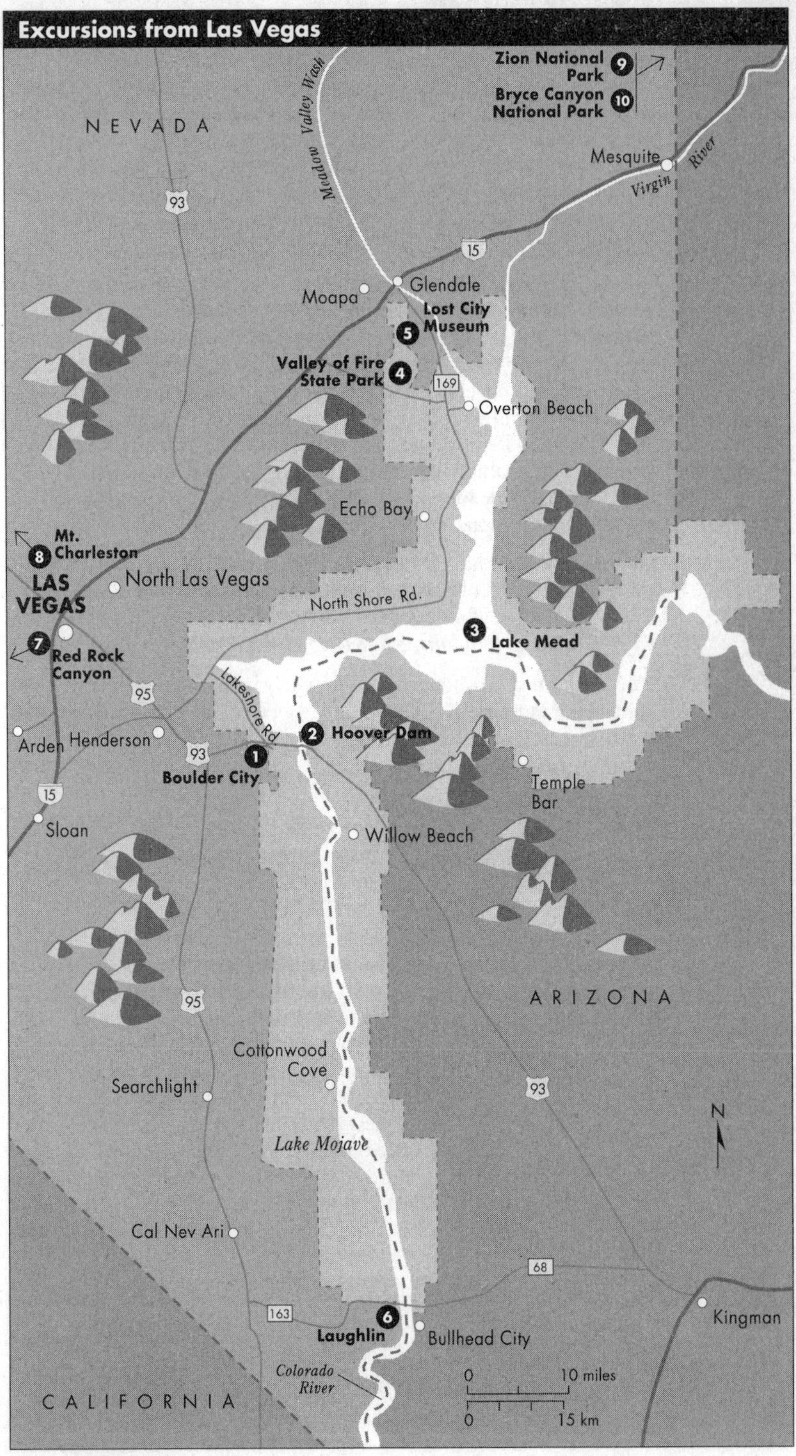
Excursions from Las Vegas
Zion National Park 9
Bryce Canyon National Park 10
NEVADA
Meadow Valley Wash
93
Mesquite
Virgin River
15
Glendale
Moapa
Lost City Museum 5
Valley of Fire State Park 4
169
Overton Beach
Echo Bay
Mt. Charleston 8
LAS VEGAS
North Las Vegas
North Shore Rd.
3 Lake Mead
7 Red Rock Canyon
95
Lakeshore Rd.
2 Hoover Dam
Arden
Henderson
93
1 Boulder City
Temple Bar
15
Sloan
Willow Beach
ARIZONA
95
Cottonwood Cove
Searchlight
93
N
Lake Mojave
Cal Nev Ari
68
163
6 Laughlin
Bullhead City
Kingman
Colorado River
0 10 miles
0 15 km
CALIFORNIA

inally called Boulder Dam, the structure was renamed for Herbert Hoover, Secretary of Commerce during the critical planning stages of the dam. More than 700,000 people a year (30 million since the tours began in 1937) take the Bureau of Reclamation's 45-minute guided tour, which leads visitors deep inside the structure for a look at its inner workings. Tours leave every few minutes from the exhibit building at the top of the dam. *Hwy. 93 east of Boulder City, ☎ 702/293–8367.* ☛ *$4 adults, $2 senior citizens, children under 11 free. Tours daily 8–6:30 in summer, 9–4:15 in winter.*

3 For the approach to **Lake Mead,** return west on U.S. 93 about 6 miles to the intersection with Lakeshore Drive. Here the **Alan Bible Visitor Center** (☎ 702/293–8906) can provide information on the history of the lake and on the accommodations available along its shore. Lake Mead's surface covers 229 square miles and its irregular shoreline extends for 550 miles. This is the largest man-made lake in the country, with Colorado River water backed up behind the dam. Come here for fishing, waterskiing, swimming, boating, sailboarding, and diving. The **National Park Service** (☎ 702/293–8906) can give you details on the lake's recreational opportunities and facilities.

Lake Mead Cruises has a 250-passenger stern-wheeler that plies the lower portion of the lake; breakfast, cocktails, and dinner with dancing are available on some of the cruises. *Lake Mead Marina, ☎ 702/293–6180. Cost: $14.50–$43 adults, $6–$12 children 3–12.*

A five-minute drive along the shore will bring you to the first marina, **Lake Mead Marina** (☎ 702/293–3484). Here you'll find boat rentals, a beach, camping facilities, a gift shop, and a restaurant. A drive of about an hour will take you along the north side of the lake, where you'll find five more marinas. When you reach the upper arm of the lake, about a mile past Overton Beach, look for the sign announcing the Valley of Fire. Turn left here, and go about 6 miles to reach the **Valley of Fire Visitor Center** (☎ 702/397–2088).

Valley of Fire

4 The 56,000-acre **Valley of Fire State Park,** dedicated in 1935, was Nevada's first state park, situated less than 2 miles west of the upper arm of Lake Mead and 55 miles northeast of Las Vegas. The Valley of Fire takes its name from its distinctive coloration, which ranges from lavender to tangerine to bright red, giving the valley an otherworldly appearance. Here the incredible rock formations that have been weathered into unusual shapes suggest elephants, domes, beehives. Mysterious signs and symbols, called petroglyphs (carvings etched into the rock) and pictographs (pictures drawn or painted on the rock's surface), are believed to be the work of the Basketmaker and Anasazi Pueblo people, who lived along the nearby Muddy River between 300 BC and AD 1150.

The visitor center has exhibits, films, lectures, slide shows, and information about the 50 campsites within the park. The park is open year-round; the best times to visit, especially during the heat of the summer, are sunrise and sunset, when the light is especially spectacular. *Hwy. 169, Overton 89040, ☎ 702/397–2088.* ⏲ *Visitor center: daily 8:30–4:30.*

5 To visit the **Lost City Museum,** head east from the Valley of Fire on Highway 169 for about 8 miles. Turn left at the "T" and continue for another 8 miles to the museum. Here you'll find on display early Pueblo Indian artifacts, Paiute basketry, weapons, and a restored Basketmaker

pit house. *721 S. Hwy. 169,* ☎ *702/397–2193.* ☛ *$2 adults.* ⏲ *Daily 8:30–4:30.*

Laughlin, Nevada

For those who'd like to see a chunk of southern Nevada and the Mojave Desert and still have a major gambling center as a destination—
6 on a river no less—**Laughlin,** Nevada, is the place. From Las Vegas, take Boulder Highway (U.S. 95/93) east, and follow U.S. 95 south almost to the California border. There, a left turn onto Highway 163 will take you east into Laughlin. It's 90 miles away and should take no more than an hour and a half to reach.

Laughlin is a classic state-line city, separated from Arizona by the Colorado River. Nevada's newest community, Laughlin has become the state's third major resort area, with 11,100 rooms added in the past 11 years. The city generally attracts retired travelers who spend at least part of the winter in Arizona, and a younger resort-loving crowd. Like Las Vegas, Laughlin draws folks who like to gamble—especially those who prefer low-pressure, low-minimum tables, cheap food, low-cost rooms, and slots galore.

If you've been shuttered in Las Vegas casinos for a few days, you'll be amazed by the big picture windows overlooking the Colorado River and the bright, airy, and open feeling that they lend to the Laughlin joints. The dealers are generally friendlier and the bettors more relaxed than in Las Vegas.

A turn to the south off Highway 163 onto Casino Drive will take you to the gambling halls: **Riverside Resort** (1650 S. Casino Dr., ☎ 702/298–2535 or 800/227–3849), **Regency Casino** (1950 S. Casino Dr., ☎ 702/298–2439), **Edgewater** (2020 S. Casino Dr., ☎ 702/298–2453 or 800/677–4837), **Colorado Belle** (2100 S. Casino Dr., ☎ 702/298–4000 or 800/458–9500), **Golden Nugget** (2300 S. Casino Dr., ☎ 702/298–7111 or 800/237–1739), **Pioneer Hotel** (2200 S. Casino Dr., ☎ 702/298–2442 or 800/634–3469), **Ramada Express** (2121 S. Casino Dr., ☎ 702/298–4200 or 800/272–6232), **Gold River** (2700 S. Casino Dr., ☎ 702/298–2242 or 800/835–7903), **Flamingo Hilton** (1900 S. Casino Dr., ☎ 702/298–5111 or 800/445–8667), and **Harrah's** (2900 S. Casino Dr., ☎ 702/298–4600 or 800/447–8700).

The **Laughlin Chamber of Commerce** (☎ 702/298–2214 or 800/227–5245) can provide further information on the area.

Red Rock Canyon and Old Nevada

For a 13-mile drive through the red rock formations and unusual high-desert scenery of southern Nevada, head west (about 16 miles) from
7 Las Vegas on Charleston Boulevard (Highway 159) to **Red Rock Canyon** and its scenic loop. The BLM Visitor Center here has exhibits of plant, animal, and desert life. *Charleston Blvd.,* ☎ *702/363–1921.* ⏲ *Daily 8–4:30. Loop open daily 7 AM–8 PM.*

Leave the loop by exiting south onto Highway 159 and go 3 miles to **Spring Mountain Ranch State Park.** This prime piece of property became a ranch in the 1860s; it was designated a state park in 1971. The red ranch house, white picket fences, long green lawns, and beautiful mountain backdrop make this a perfect place for a picnic. *Hwy. 159,* ☎ *702/875–4141.* ☛ *$4 per car.* ⏲ *Daily 8–7. Ranch house open Fri. and Mon. noon–4, weekends 10–4.*

Continue another mile on Highway 159 until you come to **Old Nevada,** a western theme park. Here the Wild West comes to life with gunfights and hangings staged in the street, silent movies, an opera house, museums, a cemetery, and a minitrain that runs around the grounds. *Hwy. 159,* ☎ *702/875–4191.* ☛ *$6.50 adults, $5.50 senior citizens, $4 children 5–11.* ⏲ *Daily 10:30–6.*

After shopping for gifts or souvenirs at Old Nevada, most folks mosey next door to the **Bonnie Springs Ranch,** which offers a duck pond, petting zoo where kids can feed baby lambs or stroke a buffalo, and small railroad that runs on weekends. Equestrians can rent horses from the ranch's large stable; guided trail rides go through the desert past cacti, yucca, and Joshua trees.

Mt. Charleston, Kyle and Lee Canyons

For a mountain retreat, head northwest from Las Vegas on Highway
8 95 about 45 miles to **Mt. Charleston,** the fifth-highest mountain in the state. At Highway 157, turn off to Kyle Canyon. In winter this area is a local skiing haven; in summer it's a welcome respite from the 115°F desert heat, as well as a place to hike, picnic, and camp. For camping information, contact the **U.S. Forest Service** (☎ 702/873–8800).

The first stop on Kyle Canyon Road is **Mount Charleston Hotel,** built in 1984. The large, lodgelike lobby has a big hearth, bar, and spacious restaurant with a mountain view. From the hotel, take Highway 157 to its intersection with Highway 158, then follow Highway 158 for 6 miles and turn left on Highway 156 toward **Lee Canyon;** here you'll find several campgrounds (at around 8,500 feet), a trail to the bristlecone forest (among the oldest living trees on Earth), and the Lee Canyon Ski Area at the end of the road (*see* Chapter 7, Sports and the Outdoors, for details). The wintertime skiing lasts from November to early March and the 9,000-foot elevation offers a peaceful view year-round.

St. George, Zion National Park, Bryce Canyon

From the neon jungle of Las Vegas, it's a journey of 116 miles north on Interstate 15 to the small, picturesque town of St. George, Utah. In getting here, you'll pass through Mesquite, one of Nevada's newest and smallest cities, whose 720-room Peppermill resort has a golf course just across the state line in Arizona.

In **St. George** you'll find an assortment of low-priced motels, bed-and-breakfast inns, an old movie theater and a new Twinplex, souvenir shops, a variety of restaurants, Mormon historical sites, and red rocks. On a wintertime visit, you might encounter snow, and in summer you can expect to find temperatures cooler than those in Las Vegas. An evening in St. George can be spent exploring the Victorian-style streets, climbing the red-rock cliffs, or looking out over the town.

Yet the red rocks of St. George are only a preview of the miles of rich
9 redness to be seen at **Zion National Park,** about 30 miles to the northeast. Follow I–15 to the first Hurricane exit, which will take you through the small town of that name. Driving up the mountain, you'll see signs directing you into the 6-mile park drive among mammoth red rocks. The Mormons believed they had found God's country when they discovered the area now called Zion National Park in 1863. In addition to giving the area its name, they christened the park's major rock formations: *Great White Throne, Angel's Landing, Cathedral Mount, Three Patriarchs,* and *Pulpit.* The elevation ranges from 3,600 feet to

8,700 feet—higher than the North Rim of the Grand Canyon. Many of the park trails are wheelchair accessible; others are narrow climbs with sheer drops that would be difficult treks for small children. *Superintendent, Zion National Park, Rte. 9, Springdale, UT 84767, ☎ 801/772–3256. ☛ $5 per vehicle for 7-day pass. ⏲ Visitor centers: daily 8–5 in winter, as late as 8 in summer.*

10 To reach **Bryce Canyon National Park** and what may seem like the prehistoric world of the Flintstones, continue east on Highway 9 to Highway 89, and turn north. Drive about 40 miles to Route 12, turn east, and another 17 miles will bring you into the park. As at Zion, red is a dominant color here, but brilliant, iridescent hues of buff and tan also appear on the fantastically shaped rocks—resembling spires, cathedrals, goblins—sculpted by the waters and weather of several million years. Most of the activity at Bryce occurs below the trail entrances, at the foot of the canyons. The park's hiking trails can be explored in wintertime on snowshoes or cross-country skis. *Bryce Canyon National Park, Bryce Canyon, UT 84717, ☎ 801/834–5322. ☛ $5 per vehicle for 7-day pass.*

6 Shopping

WHERE YOU SHOP IN LAS VEGAS will depend more on how much you want to spend—and how far you want to drive—than on what you're looking for. If you don't mind dispensing lots of money in high-rent districts, simply shop in your hotel promenade or at the Strip gift shops and shopping malls. Those not averse to doing a bit of driving might find some of the same high-ticket items at lower prices at one of the town's new factory outlet malls. And those looking for more practical items or for an excuse to drive around the greater metro area can head for the neighborhood malls, supermarkets, shopping centers, and specialty stores.

Major Shopping Districts and Malls

The Strip

The Strip is a giant shopping mall in and of itself. Here you will find two large indoor malls, as well as rows and rows of gift shops that sell Las Vegas souvenirs and sundries. Many of the hotels on the Strip have exclusive shops that sell expensive dresses, swimsuits, jewelry, and men's wear. For example, Bally's has a 40-store promenade where you can buy men's and women's high fashions, jewelry, art, and gifts. And, in addition to the adjoining Forum Shops, Caesars has the Appian Way shopping area, which features such tony retailers as Cartier, Ungaro, Ted Lapidus, and Ciro.

Las Vegas's only major shopping mall in a casino resort, the **Forum Shops at Caesars** (3500 Las Vegas Blvd. S, ☎ 702/893–4800), opened in 1992, has elevated the mall to high art—or kitsch, depending on how you see it. The 70-store complex resembles an ancient Roman streetscape, replete with immense columns and arches, two central piazzas with fountains, and a cloud-filled, domed ceiling displaying a sky that changes from sunrise to sunset in the course of three hours (perhaps inspiring shoppers to step up their pace of acquisition when it looks as if time is running out). The Festival Fountain (in the west wing of the mall) puts on its own show every hour on the hour: A robotic, pie-eyed Bacchus hosts a party for friends Apollo, Venus, and Mars, complete with lasers, music, and sound effects; at the end, the god of wine and merriment gives a sales pitch for the mall. If you can tear yourself away from the electronic wizardry, you'll find both familiar and unusual shops: Ann Taylor, Victoria's Secret, Louis Vuitton, Guess, and Gucci, along with a Warner Bros. Studio Store, where Daffy Duck and others are decked out in gladiator outfits, and a Caesars outlet selling everything from perfume to leather jackets that may bear a Caesars logo. This is also one of the city's best dining destinations: There's a branch of Wolfgang Puck's Spago (every bit as good as the original); an attractive Italian eatery, Bertolini's (*see* Chapter 8, Dining), with great gelato; and the Aspen-based Boogie's Diner (purveying casual clothes and overpriced soda fountain fare); as well as Swensen's, Stage Deli, and the upscale and excellent Palm. Visitors can glide into the Forum from the Strip on a moving sidewalk, but must exit through the Caesars Palace casino. If you try to defeat the one-way people mover, flesh-and-blood guards will quickly change your mind.

Even though it's twice as large as Caesars' retail fantasyland, the **Fashion Show Mall** (3200 Las Vegas Blvd. S, ☎ 702/369–8382) is tame by comparison. Centrally located on Las Vegas Boulevard across the street from the Desert Inn and next to the Frontier, it's hard to miss, and thus often crowded with visitors. It's very well kept, and not all the stores are overpriced. The two-story building contains 145 shops, including Neiman

Adams Western Store, **9**
Bell, Book and Candle, **6**
Belz Factory Outlet World, **22**
Bonanza "World's Largest Gift Shop," **13**
Boulevard Mall, **14**
Casino Clothiers of Nevada, **11**
Dealers Room Casino Clothiers, **14**
Ethel M. Chocolates Factory and Cactus Garden, **4**
Fashion Show Mall, **15**
Forum Shops at Caesars, **16**
Gambler's Book Club, **7**
Gamblers General Store, **3**
The Hock Shop Ltd., **8**
House of Antique Slots, **10**
Las Vegas Discount Golf, **21**
Las Vegas Factory Stores, **23**
Lucky, **19**
The Meadows, **1**
Miller Stockman, **1, 15**
Paul-Son Dice & Card Inc., **12**
Sam's Town Western Emporium, **5**
Stoney's Loan and Jewelry, **2**
Traveling Books and Maps, **17**
Union Premiums, **18**
Video Park, **20**

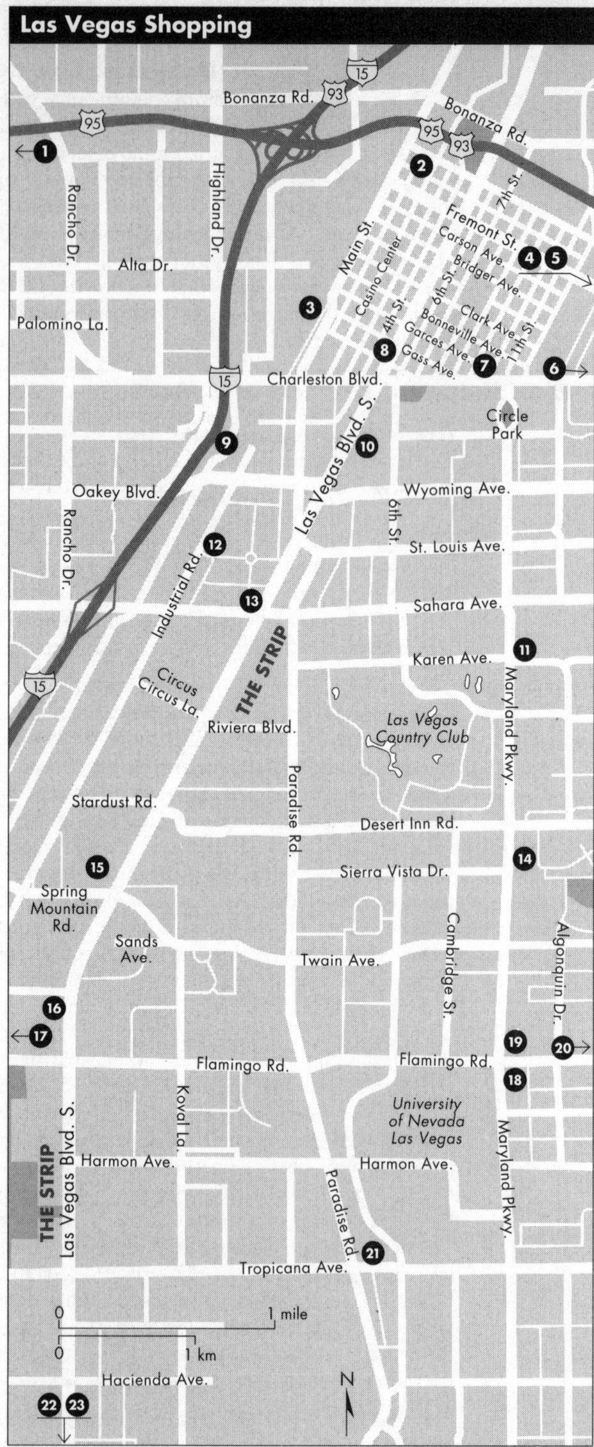

Marcus, Saks Fifth Avenue, Bullock's, May Company, and Dillards. There are also designer boutiques, Abercrombie & Fitch, and Lillie Rubin (she's the designer who makes clothes for Mary Hart of TV's "Entertainment Tonight"). One unusual mall inhabitant, the American Museum of Historical Documents, offers framed, autographed letters from Abraham Lincoln, Marilyn Monroe, and other famous people. The mall's fun food court has everything from hot dogs on a stick to Herbie Burgers; Chin's Chinese restaurant (*see* Chapter 8, Dining) offers more upscale fare. If you're in a panic about last-minute gifts, you'll find plenty of places here to buy expensive Las Vegas souvenirs; this is also the place for those who want to bring the casino experience into their homes to buy such gambling paraphernalia as gaming tables, playing cards, and dice. Waldenbooks, the only bookstore on the Strip, is also in this mall.

The other side of the Strip couldn't be more different. Inside the casinos, the gifts are elegant and expensive; outside, it's Tacky City. The endless gift shops along Las Vegas Boulevard all sell the same dice clocks, inflatable Wayne Newton dolls, jack and queen playing-card earrings, decks of used casino cards, Vegas belt buckles, key chains, and bath towels. Some stores are so schlocky you'll be embarrassed you stepped inside. **Bonanza "World's Largest Gift Shop"** (2460 Las Vegas Blvd. S, ☎ 702/385–7359), across the street from the Sahara Hotel, is the best of the bunch. It may not in fact be the world's largest, but it is the largest in town, and while it has some of the usual junk, it sells some unusual junk, too. It's so huge that you won't feel trapped, as you might in some of the smaller shops. And it's open until midnight.

Factory Outlet Stores

About 5 miles south of Tropicana Avenue on Las Vegas Boulevard South, the **Las Vegas Factory Stores** (9155 Las Vegas Blvd. S, ☎ 702/897–9090) lure inveterate bargain seekers to such stores as Mikasa, Van Heusen, Nine West, No Nonsense, Perfumania, and West Point Pepperell. On the way, you can stop off at **Belz Factory Outlet World** (7400 Las Vegas Blvd. S, ☎ 702/896–5599), one of the country's largest discount malls, where you can pick and choose from some 75 different stores, including Levi's, Bass, Geoffrey Bean, Stone Mountain, the Fragrance Outlet, and California Luggage.

Maryland Parkway

One mile east of the Strip and parallel to Las Vegas Boulevard, Maryland Parkway is the major shopping district for Las Vegas locals, with scores of fast-food outlets and stores catering to mall goers. You'll see places to shop all along this thoroughfare, but **Boulevard Mall** (3528 Maryland Pkwy., ☎ 702/735–8268) has the greatest single concentration of retailers. Less expensive than its counterparts on the Strip, Boulevard Mall boasts 140 stores, anchored by the Broadway, Sears, Dillards, and JCPenney department stores; smaller shops include Wet Seal, Express, Nature Company, Casual Corner, Harris & Frank, the Disney Store, and Sweet Factory.

The Meadows

The other major Vegas mall, **The Meadows** (4300 Meadows La., ☎ 702/878–4849), is located in a residential district west of downtown. The Meadows has 144 specialty stores in addition to the Broadway, Dillards, Sears, and JCPenney department stores.

Specialty Stores

Books

Traveling Books and Maps (4001 S. Decatur, ☎ 702/871–8082) is an attractive store that stocks Las Vegas's largest selection of guidebooks and maps, along with globes, traveling jackets, travel accessories, and more. The Southwest section is particularly comprehensive. Owner Jerry Netzky is an enthusiastic world traveler (his staff has been around, too), and can recommend the right book for the right destination.

Casino Clothes

If you've caught the gambling spirit and want to go home in a white shirt, black pants, and a big red bow tie, **Dealers Room Casino Clothiers** (3661 Maryland Pkwy. S, ☎ 702/732–3932) will be happy to sell you dealer's duds. **Casino Clothiers of Nevada** (2560 Maryland Pkwy. S, ☎ 702/732–0449) sells casino uniforms for everyone from cocktail waitresses to janitors.

Chocolates

Ethel M. Chocolates Factory and Cactus Garden (2 Cactus Garden Dr., Henderson, about 20 minutes southeast of Las Vegas, ☎ 702/458–8864; branches in most hotels). The "M" stands for Mars, the name of the family—headed by Ethel in the early days—that brought us Snickers, Milky Way, Mars bars, Three Musketeers, and M&Ms. More than 1,000 people come each day to watch the candy making at this fancy chocolate factory; free samples inspire almost all to make purchases in the adjoining shop. An adjacent cactus garden contains 2½ acres planted with more than 350 species of succulents and desert plants that are particularly colorful when they flower in spring. The factory is closed New Year's Day, Easter, Thanksgiving, and Christmas.

Film

Don't buy your film on the Strip or at the gift shops if you can help it. Instead, head to **Sahara Camera Center** (2305 E. Sahara Ave., ☎ 702/457–3333). This is also a good place to shop for camera equipment.

Food

Lucky (1300 E. Flamingo Rd., in the Mission Shopping Center, ☎ 702/733–2947) is the closest food store to the Strip—you'll have to travel several miles if you feel the need to stock up on groceries. It's open 24 hours.

Gambling Memorabilia

You won't find a better place than Las Vegas to stock up on gambling books, cards, dice, green felt, and anything else of a gaming nature you might require.

Gambler's Book Club (630 S. 11th St., ☎ 702/382–7555 or 800/522–1777) has the best collection of current and out-of-print books about 21, craps, poker, roulette, and all the other games, as well as novels about gambling and crime figures and anything else that relates to gambling and Las Vegas.

Gamblers General Store (800 S. Main St., ☎ 702/382–9903) stocks a big collection of gambling books as well as poker chips, green-felt layouts, slot and video poker machines—just about every item of gambling paraphernalia that you could imagine. It's eight blocks south of the Plaza Hotel on Main Street.

House of Antique Slots (1243 Las Vegas Blvd. S, ☎ 702/382–1520). If taking home a classic slot machine would make your trip to Las Vegas complete, you might want to stop in this shop, down the street from the Little White Chapel. But be warned: Old slots can be very expensive, with prices in the $2,000–$5,000 range, and in-home slots are legal in only 40 states. The proprietors will let you know if they are legal where you live.

Paul-Son Dice & Card Inc. (2121 Industrial Rd., ☎ 702/384–2425). Want to take home some authentic casino dice and chips? This store is a major supplier to the casinos, and also sells retail.

Lucky Charms

Bell, Book and Candle (1725 E. Charleston Blvd., ☎ 702/384–6807) is one of the most unusual shops in town, featuring a large selection of intriguing spiritual and metaphysical symbols of luck, from fast-money potions for quick casino kills to quartz crystals for power, prosperity, and romantic success. A trip to BB&C will increase your appreciation for the myriad ways that are available to propitiate the great goddess of luck—a widespread activity in this town.

Pawn Shops

Las Vegas is a great place to pick up cheap televisions, watches, and cameras pawned by local residents feeding video poker habits or visitors who needed a little extra cash to get home. **Stoney's Loan and Jewelry** (126 S. 1st St., ☎ 702/384–0819) is one of the oldest pawn shops in Las Vegas. **Super Pawn** (515 E. St. Louis, ☎ 702/792–2900) has seven locations around town, but the most convenient for visitors staying on the Strip or downtown is the address listed here.

Sporting Goods

Las Vegas Discount Golf (4405 Paradise Rd., ☎ 702/892–9999) has a large selection of golf equipment and clothing.

Video

Las Vegas may very well be the VCR capital of the world, largely because so many residents work nights and don't want to miss prime-time television. The video stores are large and well stocked.

Video Park (3230 E. Flamingo Rd., ☎ 702/451–4518) bills itself as "the world's largest video store!" and whether it is or not, it's not to be missed. When the Video Software Dealers Association meets here every year, most delegates make a trip to Video Park just for the experience. Each video genre is displayed in its own theatrical setting. To reach the horror section, for example, you have to step around a coffin complete with mannequin and sound effects. The music-video titles are placed within a 40-foot-long, 15-foot-high yellow submarine that you must climb into in order to look around.

Western Goods

Las Vegas loves its Western roots. The best Western shop in Las Vegas is **Western Emporium** (5111 Boulder Hwy., ☎ 702/454–8017) at Sam's Town, a large shopping village with boots, hats, clothing, jewelry, belt buckles, string ties, a bakery, and a barbershop. It's adjacent to Sam's Town Hotel and Casino.

Adams Western Store (1415 Western Ave., ☎ 702/384–6077) is the sort of traditional Western shop you might expect to find in Montana or Wyoming; the emphasis is on equestrian supplies and "wearing apparel." It's also the oldest Western shop in town, circa 1951, and it'll probably be the toughest for you to get to. It's off Sahara Avenue, near the freeway, appropriately enough on a backstreet named Western.

Miller Stockman (3200 Las Vegas Blvd. S, ☎ 702/737–7236; 4300 Meadows La., ☎ 702/870–2951), a higher-priced Western shop that lacks the atmosphere and old-time feel of the Western Emporium at Sam's Town, is located in both the Fashion Show Mall and the Meadows Mall.

7 Sports and the Outdoors

THE PLAYFUL SPIRIT OF LAS VEGAS, epitomized in its casinos, is also very much alive in its sports. Vegas's 13 championship golf courses host several prestigious tournaments that include a $1 million stop on the PGA tour. Many boxing superstars—Muhammad Ali, Larry Holmes, Sugar Ray Leonard, Thomas Hearns, Mike Tyson, and George Foreman—have faced each other in a Las Vegas ring.

Participant Sports and Fitness

Biking

You can rent bikes at **Bikes USA** (1539 N. Eastern Ave., ☎ 702/642–2453). Because of the intense summer heat, you won't find many cycling trails in Las Vegas, but there is one good, long jaunt: Go west on Charleston Boulevard, which will take you out of the city about 16 miles to beautiful Red Rock Canyon, where you will find a moderately difficult 13-mile scenic loop (the road is one-way). Carry lots of water.

Boating

Boats and Jet Skis may be rented at **Fun and Sun** (442 N. Water St., Henderson, ☎ 702/564–5452) and **Lake Mead Resort and Marina** (322 Lakeshore Rd., Boulder City, ☎ 702/293–3484). The fishing at Lake Mead, 30 miles from Las Vegas, is excellent (*see* Excursions *in* Chapter 5, Exploring Las Vegas).

Bowling

Many casinos offer 24-hour bowling facilities. The 106-lane **Showboat** (2800 Fremont St., ☎ 702/385–9153) is the world's largest bowling alley. Two other convenient bowling spots are the 56-lane **Sam's Town** (5111 Boulder Hwy., ☎ 702/454–8022) and the 72-lane **Gold Coast** (4000 W. Flamingo Rd., ☎ 702/367–4700).

Golf

With an average of 315 days of sunshine a year, Las Vegas's top sports recreation is golf. The only 18-hole course on the Strip is at the **Desert Inn** (3145 Las Vegas Blvd. S, ☎ 702/733–4290); it's open to the public, but resort guests get top priority and lower rates. **Los Prados** (Jones and Lone Mountain Rds., ☎ 702/645–5696) and the **Las Vegas Golf Club** (4349 Vegas Dr., ☎ 702/646–3003) are two other public options. Watch out for the hustlers who hang around the resort courses looking for an easy mark.

Health Clubs

The **Las Vegas Sporting House** (3025 Industrial Rd., ☎ 702/733–8999), behind the Stardust Hotel, has 10 racquetball courts, two tennis courts, a basketball court, a volleyball court, exercise equipment, outdoor jogging tracks, swimming pools, steam and sauna rooms, and aerobics classes; the fee is $15 a visit for guests of any hotel. The four facilities of the **Las Vegas Athletic Club** (1070 E. Sahara Ave., ☎ 702/733–1919; 3315 Spring Mountain Rd., ☎ 702/362–3720; 5090 S. Maryland Pkwy., ☎ 702/795–2582; and 3830 E. Flamingo Rd., ☎ 702/451–2526) offer racquetball courts, saunas, Jacuzzis, Nautilus and free weights, indoor and outdoor swimming pools, and aerobics classes; the fee is $10. Most hotels have health-club facilities; those at Bally's, Caesars, Desert Inn, Flamingo, Riviera, and Tropicana are open to the public for a fee.

Hiking

Hiking enthusiasts should explore the trails of Mt. Charleston, which are much cooler than the desert trails (*see* Excursions *in* Chapter 5, Exploring Las Vegas).

Horseback Riding

Bonnie Springs Ranch (1 Gun Fighter La., ☎ 702/875–4191), 18 miles from the Strip, offers a one-hour guided ride for $16.50. The cowboys at **Mountain T Ranch** (Kyle Canyon Rd., ☎ 702/656–8025), 40 miles from Las Vegas in the foothills of Mt. Charleston, lead guided trail rides lasting from one to six hours, costing $20 to $100. The six-hour deluxe tour includes lunch on the trail and a barbecue after the ride. Call ahead for reservations.

Jogging

There are jogging trails behind the **Desert Inn** and **Las Vegas Hilton,** and the **University of Nevada–Las Vegas** (4505 S. Maryland Pkwy., ☎ 702/739–3011) has a regulation track (Bill Cosby's favorite hangout when in town) from which you can see the Strip in the distance as you run. The most pleasant times to hit the streets of Las Vegas, especially in the hot months, are early morning or late afternoon.

Racquetball

Caesars Palace (3570 Las Vegas Blvd. S, ☎ 702/731–7110), the four **Las Vegas Athletic Clubs** (*see* Health Clubs, *above,* for locations and phone numbers), and the **Las Vegas Sporting House** (3025 Industrial Rd., ☎ 702/733–8999) have racquetball courts that are open to the public for a fee.

Skiing

Lee Canyon (Mt. Charleston, ☎ 702/646–0008), southern Nevada's skiing headquarters, is equipped with a 3,000-foot double chairlift and chalet. Take Highway 95 north to the Lee Canyon Exit (Highway 156), and head up the mountain. You'll know you're only 47 miles from Las Vegas when you see the slope names: Blackjack, High Roller, Keno, The Strip, Bimbo 1 and 2, and Slot Alley.

Swimming

Every hotel and most motels have large outdoor pools that are open from April to October—but only until 6 or 7 PM even when it stays light late. Hotel managements maintain that they can't afford to hire lifeguards to work through the night; in fact, they can't afford to have you lounging in the water when you could be spending your time and your money in the casino. Two **public pools** (430 E. Bonanza Rd., ☎ 702/386–6309, and 1100 E. St. Louis Ave., ☎ 702/386–6395) are open Memorial Day through Labor Day. For lake swimming, make the 30-mile drive to Lake Mead.

Tennis

Las Vegas has an abundance of tennis courts, many of them lighted for evening play. The 10 courts at **Bally's Casino Resort** (3645 Las Vegas Blvd. S, ☎ 702/739–4111) are open only to hotel guests, but nonguests may book one of the 10 courts at **Desert Inn** (3145 Las Vegas Blvd. S, ☎ 702/733–4577) if they pay a $10 court fee per person (good for the entire day). The **University of Nevada–Las Vegas** (4505 S. Maryland Pkwy., ☎ 702/739–3150) has a dozen lighted tennis courts available on a first-come, first-served (as it were) basis.

Spectator Sports

Baseball

The **Las Vegas Stars** of the triple-A Pacific Coast League play at Cashman Field (850 Las Vegas Blvd. N, ☎ 702/386–7200), north of downtown, where professional baseball made its Las Vegas debut in 1983. Winners of the league championship in 1986 and 1988, the Stars have become a successful baseball franchise and a thriving farm club for the San Diego Padres.

Basketball

The hottest tickets in town during the school year were once the basketball games of the NCAA champions, the **Runnin' Rebels** at the University of Nevada–Las Vegas (4505 S. Maryland Pkwy., ☎ 702/895–3900), but since head coach Jerry Tarkanian was fired, the Rebels—and their ticket sales—have cooled off considerably.

Bowling

Las Vegas is home to the **Showboat Invitational Bowling Tournament** (Showboat Hotel, 2800 Fremont St., ☎ 702/385–9153), the Professional Bowling Association's oldest competition, which airs on ABC-TV.

Boxing

Championship boxing came to Las Vegas in 1960, when Benny Paret took the welterweight title from Don Jordan at the Las Vegas Convention Center. Since then most of boxing's superstars have fought in Las Vegas. A title match draws the well-heeled and the well-known from all fields—and brings out the high roller in everyone. Spectators willingly fork over $200–$1,500 a seat to watch two guys pummel each other, then hang around the casinos laying down chips for the rest of the evening, sometimes for the rest of the week. Major fights are usually held at the Mirage, Caesars Palace, or MGM Grand. To learn about upcoming boxing events, look for the fight odds posted on the wall in the race and sports book of any casino. For the most comprehensive fight listings, check **Caesars Palace** (3570 Las Vegas Blvd. S, ☎ 702/731–7110) or the **Stardust Hotel and Casino** (3000 Las Vegas Blvd. S, ☎ 702/732–6111).

Golf

October brings the annual **Las Vegas Invitational golf tournament,** with top PGA golfers competing for high stakes at the Desert Inn, Las Vegas Country Club, and Spanish Trails. For more information, contact **Las Vegas Invitational** (☎ 702/382–6616).

Rodeo

When the **National Finals of Rodeo** (☎ 702/731–2115) comes to town in December, the casinos showcase country stars and the fans sport Western gear. The NFR, said to be the Super Bowl of professional rodeo, offers more than $2 million in prize money.

8 Dining

Elliot Krane, the former restaurant editor of the *Las Vegas Review-Journal*, made the selection of highly recommended restaurants.

THE RESTAURANTS OF LAS VEGAS number more than 750. The major hotel-casinos all have four or five eating places (the Las Vegas Hilton has eight), and the hotel marquees that used to announce revues and celebrity performers now proclaim food bargains: PRIME RIB $4.95! SHRIMP COCKTAIL 49¢! Dining bargains abound at the hotels, which keep the prices of meals, liquor, and rooms low in order to draw you inside and steer you toward the casino—where revenues lost by the hotels in such deals are more than made up.

Hotel restaurants serve every pocketbook, offering a variety that extends from $3 buffets to $50 gourmet meals to 49¢ breakfasts in the wee hours. The buffets at breakfast ($3–$4), lunch ($4–$6), and dinner ($6–$8) are cafeteria-style, all-you-can-eat affairs where the food is filling and there's enough variety to satisfy most any taste. Some hotels, such as the Circus Circus group, opt for the loss-leader style of buffet, where the low prices make up for the uninspired food. Most of the others, notably Harrah's, the Flamingo, and the Hacienda, put out a standard American smorgasbord, which gives you your money's worth on volume. Las Vegas's top half-dozen buffets, however, are highly competitive. The Rio's has a Mongolian barbecue; Bally's has Wong's Wok; many items at the Palace Station buffet are prepared to order; and the Golden Nugget's entrées are often high quality.

Gourmet dining has its place in Las Vegas because hotels recognize that the high roller, the player who is prepared to risk $10,000 in a weekend without blinking, expects treatment to match that largesse. No coffee shop or bargain buffet for that person, who looks for the exclusivity of the intimate, dimly lit restaurant where the diners wear a jacket and tie, the chef has been trained in Europe, and the service is attentive and professional. High rollers, of course, enjoy these meals on the house, so the paying customers also help subsidize their cost. Still, as a result, the price of a first-class dinner in Las Vegas is much lower than it is in New York or San Francisco.

Those who want to spend as little money as possible on food should eat at the cheapest buffets (Circus Circus) and snack bars (Slots A Fun, Golden Gate), take advantage of the bargain breakfasts (Plaza, Horseshoe), and stay up to try the famous $3 steak dinner (served between 10 PM and 5:45 AM at the Horseshoe). In addition, there are some excellent meal deals at regular hours: a 12-ounce porterhouse at the Fremont (6–10 PM, $8.95); prime rib at the Frontier (24 hours, $3.99); and a pound of Alaskan king crab legs at the El Cortez (5–10 PM, $9.95). What's more, coupons in the major hotel funbooks often provide further discounts on meals. The Sands, for example, features a $1-off coupon good at any hotel dining room.

The Forum Shops at Caesars has given the city its first branches of familiar big-city names. Tucked among the fancy boutiques and talking statues are Wolfgang Puck's Spago from Los Angeles, The Palm from New York and Los Angeles, and Stage Deli of Manhattan.

Outside the hotels, the many other restaurants of the city offer a variety of cuisines and the opportunity to get away from games of chance for a while. Simply arriving at a restaurant without having to walk through a noisy casino, fight off hordes of people, and wait in long lines is an attractive option for many. The prices at these places are eminently competitive with comparable hotel dining rooms and, in order to lure patrons away from the casinos, the food is often of much better quality. Generally, the waits are shorter, the service is finer, and you'll have a greater sense of "dining out."

What to Wear

The dining dress code, like nearly every other social protocol in Las Vegas, is permissive. As long as you're wearing the proverbial "shoes-and-a-shirt," you can eat in almost any restaurant in town. Wet bathing suits in the coffee shop, flip-flops and cutoffs in the buffet, cowboy hats in the steak house—no problem. Only a handful of the fanciest gourmet rooms require evening wear on the women and jackets and ties on the men; otherwise, wear your wallet and you'll be welcome.

Restaurants, both in and out of hotels, are reviewed below according to cuisine. A tip of 15% is common practice in Las Vegas restaurants, and in some circumstances you might want to slip the maître d' $5 or $10 for a special table. Except where noted, reservations are unnecessary.

CATEGORY	COST*
$$$$	over $50
$$$	$20–$50
$$	$10–$20
$	under $10

**per person for a three-course meal, excluding drinks, service, and 7% sales tax*

American

$$ **Center Stage.** The Stage's second-story view of downtown Fremont Street is incomparable, especially from the front-facing tables. The restaurant is set in a dark-green glass dome that overlooks the big neon light show outside. Steak, chicken, and veal are the principal entrées; all dinners come with soup or salad, potato, vegetable, and beverage. ✕ *Plaza Hotel, 1 Main St.,* ☎ *702/386–2512. Reservations advised. AE, D, DC, MC, V. No lunch.*

$$ **Xanadu.** Xanadu opened in 1994 to rave reviews and has remained a top choice ever since. For a fixed price of $18.95, your table is heaped with a bread bowl topped with cheese spread; a salad teeming with vegetables; assorted breads and rolls baked on the premises; side dishes of wild rice, country beans, sliced potatoes, and steamed vegetables; and a chocolate soufflé for dessert. Save room for the entrée! The two sides of the menu specify "mild" and "wild." The mild dishes include standard steaks, prime rib, and fish; the wild dishes are more interesting: towering roughy stuffed with crab, sachet of shrimp and crab in phyllo dough, tenderloin and crab cakes, stuffed chicken breast, even sushi. ✕ *Sands Hotel and Casino, 3355 Las Vegas Blvd. S,* ☎ *702/733–5000. Reservations advised. AE, D, DC, MC, V. Closed Wed. No lunch.*

$–$$ **The Broiler.** Since it opened in August of 1994, Boulder Station has emerged as one of the front-running off-Strip casinos that cater to local Las Vegans. Gambling opportunities have contributed to its popularity, but another attraction is its good, inexpensive restaurant food. The Broiler is the steak and seafood room, serving mesquite-broiled beef, fish, chicken, and veal. All entrées come with the salad bar, which is the best spread in town, complete with spring greens, Caesar and hot spinach salads, two soups, abundant breads, chunk bleu cheese, and vegetables galore. ✕ *Boulder Station, 4111 Boulder Hwy.,* ☎ *702/432–7777. Reservations advised. AE, D, MC, V.*

$–$$ **Café Michelle.** Here's a café with a European flair that makes a welcome change of pace when the casino experience has gotten to you.

Alpine Village Inn, **13**
Antonio's, **28**
The Bacchanal, **22**
Bally's Big Kitchen, **25**
Bamboo Garden, **26**
Battista's Hole in the Wall Italian Restaurant, **24**
Binion's Coffee Shop, **3**
The Bistro, **20**
The Broiler, **7**
Café Michelle, **31**
Cafe Roma, **22**
Capozzoli's, **18**
The Carnival World Buffet, **27**
Center Stage, **1**
Chin's, **17**
Circus Circus buffet, **14**
Coyote Cafe, **29**
El Sombrero, **2**
Empress Court, **22**
The Feast Buffet, **9**
Food Fantasy, **23**
The Golden Nugget Hotel buffet, **4**
The Golden Steer, **10**
Joe's Bayou, **21**
Las Olas, **25**
Le Montrachet, **12**
Lillie Langtry's, **4**
Bertolini's, **22**
Margarita's Mexican Cantina, **16**
Mary's Diner, **6**
Mikado, **20**
Palace Court, **22**
Palatium Buffet, **22**
Pamplemousse Restaurant, **11**
Paradise Buffet, **5**
Primavera, **22**
Ralph's Diner, **15**
Second Street Grille, **5**
The Silver Dragon, **33**
The Steak House, **14**
The Tillerman, **32**
Uptown Buffet, **6**
The Venetian, **8**
Xanadu, **19**
Yolie's, **30**

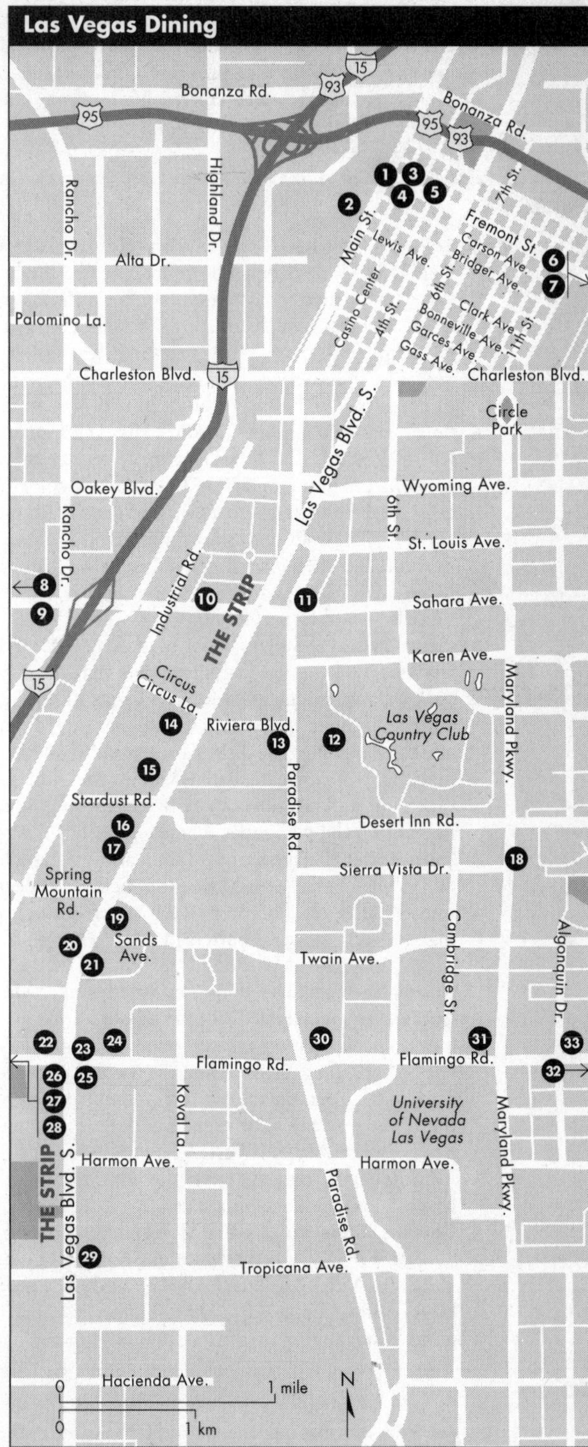

Situated in a small strip shopping mall, the café has red-and-white-checked tablecloths indoors and the traditional Cinzano umbrellas above the tables in the plaza outdoors. Omelets, crepes, seafood, and salads are the fare, with sandwiches and salads at lunchtime. ✕ *1350 E. Flamingo Rd., in the Mission Shopping Center,* ☎ *702/735–8686. AE, MC, V.*

Buffets

$ **Bally's Big Kitchen** (Bally's Casino Resort, 3645 Las Vegas Blvd. S, ☎ 702/739–4111) is believed by many to be the best buffet in town for variety and value. True to its name, the buffet is set up in what resembles a big, stainless steel, institutional kitchen; the fare is varied and ample, including roast duck, steak, prime rib, a separate serving line for fresh-cooked Chinese food, a baked-potato bar, salads, and a large variety of desserts. The dining room itself is bright and airy.

$ **Carnival World Buffet** (Rio Suites Hotel and Casino, 3700 W. Flamingo Rd., ☎ 702/252–7777) ushered in a new age in Las Vegas buffets when it opened in January 1993. The room is colorful, curvy, and always crowded; the variety and volume of food are mind-blowing; the hours are long and continuous; and the prices, believe it or not, are below average. But the pièce de résistance is the "Amazon Grill," two large Mongolian barbecues where your veggies, spices, and meat are stir-fried to order—and to perfection.

$ **Circus Circus** (2880 Las Vegas Blvd. S, ☎ 702/734–0410) has the busiest buffet on the Strip, serving more than 10,000 people every day at rock-bottom prices, even for Las Vegas. If you're looking for a buffet with an emphasis on volume and economy, as opposed to preparation and taste (most of the dishes are virtually indistinguishable), this is the place for you. Since it's Circus Circus, the food is served on pink plates in a pink-and-white room with circus tents, giraffes, and elephants painted on the wallpaper. There's usually a long line to get in.

$ **Feast Buffet** (Palace Station Hotel and Casino, 2411 W. Sahara Ave., ☎ 702/367–2411) introduced the "action" concept—where your eggs, burgers, fish, etc., are prepared by short-order cooks behind the serving line—to Las Vegas buffets in 1988. Though Bally's Big Kitchen and the Rio's Carnival World buffets have taken the concept a step or two further, the Feast is still among the tops in town.

$ **Golden Nugget Hotel** (129 E. Fremont St., ☎ 702/385–7111) has the most expensive buffet in town; you won't find the Velveeta cheese, three-bean salad, or other staples of the less pricey places. Here, the eggs are cooked to order, the cheese and cold cuts are appealing, and the salad bar is always fresh. The bread pudding is renowned far and wide. The Sunday night buffet is best: You get the best of Sunday brunch (eggs, lox and bagels, herring, etc.), plus the dinner entrées. The Nugget buffet costs half again as much as any of the others, but it's worth it.

$ **Uptown Buffet** (Sam's Town Hotel and Casino, 5111 W. Boulder Hwy., ☎ 702/456–7777), the **Palatium Buffet** (Caesars Palace, 3570 Las Vegas Blvd. S, ☎ 702/731–7449), and the **Paradise Buffet** (Fremont Hotel and Casino, 200 E. Fremont St., ☎ 702/385–3232) are other good buffet options.

Cajun

$$ **Joe's Bayou.** Among the Cajun, Creole, and other southern dishes at Joe's are Louisiana chicken gumbo, Natchez prime rib, shrimp Creole, St. Louis steak, and Memphis barbecue (with slow preparation over mesquite). All dinners include plantation greens, cornbread, and salad. The quiet, dark room has a nautical theme; the statue of a sea captain greets diners up front, and a collection of oars, ships' clocks, and nets hangs from the ceiling. ✕ *Harrah's Hotel and Casino, 3475 Las Vegas Blvd. S,* ☏ *702/369–5000. Reservations advised. AE, D, DC, MC, V. No lunch.*

Chinese

$$$$ **Chin's.** An upscale Chinese restaurant with a bright, contemporary decor, Chin's specializes in original Hong Kong–style cuisine. The specialties here are the likes of deep-fried chicken in strawberry sauce and steamed scallops with black beans on baby abalone shells; try the dim sum plate for lunch. Service is somewhat formal. The restaurant is on the Strip, in front of the Fashion Show shopping mall. ✕ *3200 Las Vegas Blvd. S,* ☏ *702/733–8899. Reservations advised. AE, D, DC, MC, V.*

$$$$ **Empress Court.** "We don't serve chop suey here," the tuxedoed maître d' exclaims, "no moo shu pork or cashew chicken either, just traditional Hong Kong–style cuisine." Welcome to the newest addition to the Caesars Palace family of restaurants, a $4 million rest stop for the wealthy Asian gamblers who drop megabucks in the Caesars casinos. The theme is water and the animal life that inhabits it. A two-story staircase has a koi pond at its center; etchings of fish decorate the glass panels in the main dining room; patterns of blue fish swim in the carpeting; and a large aquarium of exotic fish occupies the middle of the room. The food is exotic: braised shark's fin with crabmeat, imperial Peking duck, and double-broiled bird's nest. The Emperor, a set menu for two, includes Cantonese roast duck salad in sesame sauce, velvet chicken soup with mushrooms, prime sirloin strips with rainbow vegetables, braised abalone with sea cucumber, and ginger ice cream and cookies. ✕ *Caesars Palace, 3570 Las Vegas Blvd. S,* ☏ *702/731–7888. Reservations advised. Jacket and tie. AE, D, DC, MC, V. Closed Tues., Wed. No lunch.*

$$$ **Lillie Langtry's.** This elegant restaurant was replaced for a while by Elaine's, which featured California-Continental cuisine, but was brought back by popular demand. Lillie's is as close to Chinese gourmet as you'll get this side of Canton. The dishes are exotic Cantonese with a little Szechuan spiciness. Start out with the Great Combination Plate, and maybe sample some shark's fin soup. The black-pepper steak will send charcoal freaks to culinary heaven, and the almond chicken is a classic. Don't miss the dragon-eye fruit for dessert. ✕ *Golden Nugget, 129 E. Fremont St.,* ☏ *702/385–7111. Reservations advised. AE, D, DC, MC, V. No lunch.*

$$ **Bamboo Garden.** Don't let the modest setting in a Flamingo Road shopping center and the reasonable prices fool you: Bamboo Garden has some of the most unusual Oriental cuisine around. Dishes include cream of seafood soup, Mongolian lamb, firecracker beef, clams Dou Chi, Hunan eggplant, and more. The room is elegant, with a bamboo motif, and the service is superb. ✕ *4850 Flamingo Rd.,* ☏ *702/871–3262. Reservations advised. AE, D, DC, MC, V.*

$$ **Silver Dragon.** On Flamingo Road, 2 miles east of the Strip (and two blocks east of Maryland Parkway), stands this Las Vegas landmark, a replica of a Peking palace. If you seek a less crowded restaurant than many of those on the Strip, or if you have a yen for sweet-and-sour at an unlikely hour, the Silver Dragon, open until 4 AM, has traditional Chinese fare and moderate prices as well. ✕ *1510 E. Flamingo Rd.,* ☏ *702/737–1234. AE, MC, V.*

Coffee Shops

$$ **Binion's Coffee Shop.** There always used to be a long line of people waiting to get into this coffee shop, which serves low-priced "just good food"

in large portions. Then the steak house next door was removed and the coffee shop expanded to fill the entire basement of Binion's. Unfortunately the line is still long. The specialties include Benny Binion's Natural (two eggs; ham, bacon, or sausage; home fries; toast; jelly; and coffee), which is considered by many to be the best breakfast bargain in town, and Binion's Delight (hamburger, cheese, lettuce, tomato, dressing, and fries). Chili, steaks, and soups fill out the menu. This is also where you'll find the famous $3 steak dinner (10-ounce New York strip, salad, baked potato, roll and butter), served between 10 PM and 5:45 AM, Las Vegas dining's value icon for almost 20 years now. Westernabilia and keno boards cover the walls. ✕ *Binion's Horseshoe Hotel and Casino, 128 Fremont St.,* ☎ *702/382–1600. AE, D, DC, MC, V.*

$–$$ **Cafe Roma.** Less expensive than the other restaurants of Caesars Palace, Cafe Roma continues the hotel's Roman theme in a two-tiered dining room with large columns and gold walls. An American menu is available 24 hours, a Chinese menu after 5 PM. Portions are large and the atmosphere pleasant. Cafe Roma serves one of the best grilled-cheese sandwiches in town, extra large, cut into thirds, with a hefty side of fries. A large basket of crackers and bread comes with every meal. ✕ *Caesars Palace, 3570 Las Vegas Blvd. S,* ☎ *702/731–7534. AE, D, DC, MC, V.*

$ **Food Fantasy.** Food Fantasy lets you serve yourself, cafeteria-style, while your eggs or hamburgers or roast-beef sandwiches are prepared to your specifications. This is one of the rare hotel (nonbuffet) restaurants that has a salad bar, and it is well stocked. Waffle fans take note: Extra-large, piping-hot waffles are made right before your eyes—a terrific evening treat when topped with vanilla ice cream. ✕ *The Flamingo Hilton and Tower, 3555 Las Vegas Blvd. S,* ☎ *702/733–3111. AE, D, DC, MC, V.*

Diners

$ **Mary's Diner.** Another venture of the Boyd Group, Mary's Diner at Sam's Town follows the same formula as Ralph's Diner at the Stardust (*see below*). ✕ *Sam's Town Hotel and Casino, 5111 W. Boulder Hwy.,* ☎ *702/454–8073. AE, D, DC, MC, V.*

$ **Ralph's Diner.** The folks who run the Boyd Group of hotels (California, Fremont, Sam's Town, and the Stardust) can spot a good American trend as well as anyone, and they responded quickly when the diner craze arrived. At Ralph's, jukes are on the tables; the music is 1950s; and an old-fashioned soda fountain serves up milk shakes, sodas, banana splits, and ice-cream sundaes. Daily Blue Plate Specials start at $3.95. The linoleum, of course, is black-and-white checkerboard. ✕ *Stardust Hotel and Casino, 3000 Las Vegas Blvd. S,* ☎ *702/732–6580. AE, D, DC, MC, V.*

Dinner Shows

At one time nearly all of the major Las Vegas hotel-casinos offered dinner with their shows. These days, only a few hotels accompany their entertainment with food—most likely because few patrons seem to want it. But for those who do, dinner shows are still a great bargain. The hotels accompanying their glitter with grub are: **Tropicana** ("Folies Bergere"), **Excalibur** ("King Arthur's Tournament," where eating with your hands is part of the medieval fun), and **Rio** ("Conga").

French/Continental

$$$$ **Palace Court.** Popularly regarded as the best white-glove restaurant in town and winner of four Mobil stars every year for the past 15, the

Court offers excellent food served on fine china to the accompaniment of gently tinkling crystal. A stained-glass skylight domes the rotunda-style dining room and is illuminated by dozens of golden bulbs when the sun descends. Recent menu selections have included tournedos of beef, potato-crust salmon, breast of duck with pink peppercorn sauce, fresh Maine lobster, and rack of lamb. The caviar appetizer is out of this world. The wine list is extensive, presented by one of only three sommeliers in Las Vegas. Dinner seatings at 6–6:30 PM and 9–9:30 PM. ✕ *Caesars Palace, 3570 Las Vegas Blvd. S,* ☎ *702/731–7547. Reservations required. Jacket required. AE, D, DC, MC, V.*

$$$–$$$$ **Pamplemousse Restaurant.** A small, quiet room that seats just 70, the Pamplemousse is popular with the convention trade—in fact, management suggests you make your reservations even before you start out for Las Vegas. The dominant color is red, orchestral music can be heard on the stereo system, and the food is classic French cuisine. Because the entrées change from day to day, there is no printed menu; the waiter recites the bill of fare (and the prices, but only if you ask). Specialties of the house include veal medallions in cream sauce with Dijon mustard, and roast duckling in red wine and banana rum sauce. All dinners include salad, a basket of breads, steamed vegetables, and crudités. ✕ *400 E. Sahara Ave.,* ☎ *702/733–2066. Reservations required. AE, D, DC, MC, V. Closed Mon. No lunch.*

$$$ **The Bistro.** All of the restaurants at the Mirage are imaginative set pieces with superb food and ultrahigh prices, but the Bistro is possibly the best of the bunch. The many-windowed room is appointed with wood, brass, flowers, statues, and murals and is peaked by a stained-glass dome. The menu features escargot, duck pâté, lobster with truffles, duck in peach sauce, rack of lamb with a honey-mustard crust, venison, pheasant, and more. ✕ *The Mirage, 3400 Las Vegas Blvd. S,* ☎ *702/791–7111. Reservations advised. AE, D, DC, MC, V. No lunch.*

$$$ **Le Montrachet.** An elegant room with soft peach lighting, paintings of pastoral scenes, elaborate table settings, and fine linen, Le Montrachet gives you no indication that you're in Las Vegas. The menu changes with the season, approximately every three months. A recent bill of fare offered strudel-wrapped lobster, tenderloin of rabbit, broiled veal chops in Madeira sauce, and venison with blackened mushrooms. Sorbets are served between courses. You won't find cigarette girls or gambling paraphernalia here, but you will find fresh flowers at every table and a wine list with 400 selections. ✕ *Las Vegas Hilton, 3000 W. Paradise Rd.,* ☎ *702/732–5111. Reservations advised. AE, D, DC, MC, V. Closed Tues. No lunch.*

German

$$ **Alpine Village Inn.** If you don't have a reservation, the wait can be up to 90 minutes for this Las Vegas favorite, across the street from the convention center. The upstairs full-service restaurant is decked out as a Swiss chalet: "snow" tops the "huts" that serve as booths, there's a giant replica of a gingerbread house in the middle of the room, and the servers wear lederhosen or dirndls. In addition to substantial German entrées such as Schweinebraten (pork roast), sauerbraten (marinated beef), Wiener schnitzel (veal cutlet), or Bratpfanne (roast chicken), dinners include a relish bowl, hors d'oeuvres, soup, salad, cabbage, potatoes, a bread basket, cinnamon rolls, dessert, and a beverage. The downstairs collegiate rathskeller features an organist who leads sing-alongs, peanuts on the tables (and shells on the floor), and an interesting menu of German pizza, game sausage, buffalo burgers, and kids' meals. There's a gift shop if you want a memento of your dining experience.

✕ *3003 W. Paradise Rd., opposite the Las Vegas Hilton,* ☎ *702/734–6888. Reservations advised. AE, D, DC, MC, V.*

Italian

$$$ **Primavera.** Homemade pasta and the Primavera hamburger are perfect for an afternoon in this pleasant, bright setting overlooking the enormous Garden of the Gods swimming pool at Caesars Palace. At dinnertime the mood is more restrained, the lights low, and, with seating for only 75, the tables hard to come by. The specialty of the house is fettuccine Primavera, tossed with sautéed vegetables, sweet butter, fresh cream, and Parmesan cheese. The dessert tray is outstanding, but if you don't have room, you might try one of the fine after-dinner grappas, bottled exclusively for this restaurant. ✕ *Caesars Palace, 3570 Las Vegas Blvd. S,* ☎ *702/731–7568. Reservations advised. AE, D, DC, MC, V.*

$$–$$$ **Antonio's.** This quiet restaurant is popular with locals as well as tourists. Small, with marble walls and murals depicting Italian scenes and crystal chandeliers, Antonio's has an open kitchen at one end. The long menu offers well-prepared Northern Italian cuisine, as well as such old favorites as cioppino (seafood cooked with tomatoes, wine, and herbs, and spices) and eggplant Parmesan. If it's available, order the five-onion soup—and you can ask the waiter for the recipe. ✕ *Rio Suites Hotel and Casino, 3700 E. Flamingo,* ☎ *702/252–7777. Reservations advised. AE, DC, MC, V. No lunch.*

$$ **Battista's Hole in the Wall Italian Restaurant.** A local institution that was featured often on TV's "Vegas," Battista's is a Hollywood Las Vegas restaurant, one with celebrity photographs on the walls, alongside the wine bottles, garlic, and peppers. The fare is your basic Italian—pizza, ravioli, lasagna, and other pastas. All dinners include minestrone, garlic bread, salad, a pasta side dish, wine, and cappuccino. You'll hear opera on the stereo, and sometimes Battista Locatelli himself roams the restaurant, singing. His house rules prohibit tank tops and children under four. ✕ *4041 Audrie St. at Flamingo Rd.,* ☎ *702/732–1424. AE, D, DC, MC, V. No lunch.*

$$ **Bertolini's.** Tables at this "sidewalk" café inside the Forum Shops at Caesars are set up in the piazza surrounding the Fountain of the Gods. The outside section is very noisy; if you want to talk, take a table in the dark and clubby interior, where booths line the black-and-yellow antiqued walls and an open kitchen stands at the back, turning out pasta and rice dishes, single-portion pizzas, soups and salads, and chicken, sausage, and fish. Save room for dessert: A gelato bar offers some of the most mouthwatering ice cream and sorbet around. ✕ *Forum Shops at Caesars,* ☎ *702/735–4663. No reservations. AE, MC, V.*

$$ **The Venetian.** You can't miss this landmark Italian restaurant, which opened in 1955 as the first pizza place in Las Vegas: Murals of Venice grace the exterior (and interior) walls. The traditions here are the jumbo bowl of pork neck bones served, as an appetizer, in a wine marinade (use the bib!), and Venetian greens served on a bed of pasta. You can't go wrong with any dishes that have a "p" in the name: pasta, parmigiana, eggplant, pizzaiola, scaloppine, peppers. Also, the selection of homemade bread is outstanding. Early-bird specials are served between 4 and 6 PM. ✕ *3713 W. Sahara Ave.,* ☎ *702/876–4190. Reservations advised. AE, D, DC, MC, V. No lunch.*

$–$$ **Capozzoli's.** A lighthouse stands at the entrance to this small yet comfortable Italian restaurant in a minimall a little more than a mile east of the Strip. Capozzoli's, which stays open until 4 AM, is popular with local residents. The decor consists of red-and-white tablecloths and wine bottles on the ceiling; the menu offers veal Parmesan, chicken, and tripe, with soups, salads, and breads made fresh daily. Sandwiches, subs, and pizzas are the lunchtime fare. The place tends to be jammed on weekends and during conventions. ✕ *3333 S. Maryland Pkwy.,* ☎ *702/731–5311. Reservations advised. AE, DC, MC, V.*

Japanese

$$$ **Mikado.** Just a few steps from The Mirage's noisy casino, this restaurant provides as much of an oasis as is possible amid the city's madness; it's relatively soothing if you're seated far from the door, near the placid streams, gardens, and murals. The menu consists of standard Japanese fare: steak, chicken, and shrimp prepared teppan-yaki (chopped, diced, and barbecued on a hot grill) or tempura (deep-fried) style; yaki-tori (grilled beef in a thick-noodle soup); plus sushi and sashimi from the sushi bar in the corner. ✕ *Mirage Hotel and Casino, 3400 Las Vegas Blvd. S,* ☎ *702/791–7111. Reservations advised. AE, DC, MC, V. No lunch.*

Mexican

$$ **Las Olas.** This is by far the best Mexican restaurant in a casino in Las Vegas. Las Olas means "the waves," and the biggest wave-in-a-container you've ever seen is behind the bar—it's hypnotic if you stare at it while indulging in intoxicants. Dinner starts with an avocado-bacon-cilantro salsa and chips. The albóndigas (meatball) soup is excellent. The combo plates and enchiladas are fairly standard (served in red or green chili sauce), but the imaginative dinner specialties (chicken, steak, scampi) are well worth the extra few dollars. The filet-and-scampi combo takes top honors. ✕ *Bally's Hotel and Casino, 3645 Las Vegas Blvd. S,* ☎ *702/739–4111. Reservations advised. AE, D, DC, MC, V. No lunch.*

$–$$ **Margarita's Mexican Cantina.** This was a steak house until Margaret Elardi bought the Frontier and turned it into a grind joint. What do slot players like best? she asked. Not chops but tacos and margaritas. The decor is classic Southwest, with turquoise and pink tiles, hardwood chairs, and pink and purple neon shading the ceiling—authentic except for the keno boards on the wall and the keno tickets and crayons at every table. The cuisine is good Tex-Mex: tacos, enchiladas, chimichangas, burritos. At the tortillerùa up front, the chef prepares fresh tortillas that you can smell throughout the casino; they're served with salsa, guacamole, and bean dip in lieu of chips. For dessert try the Burrito Tropical, a deep-fried tortilla stuffed with fresh fruit, ice cream on the side, and a rich sauce topping. ✕ *Frontier Hotel, 3120 Las Vegas Blvd. S,* ☎ *702/794–8200. AE, D, DC, MC, V.*

$ **El Sombrero.** One of the oldest restaurants in Las Vegas, this tiny Mexican eatery has been run by the same family since 1952. It's in a somewhat depressed section of the city (south of downtown, across from the St. Vincent de Paul thrift shop), but sombrero and serape decorations make it cheerful inside. Offerings include such typical Mexican dishes as burritos and tacos, enchiladas, and tamale combinations. The sopapillas are renowned. ✕ *807 S. Main St.,* ☎ *702/382–9234. AE, MC, V. Closed Sun.*

Only in Las Vegas

$$$$ **The Bacchanal.** Caesars Palace's most elaborate restaurant turns food service into showbiz. To re-create a Roman feast in the atmosphere of a private villa, male guests are served wine by toga-clad "wine goddesses," who also deliver a massage before dessert (a toke is expected).

Two stone lions guard the room, and a lighted pool occupies the center. Spectacle and gluttony are the operating principles here: The $65 prix-fixe dinner includes two types of appetizers; soup; salad; a pasta course; a main dish, such as filet mignon, rack of lamb, or prime rib; dessert; coffee; and all the wine you can drink. Don't expect refined dining; it's best to share the three-hour Bacchanalian food orgy experience with a large group. What with the rowdy conversation and the wine goddesses refilling your cup every minute, you'll hardly notice that the food is fairly mundane. ✕ *Caesars Palace, 3570 Las Vegas Blvd. S,* ☎ *702/731–7525. Reservations advised. Dinner seatings at 6–6:30* PM *and 9–9:30* PM. *AE, D, DC, MC, V. Closed Sun., Mon.*

Seafood

$$$ Second Street Grille. This is a fine dining room that serves "contemporary American" food such as steaks, lamb chops, and veal, with strong European, Asian, and Hawaiian influences. But the best food here is the seafood, with the daily specials flown in fresh from Hawaii. A good way to start out is with the Mongolian seafood pot (filled with fish, clams, crab, and scallops), the ahi sashimi, Maryland crab cakes, or seared sea scallops. Follow it up with 24 ounces of king crab legs in a lime-ginger sauce, sautéed soft-shell crab, thick swordfish steak, or wok-charred salmon with king crab hash. The room is dark and intimate, the service is professional but not pretentious, and best of all, Second Street Grille is fairly unknown in the Las Vegas fine-dining firmament, so you can count on same-day reservations. ✕ *Fremont Hotel and Casino, 200 E. Fremont St.,* ☎ *702/385–3232. Reservations advised. AE, D, DC, MC, V. Closed Tues., Wed. No lunch.*

$$ The Tillerman. Its location on Flamingo Road, almost 3 miles east of the Strip, makes the Tillerman a quiet refuge from the casinos and a favorite with convention delegates. The garden setting—the restaurant is built around a huge ficus growing in the center of the room—places you under an open skylight on hot desert nights. A dozen different, well-prepared seafood selections are offered each night, and the steaks are always done just right. ✕ *2245 E. Flamingo Rd.,* ☎ *702/731–4036. AE, D, DC, MC, V. No lunch.*

Southwestern

$$$–$$$$ Coyote Café. The Coyote describes itself as "gourmet Southwestern." The café out front offers an excellent alternative to the crowded buffet and coffee shop for breakfast; you'll walk right in, sit right down, and be served one of six breakfasts, such as huevos rancheros, quiche, or fruit and yogurt. The fine dining room in the back serves lunch and dinner from a somewhat limited, but excellent, menu. Appetizers, such as Southwestern painted soup and Huitlacoche tamales, complement entrées like Howlin' Chile Relleno and Cowboy Rib Chop, served with onion rings. ✕ *MGM Grand Hotel and Casino, 3805 Las Vegas Blvd. S,* ☎ *702/891–7349. Reservations advised for dinner. AE, D, DC, MC, V.*

Steak Houses

$$$ Golden Steer. In a town where restaurants come and go almost as quickly as visitors' cash, the longevity of this steak house, opened in 1962, is itself a high recommendation. Over the years, folks have been coming here for the relaxed atmosphere and, especially, for the huge slabs of well-prepared meat: Steak, ribs, and roast beef are particularly popular. Although you wouldn't know it from the outside, the Steer is cav-

ernous; however, lots of small, intimate rooms—done in San Francisco Barbary Coast–style, with red leather chairs, polished dark wood, and stained-glass windows—break up the space. The namesake's image, a big fat yellow cow, beckons from a sign out front. ✕ *308 W. Sahara Ave.,* ☎ *702/384–4470. Reservations advised. AE, D, DC, MC, V. No lunch.*

$$–$$$ **Steak House.** Believe it or not, the steak house set within the craziness of Circus Circus is one that many local residents contend is the best in town. The atmosphere here is totally unlike that of the rest of Circus Circus; the wood paneling and antique brass furnishings adorn a dark, quiet room reminiscent of 1890s San Francisco. The beef—aged 21 days—is displayed in a glassed-in area at the side; the cooking takes place over an open-hearth charcoal grill in the middle of the room. Steaks, chops, and roast beef make up the menu, and all entrées are accompanied by soup or salad, fresh bread, and a giant baked potato. ✕ *Circus Circus, 2880 Las Vegas Blvd. S,* ☎ *702/734–0410. Reservations advised. AE, D, DC, MC, V. No lunch.*

$$–$$$ **Yolie's.** If you like your meat marinaded, mesquite-broiled, and served rodizio-style (sliced continuously from the skewer onto your plate by a waiter in the fashion of a churrascaria, or Brazilian house of meat), then this is definitely the place for you. The fixed price of $22.95 ($12.95 for lunch) gets you bread, soup, sides, and all-you-can-eat slices of turkey, lamb, brisket, chicken, sausage, and steak, all grilled over a mesquite-fired, glass-enclosed rotisserie in view of the dining room. It's a fun place to eat. Live it up—you're in Las Vegas! ✕ *3900 Paradise Rd.,* ☎ *702/794–0700. Reservations advised. AE, D, DC, MC, V. No lunch weekends.*

9 Lodging

FOR MANY YEARS, the guiding principle in Las Vegas hotel construction was to make the rooms as loud but minimalist as possible, with no modern amenities such as TV sets or clocks. The goal was to keep the guest out of the room and in the casino. While some hotels still subscribe to that theory, most Las Vegas lodging houses have entered the modern age and now offer TVs and pay-TV movies, AM/FM radio, direct-dial telephones, and soft color schemes. High-roller suites, provided by the casino-hotels for those who agree to risk a minimum specified amount of money at the tables, are the ultimate in luxury accommodations. No-smoking floors or rooms are generally available these days, too.

Rooms, especially at the older properties, are often distinguished by the terms "garden," in older, low-rise wings, and "tower," in newer, high-rise buildings. Many hotels, such as the Alexis Park, Rio, Lady Luck, and Frontier, have "minisuites," which are larger and more comfortable than routine hotel rooms. Others, like the Westwood Ho and Residence Inn, have two-bedroom apartments for families or larger parties. A number of motels, such as Sun Harbor Budget Suites, feature complete kitchenettes and weekly rates.

To reserve a room in any property in this chapter, you can contact **Fodor's new toll-free lodging reservations hot line** (☎ 1–800–FODORS–1 or 1–800–363–6771; 0800–89–1030 in Great Britain; 0014/800–12–8271 in Australia; 1800–55–9101 in Ireland).

Hotels

Las Vegas is now home to nine of the 10 largest hotels in the world. The largest hotels, in order, are: the MGM Grand, Excalibur, Flamingo Hilton, Las Vegas Hilton, Mirage, Treasure Island, Bally's, Circus Circus, and Imperial Palace. There are now nearly 90,000 hotel and motel rooms in Las Vegas. If that seems like a lot, consider that the 1996 visitor volume is projected to surpass 24 million, which divides into a little more than a half-million visitors a week—the equivalent of every man, woman, and child in Honolulu, Hawaii, being suddenly transported to Las Vegas. In short, accommodations fill up fast around here, even when no major conventions or events are scheduled.

When it's time for a major convention, it's not unusual for Las Vegas to sell out completely. Nearly two dozen conventions a year each attract more than 25,000 participants. Combine those with three-day weekends, holidays, large sporting events, and normally crowded weekends, and it's wise to make your lodging arrangements as far ahead of your visit as possible. On the other hand, things change quickly in Las Vegas. If you arrive at the last minute without accommodations, you'll almost always be able to find a room somewhere in town. And if your original room is not to your liking, you can usually upgrade it around checkout time the next day.

In general, rates for Las Vegas accommodations are far lower than those in most other American resort and vacation cities. In addition, there are often further discounts and package deals. When business is slow, many hotels offer reduced rates on rooms in their least desirable sections, sometimes with a buffet breakfast or even a show included. Most "sales" occur from December through February and July through August, the coldest and hottest times of the year. Imperial Palace, for example, often advertises rooms at $10 a night for Sunday through Thursday stays in December.

One useful guide to bargain rates is the Sunday "Calendar" section of the Los Angeles Times, where most Las Vegas hotels advertise. Another way to learn about specials is to call a hotel's toll-free number and ask what package deals it has for your vacation dates. When the hotel reservations clerks continually tell you they're sold out, try the Las Vegas Tourist Bureau (☎ 702/739–1482) or the Las Vegas Hotel Reservation Center (☎ 702/736–6766). One of them may be able to place you in the hotel of your choice.

CATEGORY	COST*
$$$$	over $120
$$$	$80–$120
$$	$50–$80
$	under $50

**All prices are for a standard double room, excluding service charge and 8% tax.*

Hotels

$$$$ **Caesars Palace.** If the opulent entrance, fountains, Roman statuary, bas-reliefs, roaming centurions, and handmaidens all look vaguely familiar to you, it's because you may have seen this quintessentially Las Vegas hotel in such movies as *Electric Horseman* and *Rain Man.* With 1,518 rooms, Caesars is not one of the largest hotels in the city, but it has always gone after quality rather than quantity. In recent years, the hotel has expanded its casino and added a lavish shopping mall, the Forum Shops (*see* Chapter 6, Shopping). The restaurants are among the most expensive and extravagant in town: along with the excellent Palace Court, Primavera, Cafe Roma, Empress Court, Palatium Buffet, and the showy Bacchanal (*see* Chapter 8, *Dining,* for all six), the hotel boasts three other restaurants; Cleopatra's Barge lounge is one of a kind. The hotel is the home of world-class sporting events and top superstars, such as David Copperfield and Diana Ross. Its Omnimax theater, a huge geodesic dome, shows movies specially made for the 70mm process. *3750 Las Vegas Blvd. S, 89109, ☎ 702/731–7110 or 800/634–6661, FAX 702/731–6636. 1,518 rooms and suites. 9 restaurants, lounge, 2 pools, 4 tennis courts, health spa, squash court, shopping mall, showroom. AE, D, DC, MC, V.*

$$$$ **The Mirage.** Steve Wynn's $630 million South Seas–theme resort is appropriately named. This desert property—comprising a rain forest with 3,000 tropical plants, palm and banana trees, and lagoons; six Himalayan white tigers; a 53-foot-long aquarium filled with tropical fish, including baby sharks; seven dolphins frolicking in the largest saltwater pool in the world; and a 50-foot waterfall that becomes an exploding volcano after dark—seems at times to have been created by resident master illusionists Siegfried and Roy. Gleaming white marble and high-quality wood throughout the public areas add to the fantasy atmosphere. But there are many down-to-earth reasons to stay at the Mirage, not the least of which is the high quality of the service. The staff seems to actually like working here, and the hotel to want your business. The accommodations are pleasant in all price ranges. Immaculate rooms feature bright colors and attractive if simple furnishings; make sure to get one (no extra charge) with an eye-popping view of the Strip, including the volcano. Suites, though pricey, are worth a special-occasion splurge: They have Jacuzzi bathtubs, loads of amenities, hidden TVs that rise from out of nowhere, and enough space to throw a real party. The food in the hotel's buffet restaurant is a cut

Aladdin, **15**
Alexis Park, **13**
Bally's, **14**
Barbary Coast, **18**
Binion's Horseshoe, **42**
Buffalo Bill's, **4**
Caesars Palace, **17, 42**
Circus Circus, **32**
El Cortez, **44**
Excalibur, **11**
Fitzgeralds, **41**
Flamingo Hilton Las Vegas, **19**
Four Queens, **40**
Frontier, **28**
Gold Spike, **43**
Gold Strike, **2**
Golden Nugget, **39**
Hacienda, **6**
Harrah's, **22**
Imperial Palace, **21**
Lady Luck, **38**
Las Vegas Club, **37**
Las Vegas Hilton, **34**
Luxor, **8**
Maxim, **20**
MGM Grand, **12**
The Mirage, **23**
Motel 6, **9**
Nevada Landing Hotel and Casino, **3**
Plaza, **36**
Primadonna, **5**
Residence Inn by Marriott, **26**
Rio Suite, **16**
Riviera, **33**
Royal Oasis, **7**
Sahara Las Vegas, **35**
Sam's Town, **45**
Sands, **25**
Sheraton Desert Inn, **27**
Stardust, **29**
Sun Harbor Budget Suites, **30**
Treasure Island, **24**
Tropicana, **10**
Westward Ho, **31**
Whiskey Pete's, **1**

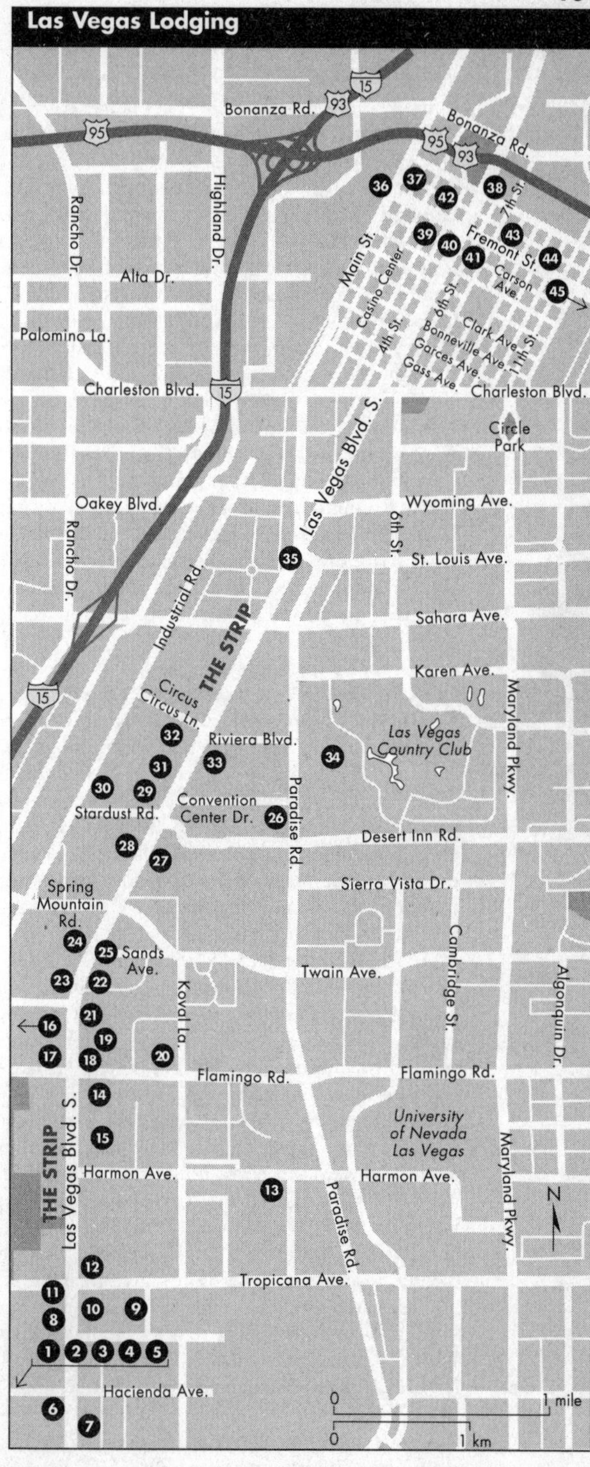

above the usual, and Moongate is the prettiest Chinese restaurant in town. ⌂ *3400 Las Vegas Blvd. S, 89109,* ☎ *702/791–7111 or 800/627–6667,* FAX *702/791–7446. 2,825 rooms, 224 suites. 7 restaurants, lounge, pool, golf course, 4 tennis courts, health spa, shopping arcade, showroom. AE, D, DC, MC, V.*

$$$$ **Sheraton Desert Inn Hotel & Country Club.** One of the classiest and best-laid-out in town, the DI was once the home and property of the late Howard Hughes. Hughes was staying on the ninth floor, so the story goes, when the hotel staff asked him to move out to make room for some high rollers. He promptly bought the place instead. This relatively small hotel, comprised of two low-rise buildings and one taller one, has always gone for an upscale clientele who like to play golf and gamble. If you get a room with smoked-glass windows overlooking the PGA championship golf course, you could almost forget you're in Las Vegas—no neon signs, tall buildings, or traffic jams in the view (other rooms do face the Strip, however). Each year the hotel hosts three major Tour events: the Desert Inn–LPGA International, the Las Vegas Senior Classic (Senior PGA Tour), and the Las Vegas International (PGA Tour). Rooms have a southwestern feel, many with separate dining or lounging areas; some suites even have private swimming pools. The Crystal Room Showroom alternates between headliners and Broadway theater productions. There are three gourmet restaurants on the premises, a deli, and a 24-hour coffee shop. ⌂ *3145 Las Vegas Blvd. S, 89109,* ☎ *702/733–4444 or 800/634–6906,* FAX *702/733–4774. 821 rooms, including 95 suites. 5 restaurants, lounge, pool, 18-hole golf course, 10 tennis courts, health spa, showroom. AE, D, DC, MC, V.*

$$$$ **Alexis Park Resort Hotel.** Would businesspeople and couples come to a luxury hotel in Las Vegas that had no neon, no gaming tables, and no slots? The Alexis Park opened in 1984 and discovered that the answer was yes. Two miles from the convention center, this is a favorite spot for convention delegates who want as "normal" a living experience as possible during their business trip. The individual buildings of the all-suite desert hotel are two-story, white-stucco blocks with red-tile roofs, all set in a water garden. Views are of either a rock pool or a lawn. Every room has a wet bar; some have fireplaces or Jacuzzis. ⌂ *375 E. Harmon Ave., 89109,* ☎ *702/796–3300 or 800/453–8000,* FAX *702/582–2228. 500 suites. 3 restaurants, lounge, 3 pools, 9-hole putting green, 2 tennis courts, health spa. AE, D, DC, MC, V.*

$$$–$$$$ **Las Vegas Hilton.** Barbra Streisand opened this hotel with a four-week gig and was followed by Elvis Presley, who made the Hilton his official Las Vegas venue throughout the 1970s; you can still stay in the Elvis Suite on the 31st floor, where the King of Rock and Roll resided when he played here. Though the Hilton, which is adjacent to the Las Vegas Convention Center, no longer holds the title of largest hotel in town, it's still a sight to see—best of all by standing at its foot and staring up at the 375-foot tower, 29 floors, and three wings. The rooms are spacious, with soft colors, large beds, and telephones in the lavatories; those on the higher floors have great views of the city. They can also be hard to find; the numbering system goes from hundreds to thousands and varies from wing to wing. Andrew Lloyd Webber's "Starlight Express" plays in the showroom, the lounge seats 900, and the buffet features all the cold king crab you can eat. ⌂ *3000 Paradise Rd., 89109,* ☎ *702/732–5111 or 800/732–7117,* FAX *702/794–3611. 2,950 rooms, 224 suites. 8 restaurants, lounge, pool, putting green, 6 tennis courts, health spa, showroom. AE, D, DC, MC, V.*

$$$–$$$$ **Residence Inn by Marriott.** This town-house-style all-suite hotel on nicely landscaped grounds is across the street from the Convention Center and a short cab ride away (1¼ miles) from the Strip. Guests are served

a complimentary breakfast and a complimentary weekday dinner buffet. The studios and two-bedroom suites all have kitchens. Curbside parking is a plus. *3225 Paradise Rd., 89109, 702/796–9300 or 800/331–3131, FAX 702/796–9562. 144 studios, 48 2-bedroom suites. Pool, tennis court. AE, D, DC, MC, V.*

$$$ Bally's Casino Resort. With nearly 3,000 rooms on the busiest corner of the Strip, the hotel calls itself "A City Within a City," and this is not much of an exaggeration. Bally's is the only hotel with two major showrooms: Headliners like George Carlin are featured in one, and the $10 million spectacular "Jubilee!" (*see* Chapter 10, Nightlife) is offered twice a night in the other. The hotel also has a huge casino, a comedy club, a 40-store shopping arcade that sells everything from fine furs to ice cream, 10 tennis courts, separate health spas for men and women, an attractively landscaped outdoor pool, and a terminal for the monorail to MGM Grand. Since the front parking lot was transformed into "Bally's Garden," visitors no longer have an arduous long walk from the Strip to the casino; instead, they can hop on a people-mover for a five-minute ride through a series of special effects. All 2,800 rooms have now been upgraded, and dozens are now equipped for guests with disabilities. *3645 Las Vegas Blvd. S, 89109, 702/739–4111 or 800/634–3434, FAX 702/739–4405. 2,832 rooms, 265 suites. 6 restaurants, lounge, pool, 10 tennis courts, health spas, comedy club, 2 showrooms. AE, D, DC, MC, V.*

$$$ Flamingo Hilton Las Vegas. The Fabulous Flamingo that opened in 1946 with everyone—from Bugsy down to the janitors—dressed in a tuxedo, was a 98-room oasis with palm trees imported from California. The Flamingo has changed a lot since then: Today its six towers overlook a new 15-acre pool area where the original motor lodges once stood. The Flamingo is pervasively pink, from the outside neon sign to the in-room vases and pens and the lobby carpeting. The spacious rooms in the towers offer expansive views of the Strip. The swimming pool area is one of the largest and prettiest in town, and, an unusual feature, the registration area is on the side of the hotel near the elevators, so you won't have to carry your luggage through the casino. Package rates for special tours keep this large hotel and casino bustling. *3555 Las Vegas Blvd. S, 89109, 702/733–3111 or 800/732–2111, FAX 702/733–3353. 3,580 rooms, including 348 suites. 5 restaurants, lounge, 3 pools, 4 tennis courts, health spa, showroom. AE, D, DC, MC, V.*

$$$ Golden Nugget Hotel. The Nugget was only a gambling hall with sawdust on the floors and no hotel rooms when Steve Wynn took it over in the 1970s and decided to go after high rollers. Now red rugs flow over white marble, leading you to the lobby and a large public area with columns, etched-glass windows, and fresh flowers in gold-plated vases. Almost everything here is gold—the telephones, the slots, the elevators. The large, Victorian-style rooms have four-posters, period mirrors and furniture, and dining areas. In addition to the standard double rooms, the Nugget has 27 duplex suites—some with a personal room-service waiter—and six two-bedroom apartments, each decorated in a different style. "Country Fever," the hottest country-western show in town, plays in the showroom. *129 E. Fremont St., 89101, 702/385–7111 or 800/634–3454, FAX 702/386–8362. 1,805 rooms, 106 suites. 5 restaurants, lounge, pool, health club, showroom. AE, D, DC, MC, V.*

$$$ MGM Grand Hotel and Theme Park. This is the largest hotel in the world, a vast entertainment megaresort on 112 acres occupying the grounds of the former Tropicana golf course and Marina Hotel. Four emerald-green, Wizard of Oz–theme towers, three of them 30 stories high, house

5,005 guest rooms, including 733 Hollywood-inspired suites—a full 1,000 rooms larger than the world's second largest hotel, Excalibur, across the street. Also here are the world's largest casino, eight restaurants (not including the fast-food court or theme park eateries), two showrooms, a special-events arena, a 23,000-square-foot swimming pool, three sprawling kids' arcades, a complete day-care facility, and, of course, the 33-acre amusement park. And that's not all. The valet check-in area has 16 lanes. The lobby is breathtaking, centered on a wall of synchronized video monitors. Rooms are average size, with Hollywood decor and picture windows. *3805 Las Vegas Blvd. S, 89109, 702/891–1111 or 800/929–1111, FAX 702/891–1030. 5,005 rooms. 9 restaurants, 2 lounges, pool, tennis courts, health club, 2 showrooms.*

$$$ **Rio Suite Hotel and Casino.** Opened in 1990, the Rio is the first all-suite hotel in Las Vegas with a casino. The striking blue-and-red, 21-story, three-tower hotel is off the Strip (west of the I–15 freeway)—a good location if you prefer quieter surroundings—and has a Brazilian theme, including the sandy beach beside the pool. While suites here don't have separate sitting rooms, they're spacious and feature extra-large sofas, sitting areas, dining tables, and floor-to-ceiling windows. The rooms in the new tower have an interesting amenity: a window in the shower looks out onto the suite, which, with its big picture windows, has an expansive view. These are the only rooms in Las Vegas with a view of the mountains or Strip from the shower! *3700 W. Flamingo Rd., 89109, 702/252–7777 or 800/888–1808, FAX 702/253–6090. 861 suites. 7 restaurants, lounge, pool, health spa, beach, showroom, free shuttle to Strip. AE, D, DC, MC, V.*

$$$ **Treasure Island.** Developed by the Mirage group and opened in November 1993, Treasure Island is a hotel-casino whose design is based on the stories of Robert Louis Stevenson. The casino wraps around Buccaneer Bay, a marvelously detailed replica of a South Seas pirate village, where once every 90 minutes (starting at 4 PM and weather permitting), you can see pirates and sailors duke it out aboard the *Hispaniola* and H.M.S. *Britannia.* The Cirque du Soleil production "Mystere" has a permanent home here. The hotel and casino are a miniature (and less opulent) version of the Mirage next door, though Treasure Island has nearly the same number of rooms. This means that there are essentially the same number of guests, visitors, and employees, but they're all crowded into half the space. The rooms are pint-size but functional, with soft hues, minimalist furniture, and good high sinks. The size of the rooms is evident from outside by looking at the windows: each window is shared by four rooms. A monorail connects the sister hotels for easy access to the Mirage. *3300 Las Vegas Blvd. S, 89109, 702/894–7111 or 800/944–7444, FAX 702/894–7446. 2,941 rooms. 5 restaurants, lounge, pool, health club, showroom. AE, D, MC, V.*

$$ **Aladdin Hotel and Casino.** In 1985 the Aladdin was purchased for $51.5 million by Ginsu Yasuda, the late Korean-born Japanese resident who liked to shoot craps in Las Vegas. He moved his family here, took over the penthouse, and sunk more millions into the hotel on a remodeling spree of the 1,100 rooms. Unfortunately, Yasuda ran the Aladdin into the ground, and it went through several years of bankruptcy. But it has emerged from those dark days, and has recently come a long way up, both in service and facilities. The rooms are fairly standard, with low-key tan walls, dark-pink carpeting and bedspreads, and a view of the Strip. Elevators opposite the registration area make long walks unnecessary. The showroom has the biggest country-western-style revue on the Strip, and, behind the hotel, the 10,000-seat Aladdin Theatre for the Performing Arts (*see* Chapter 10, *Nightlife*) hosts headliners, rock groups, and touring theater troupes. *3667 Las Vegas Blvd. S,*

89109, ☎ 702/736–0111 or 800/634–3424, FAX 702/734–3583. 1,100 rooms, 44 suites. 6 restaurants, lounge, 2 pools, 3 tennis courts, shopping arcade, showroom. AE, D, DC, MC, V.

$$ **Barbary Coast Hotel and Casino.** The Barbary Coast has one of the most central locations in Las Vegas, across from Caesars and next door to the Flamingo Hilton. It's a fun place with a San Francisco Gold Rush theme—the Victorian-style rooms have brass four-posters with canopies, old-fashioned lamps, lacy curtains, separate eating areas—and good rates. The views are of the Strip or the Flamingo Hilton. Because there are only 200 rooms here, it's not always easy to get one. *3595 Las Vegas Blvd. S, 89109, ☎ 702/737–7111 or 800/634–6755, FAX 702/737–6304. 196 rooms, 12 suites. 3 restaurants, lounge. AE, D, DC, MC, V.*

$$ **Binion's Horseshoe Hotel and Casino.** You'll look in vain for the brilliant red neon sign of the old Mint Hotel on Fremont Street; it was taken down in 1988 when the Horseshoe's founder, Benny Binion, bought the Mint, tore down the walls between the two casinos, and created a larger Horseshoe. The new neon signs are a turquoise Horseshoe legend and, up top, a revolving neon horseshoe. Inside, staff members speak of the old Mint building as the "West" Horseshoe, the original Horseshoe as the "East" side. Before the expansion, the Horseshoe had just 80 rooms upstairs and they were hard to get. "We don't take reservations," Binion said once. "If I know you, you got a room. If I don't, you don't have a room." The 26-story hotel and casino, now run by Binion's son, Jack, and daughter, Becky, has 300 rooms with some of the best views of downtown. These rooms are available to the public, though on a limited basis, since they are often reserved for the hotel's biggest gamblers. On the west side are modern, medium-size rooms decorated in light colors. The east-side rooms, which you may never see, reflect the western style of the Horseshoe: They have Victorian-style wallpaper and brass beds with quilted spreads. The pool is on the roof. The snack bars have down-to-earth food and prices. *128 E. Fremont St., 89101, ☎ 702/382–1600 or 800/237–6537, FAX 702/384–1574. 380 rooms. 4 restaurants, pool. AE, DC, MC, V.*

$$ **Excalibur Hotel and Casino.** Before they opened this spectacular 4,032-room hotel in 1990, Circus Circus execs visited the castles of England, Scotland, and Germany. The result might be described as King Arthur does Las Vegas. (A local "name-the-hotel" contest received many votes for Castle Castle.) The hotel's seven restaurants and 23-shop Medieval Village have an Arthurian theme, complete with strolling Renaissance performers, and the megaresort is the home of Las Vegas's most unusual entertainment extravaganza, "King Arthur's Tournament" (*see* Chapter 10, *Nightlife*). At the wedding chapel, you can tie the knot with all the trappings of King Arthur and Lady Guinevere. Merlin's Magic Motion Machine, a simulated thrill ride with a big screen, state-of-the-art sound, and synchronized seats, is pure modern Las Vegas, as is the 100,000-square-foot casino. The Excalibur is also notable for its good-value accommodations; the occupancy rate is almost always 100%. *3850 Las Vegas Blvd. S, 89119, ☎ 702/597–7777 or 800/937–7777, FAX 702/597–7040. 4,032 rooms. 7 restaurants, 2 pools, shops, theater, showroom, wedding chapel. AE, DC, MC, V.*

$$ **Four Queens Hotel and Casino.** This prominent downtown hotel has one amenity you'll find nowhere else in Las Vegas: Security guards stand at the elevators 24 hours a day and ask to see your room key before you enter. The Queens rooms are furnished in New Orleans style with turn-of-the-century wallpaper, vintage lamps, four-posters, and views of Fremont Street, Fitzgeralds, or the Golden Nugget. Jazz is performed in the French Quarter lounge on Monday evening. *202 E.*

Fremont St., ☎ *702/385–4011 or 800/634–6045,* FAX *702/387–5133. 720 rooms. 4 restaurants, lounge. AE, DC, MC, V.*

$$ Frontier Hotel. While the Frontier of today stands on the same property as the original 1942 hotel, it bears little resemblance to the old place, as depicted in mementos on the second-floor walls of the executive offices. In 1988, without disturbing the basic cowboy character of the place, a new owner lowered the room rates, reduced the gaming table minimums, and converted the showroom into a buffet. An Early West motif prevails, but the rooms have been upgraded and you won't find cactus or branding irons on the walls as in the original hotel. The new Atrium Tower has 580 minisuites, decorated in earth tones, with separate dining areas and views of the Strip or the Frontier garden area; the center of the 14-story tower is open to the sky, which is unique in Las Vegas. *3120 Las Vegas Blvd. S, 89109,* ☎ *702/794–8200 or 800/634–6966. 986 rooms. 4 restaurants, lounge, pool, putting green, 2 tennis courts. AE, D, DC, MC, V.*

$$ Hacienda Hotel and Casino. The first big hotel you see from the freeway if you're driving in from southern California, the Hacienda is a refreshing alternative to some of its bigger, more impersonal competitors up the Strip. In early 1991, 400 rooms were added and the casino space was doubled; Circus Circus bought the Hacienda in early 1995. Rooms are standard, with white walls, twin beds, and eating areas; the views take in Las Vegas Boulevard or the freeway. The showroom hosts an illusion act. The hotel's Little Church of the West, one of the oldest wedding chapels in town, was originally built in 1942 on the property of the Last Frontier Hotel. The courtyard rooms, now some of the last of the original 1950s' low-risers, surround the lush, tranquil, 40-year-old pool area. *3950 Las Vegas Blvd. S, 89119,* ☎ *702/739–8911 or 800/634–6655,* FAX *702/798–8289. 985 rooms, 65 suites. 3 restaurants, lounge, pool, 6 tennis courts, showroom, wedding chapel, RV park. AE, D, DC, MC, V.*

$$ Harrah's Hotel and Casino. You can't miss the 450-foot-long Mississippi River gambling boat affectionately known as the "Ship on the Strip"; even before you see it, you can hear it tooting its foghorn. Originally a Holiday Inn when it opened in 1973, it has sailed under Harrah's flag since 1992. While the casino is as red and bawdy-looking as it can be, the rooms are modest and have lavender doors, gray walls, blue bedspreads and matching curtains, and dark-wood furniture. Jackson Square shopping center outside the hotel furthers the New Orleans French Quarter theme, with such shops as Holiday Jazz, Louisiana Limited, and Cajun Spice. *3475 Las Vegas Blvd. S, 89109,* ☎ *702/369–5000 or 800/634–6765,* FAX *702/369–5008. 1,686 rooms, 39 suites. 5 restaurants, lounge, pool, health club, showroom. AE, D, DC, MC, V.*

$$ Imperial Palace Hotel & Casino. The Imperial Palace was the first hotel built in Las Vegas around an Oriental theme, featuring crystal, jade, and carved wood. Located in the heart of the Strip, it's home to one of Las Vegas's most popular long-running shows, "Legends in Concert" (*see* Chapter 10, *Nightlife*), and to one of Las Vegas's most popular tourist attractions, the Automobile Museum (*see* Tour 1 *in* Chapter 5, Exploring Las Vegas). The hotel offers eight restaurants and two buffets, the only multitiered sports book in Las Vegas, its own wedding chapel, and, of course, the famous Antique Auto Collection. Imperial Palace has the best facilities for people with disabilities in Las Vegas. *3535 Las Vegas Blvd. S, 89109,* ☎ *702/731–3311 or 800/634–6441,* FAX *702/735–8578. 2,412 rooms, 225 suites. 8 restaurants, lounge, pool, shopping arcade, showroom, wedding chapel. AE, DC, MC, V.*

$$ Lady Luck Casino and Hotel. The addition of a 25-story, 400-room tower in 1989 made this the third-largest hotel property downtown. The new tower is across the street from the 17-story tower that opened in 1986, and visitors travel from the old Lady to the new Lady via a glass-enclosed pedestrian bridge on the third-floor level. Lady Luck has small, bright rooms with white walls and half windows that look out on Ogden Street. There are also 115 "junior suites" and a number of "senior suites," too, for the Lady's many high rollers. (Why are there so many high rollers at the Lady Luck? Because the casino has some of the least demanding comp criteria in town.) ☐ *206 N. 3rd St., 89109,* ☎ *702/477–3000 or 800/634–6580,* FAX *702/477–3002. 800 rooms. 4 restaurants, pool, showroom. AE, D, DC, MC, V.*

$$ Las Vegas Club Hotel and Casino. Here, a sports theme prevails everywhere but in the guest rooms. The coffee shop is the Dugout, the lobby walls display baseball and basketball photos and memorabilia, and a gift shop offers a wide selection of baseball shirts. The small rooms have a light-brown finish, the beds have small awnings, and the tiny half windows overlook Fremont and Main streets. ☐ *18 E. Fremont St., 89109,* ☎ *702/385–1664 or 800/634–6532,* FAX *702/387–6071. 224 rooms. 2 restaurants, lounge. AE, DC, MC, V.*

$$ Luxor. The folks at Circus Circus, who also developed Excalibur, have built one of the modern wonders of the world right next door. Luxor, a 2,521-room, 30-story, pyramid-shape hotel-casino, completed in October 1993, can now lay claim to the most completely rendered theme of all the themed hotels in Theme City. The pyramid, to start, is pure Egyptian. The most impressive artifacts from King Tut's tomb have been impressively reproduced by Egyptian craftsmen and displayed in Luxor's museum. The River Nile boat ride around the inside edge of the pyramid comes with a narrated tour through Egyptian mythology and theology. Four "inclinators" travel the 39-degree incline of the pyramid to the guest rooms; "hallways" to the rooms overlook the world's largest atrium. Rooms are large, decorated in an Egyptian motif, and have the most unusual windows in town. The video arcade is on two levels, with interactive race cars, small motion simulators, state-of-the-art video, and a roomful of air-hockey games. Palm trees grow up right out of the pool. ☐ *3900 Las Vegas Blvd. S, 89119,* ☎ *702/262–4000 or 800/288–1000,* FAX *702/262–4452. 2,521 rooms. 6 restaurants, lounge, pool, showroom, 3 theaters. AE, D, MC, V.*

$$ Maxim Hotel and Casino. Situated just two blocks off the Strip, the Maxim is a good place to try when other establishments have no room, and even when they do. This is a very friendly, low-end-gambler-oriented joint, with a good coffee shop, a nice little gourmet room, a comedy club, and a rooftop pool. The older rooms sport earth tones and are decorated with Las Vegas prints. The newer rooms (all medium-size) have a southwestern flair. ☐ *160 E. Flamingo Rd., 89109,* ☎ *702/731–4300 or 800/634–6987,* FAX *702/735–3252. 795 rooms. 3 restaurants, lounge, pool, showroom. AE, D, DC, MC, V.*

$$ Plaza Hotel. Those taking Amtrak to town will step off the train into the Plaza. Opened in 1971, the Plaza anchors Fremont Street and can be seen in the center of nearly every photo of it. The hotel's roof is the base of activities for broadcasts of the Las Vegas New Year's celebrations. The Plaza almost always has a room, even during big conventions. A green decor and mirrors above the bed characterize the medium-size rooms. Be sure to ask for one overlooking Fremont Street; otherwise you'll have a view of the railroad tracks. ☐ *1 Main St., 89109,* ☎ *702/386–2110 or 800/634–6575,* FAX *702/382–8281. 1,037 rooms. 3 restaurants, lounge, pool, 4 tennis courts, showroom, wedding chapel. AE, D, DC, MC, V.*

$$ Riviera Hotel. Once upon a time there was a nice nine-story hotel-casino on the Strip that styled itself after the Miami resorts of the 1950s and tried to capture the feeling of the French Riviera. As time went on, an owner decided to expand by adding a tower. Then a new owner added another tower and enlarged the casino. Still another owner tacked on two more towers and moved the casino walls yet farther apart. It could be argued that one of them should have torn it all down and started from scratch, but what's done is done, and the Riviera won't be expanding again for a while. Though the casino itself has become less of a maze since the completion of the last expansion in 1991 (it's now basically one huge room), it's still a ramble to locate the proper elevator to the correct tower to your room. Most of the accommodations are large, modern affairs with maroon bedspreads and carpeting, teak furniture, and dining areas (be sure to ask for a room overlooking the Strip). Four showrooms showcase female impersonators, a hot production show, a comedy club, and a topless dance revue. ☒ *2901 Las Vegas Blvd. S, 89109,* ☎ *702/734–5110 or 800/634–6753,* FAX *702/794–9451. 1,959 rooms, 150 suites. 4 restaurants, pool, 2 tennis courts, health club, 4 showrooms. AE, DC, MC, V.*

$$ Sahara Las Vegas Hotel. The oasis theme, established in 1952 when the Sahara opened for business, still remains more than 40 years later—an eternity in Las Vegas. Like many of its neighbors, the Sahara began as a small motor hotel and built itself up by adding towers, towers, and more towers. Unlike many of its neighbors, however, the Sahara has retained a small, gardenlike ambience. A walk through the lobby will take you past the pool, with its sunbathers and huts where you can sit and have a drink. The original rooms are small, in the motor-hotel style, with a dining area, a medium-size window, and utilitarian furniture; all the old garden rooms overlook the pool, greenery, and artificial grass. The tower rooms are larger, with king-size beds and mauve colors; they overlook the Strip or Paradise Road. ☒ *2535 Las Vegas Blvd. S, 89101,* ☎ *702/737–2111 or 800/634–6666,* FAX *702/791–2027. 1,961 rooms, 75 suites. 5 restaurants, lounge, 2 pools, health club, showroom. AE, D, DC, MC, V.*

$$ Sands Hotel and Casino. This 750-room hotel, with its famous 16-story cylindrical tower poking up from the Strip like a periscope, is rich in history. The pool, shaped like a *V* (for Vegas), with a platform in the middle for sunbathers, was the setting for the classic 1950s Vegas publicity photograph that showed a group of fun-loving men and women shooting dice in it—truly a "floating" crap game. And in the swinging 1960s, the Sands was headquarters for Frank Sinatra, Sammy Davis, Jr., Dean Martin, Peter Lawford, and Joey Bishop, who came out here to make the quintessential Las Vegas film, *Ocean's 11.* The distinctive circular tower and casino underneath it were completed in 1967, though the original 11 low-rise 1950s buildings clustered around the pool remain. An 11-acre convention center opened here in 1990. Tower rooms are twice the size of garden rooms, with red bedspreads, walls, and curtains; the upper-story rooms have sliding-glass doors that open onto some of the only open-air balconies on the Strip. Presidents Kennedy, Nixon, and Reagan were guests in the Sands Presidential Suite. ☒ *3355 Las Vegas Blvd. S, 89109,* ☎ *702/733–5000 or 800/634–6901,* FAX *702/733–5624. 715 rooms. 4 restaurants, lounge, 2 pools, putting green, 6 tennis courts, health club, showroom, convention center. AE, D, DC, MC, V.*

$$ Stardust Hotel and Casino. The vision for the Stardust came from the mobster Tony Cornero, who in the 1930s ran gambling ships off the southern California coast; he owned a small club out on Boulder Highway and dreamed of building the biggest, classiest casino in town. He didn't live long enough to realize his dream, however; one morning, while shooting craps at the Desert Inn, he had a heart attack, dying with the dice in his hands. Today the Stardust belongs to the Boyd Group, the operators of middle-market hotels (Sam's Town, Fremont, California) that emphasize slots, low table minimums, and good deals on food. The Stardust added a new casino and 32-story high-rise in 1990, which more than doubled the number of its rooms. The tower rooms offer a great view of the Strip or the hotel garden and pool area and are among the largest and most attractive in town. *3000 Las Vegas Blvd. S, 89109, ☎ 702/732-6111 or 800/634-6757, FAX 702/732-6257. 2,500 rooms. 5 restaurants, lounge, pool, 2 tennis courts, showroom. AE, DC, MC, V.*

$$ Tropicana Resort and Casino. The Tropicana ads refer to it as "the Island of Las Vegas," but in reality the property surrounds the water, rather than the water surrounding the property. Still, it is a beautifully landscaped hotel-casino, including 35-foot Easter Island–like sculptures; Polynesian totems; a longhouse bridge; waterfalls; and a meandering swimming pool boasting swim-up blackjack tables, swim-up bars, and a 110-foot-long water slide. The theme of the Tropicana is, as you would expect, tropical, with neon palms and colorful birds on the "Wildlife Walk" between towers; rooms have rattan furnishings and flowered bedspreads. The hotel is also home to the longest-running show in Las Vegas, "Folies Bergere" (*see* Chapter 10, Nightlife). *3801 Las Vegas Blvd. S, 89109, ☎ 702/739-2222 or 800/468-9494, FAX 702/739-2448. 1,708 rooms, 200 suites. 6 restaurants, lounge, 3 pools, 4 tennis courts, health club, racquetball, showroom. AE, D, DC, MC, V.*

$ Circus Circus. You can always find a room at Circus Circus; if they don't have one for you at their own hotel, they'll locate one in another. But beware, this place is both a madhouse and a maze. Circus Circus has expanded several times over the years; now it can be hard to figure out where you're going, and you'll run into crowds of similarly confused people while you try. The registration area is in the front of the hotel under the pink porte cochere, but the room elevators are all the way at the back, necessitating a long jostling stroll through the casino. Upstairs you'll find painted circus tents in the hallway and some of the most garishly appointed guest rooms in Las Vegas: bright-red carpets, matching red chairs, pink walls and, on one wall, red-, pink-, and blue-striped wallpaper. The casino attracts so many visitors that drivers will find it a major achievement just getting into the parking lot. On a Saturday night, the stretch of Las Vegas Boulevard leading up to Circus Circus is often gridlocked; the valet parking sign reads FULL (though you may be able to get help—for a toke) and the nearest parking space is halfway to Arizona. (If you spend a few minutes learning the back way in, from Industrial Road, and locating alternative parking, you'll save yourself a lot of grief.) Circus Circus is a favorite of families: Parents can drop the kids off at the midway to play games or watch the circus acts while the adults hit the slots; five-minute circus acts are performed every 20 minutes from 11 AM to midnight. The most recent boon to families is Grand Slam Canyon, a 5-acre theme park opened in August 1993 directly behind the hotel, offering a flume ride, a roller coaster, bumper cars, laser tag, and kiddie rides. Some of the kitschiest gift shops in Vegas are at this hotel; you can buy Elvis decanters, $80 slot replicas, Vegas bells, toothpick holders, and thimbles here. *2880 Las Vegas Blvd. S, 89109, ☎ 702/734-0410 or 800/634-3450, FAX 702/734-2268. 2,793 rooms. 5 restaurants, 3 pools, wedding chapel, RV park. AE, D, DC, MC, V.*

$ El Cortez Hotel. Here is a good deal in lodging: a room for two in the downtown area for $23 a night—available on a walk-in basis only, and not on Saturday. The two floors of tiny rooms have twin beds, a small TV, and a narrow window with a view of Fremont Street. Rooms in the tower are newer, larger, and only a little more expensive—up to $40. *600 E. Fremont St., 89109, 702/385–5200 or 800/634–6703, FAX 702/385–1554. 315 rooms. 2 restaurants. AE, D, DC, MC, V.*

$ **Fitzgeralds Hotel and Casino.** The decor of this 34-story hotel (the tallest building in Nevada for 15 years, until it was eclipsed by the Stratosphere Tower) perpetuates the Irish theme of the casino. The marquee is green, the bellmen sport green pants and green ties, the cocktail waitresses wear green dresses, and you'll walk to your room on—you guessed it—green carpeting. But when you reach your room, you'll find that the door is orange, the bedspreads tan, and the walls light brown—to complement the green curtains and carpets. The views are of Fremont Street or the neighboring Four Queens. *301 E. Fremont St., 89109, 702/388–2400 or 800/274–5825, FAX 702/388–2181. 650 rooms. 3 restaurants, lounge, health spa. AE, D, DC, MC, V.*

$ **Gold Spike Hotel and Casino.** Jackie Gaughan owns both El Cortez and the Gold Spike. The hotel is billed as "Las Vegas as it used to be," with penny slots, 40¢ live keno, and $1 blackjack tables. The Spike charges only $20 a night, every night, for a small, plain double room with twin beds, a nightstand, a TV, and a view of East Ogden Avenue. A suite for $30 a night adds a four-poster, couch, and balcony. All rates include breakfast for each guest. *400 E. Ogden Ave., 89109, 702/384–8444 or 800/634–6703. 110 rooms. Coffee shop. AE, D, DC, MC, V.*

$ **Sam's Town Hotel and Casino.** Sam's Town is named for Sam Boyd, the pioneer gambler and owner who built a small grubstake into one of the largest casino companies—a closely held corporation of family and friends—in Nevada; he died in 1993 at the age of 86. His Boyd Group now owns Sam's, the Fremont, the California, and the Stardust in Las Vegas, and the Eldorado and new Joker's Wild in Henderson. This property is far from the center of activity and close to the desert, which gives its Old West decor some authenticity. Indeed, Sam's excels at perpetuating the western theme: Everyone wears garters and string ties; the food is good, plentiful, and inexpensive; and there's a big western-wear store on the property. Sam's Town recently completed a major expansion and total renovation of the property that resulted in 450 new rooms, a nine-story glass-roof atrium complete with tall live trees, cobblestone paths, rock waterfall and babbling brooks traversed by wooden bridges. There's also a free laser-and-dancing-waters musical show (8 and 10:30 PM). The $100 million expansion also added two new al fresco restaurants, an improved pool area, and the best sports bar in town (half-court basketball, anyone?). *5111 W. Boulder Hwy., 89109, 702/456–7777 or 800/634–6371, FAX 702/454–8014. 650 rooms. 6 restaurants, lounge, pool, bowling, RV park. AE, D, DC, MC, V.*

Out of Town

Five casino hotels on I–15 serve those traveling the Los Angeles to Las Vegas route who want a break from driving.

$ **Gold Strike Hotel and Gambling Hall.** Only 30 minutes west of Las Vegas (on I–15 near the California–Nevada border), the Gold Strike has rooms for $19–$31 a night and a weird white-and-orange facade that has to be seen in full daylight to be appreciated. The casino has a strong Old West ambience. *1 Main St., Jean 89019, 702/477–5000 or 800/634–1359, FAX 702/874–1583. 813 rooms. 3 restaurants, lounge, pool. AE, D, DC, MC, V.*

$ Nevada Landing Hotel and Casino. A carbon copy of the Gold Strike, except for the riverboat exterior, Nevada Landing is right across I–15 (on the westbound side). Both were sold to Circus Circus in spring 1995. *2 Goodsprings Rd., Jean 89019, 702/387–5000 or 800/628–6682, FAX 702/874–1583. 303 rooms. 3 restaurants, lounge, pool. AE, D, DC, MC, V.*

$ Buffalo Bill's Hotel and Casino. This is one of the three Primm family hotel-casinos 40 miles west of Las Vegas on I–15 right at the California state line. It opened in August 1994 to join Whiskey Pete's and the Primadonna. The trio of casinos are a little world all their own, connected by a free monorail (across the freeway between Pete's and Primadonna) and a free elevated train (between Bill's and Primadonna). A free Ferris wheel fronts Primadonna and a flume ride (admission) meanders through the casino and around the grounds of Buffalo Bill's. But the main attraction here is Desperado, as ferocious a roller coaster as you're likely ever to ride: a 225-foot 60-degree drop, during which your car reaches speeds of 85 miles per hour. To get people out here from Las Vegas, Bill's has to make it worth their while, and does so with $21 rooms, very inexpensive food, and excellent funbooks; a family of four would be hard-pressed to spend $100 for an overnight stay, even if they did everything there was to do. *I–15 South at Stateline, 702/382–1111 or 800/367–7383, FAX 702/874–1749. 618 rooms. 4 restaurants, lounge, pool, showroom. AE, D, DC, MC, V.*

$ Primadonna. A Ferris wheel out front and a full-size working carrousel in the children's arcade are the focal points of the Primadonna's carnival theme. Like its sister properties, rooms are cheap and large, with king-size beds and cable TV, and furnishings are brightly colored. The casino gets busy, and bands play in the showroom. *I–15 South at Stateline, 702/382–1111 or 800/367–7383, FAX 702/874–1749. 618 rooms. 4 restaurants, lounge, pool, showroom. AE, D, DC, MC, V.*

$ Whiskey Pete's Casino and Hotel. A laser rainbow pierces the black night sky from Pete's. Inside you'll find a noisy, surprisingly busy, state-line casino, with lounge bands, cheap food, and rooms for only $19–$31. The rooms are large, with king-size beds, cable TV, direct-dial phone, and small bathrooms. When you're headed for Las Vegas from the west, an overnight stop at Pete's will leave you 45 minutes of driving time in the morning. *I–15 South at Stateline, 702/382–4388, FAX 702/874–1079. 600 rooms. 6 restaurants, lounge, pool. AE, D, DC, MC, V.*

Motels

Motels offer you the opportunity to save some money and the chance to park just outside your room. Those who dread having to search for a parking space and then jostle through crowded casinos, ride up slow elevators, and trek down long halls to reach their bed may prefer the compactness of a motel. Don't be concerned that staying in a motel will take you away from the action; all the motels listed here are near casinos, so when you have the gambling urge, you can cross the street and start firing it up with quarters—or hundred dollar bills.

$ Motel 6. Welcome to the largest Motel 6 in the United States, with 877 rooms, a pool, and a big neon sign. Rooms here look like those of any other Motel 6, but when travelers think in terms of cheap accommodations, they think of this chain, so the place tends to get booked up fast. *195 E. Tropicana Ave., 89109, 702/798–0728, FAX 702/798–5657. 877 rooms. Pool. AE, D, DC, MC, V.*

$ Royal Oasis. This is the quintessential 1960s Las Vegas motel: on a large piece of property at the south end of the Strip (across from the

Hacienda) with "old-growth" landscaping, well-used rooms (a bit tattered around the edges), a friendly staff, and rates under $25 (under $40 on weekends). What sets the Royal Oasis apart is its no-reservations, first-come, first-served policy. This is very handy for people who blow in without a room booked; it's also nice to know when you're settled into a room that you won't get asked to leave on Saturday night because the motel is sold out with reservations (a common occurrence in other places). Local calls are free. *4375 Las Vegas Blvd. S, 702/739–9119. Pool, laundry. MC, V.*

$ **Sun Harbor Budget Suites.** An excellent and nearby alternative to the Westward Ho (often crowded with conventioneers, slot-club members, and tournament players) is this sprawling complex on the corner of Industrial and Stardust roads. Every room here is a minisuite, with a living-dining room, a small separate bedroom, and a full kitchenette; the TV fills an open window between the living room and bedroom. Weekly rates offer a good discount; rooms are least expensive on the second and third floors, and cheaper if you bring your own linens and towels. The Frontier, Desert Inn, Stardust, Riviera, and Circus Circus are all within walking distance. *1500 Stardust Rd., 89109, 702/732–1500 or 800/752–1501,* FAX *702/732–2656. 639 rooms. Pool, spa. AE, MC, V.*

$ **Westward Ho Motel and Casino.** The largest motel in the world, with seven swimming pools and a casino, the Ho is strategically located between the Stardust and Circus Circus. The location is also a drawback, however: On Saturday night, this part of town is gridlocked, and returning to your room by car will take considerable time—unless you learn the shortcut from Industrial Road through the Stardust parking lot. *2900 Las Vegas Blvd. S, 89109, 702/731–2900 or 800/634–6803,* FAX *702/731–6154. 1,000 rooms. Restaurant, 7 pools. MC, V.*

10 Nightlife

THE VERY NAME "LAS VEGAS" has come to be synonymous with a certain style of showbiz, ever since Jimmy Durante first headlined at Bugsy Siegel's Fabulous Flamingo Hotel in 1946 and "Minsky Goes to Paris" introduced topless showgirls at the Dunes in 1957. In those days, the lounges gave up-and-coming entertainers a chance to polish their acts on their way to the showrooms, where the camaraderie and informality lent an anything-can-happen-here-tonight air to the entertainment. Over the years, the Entertainment Capital of the World has weathered a number of changes in its stage presentations, policies, and prices, but one thing has remained consistent for the past 50 years: style.

Headliners such as Frank Sinatra, Wayne Newton, Bill Cosby, Ann-Margret, Tom Jones, and David Copperfield still sell out the 1,200-seat showrooms. Extravagant revues like "EFX," "Folies Bergere," and "Jubilee" still stage spectacular productions, with outrageous sets, costumes, variety acts, and song and dance. Young and exuberant shows like "Splash" and "Enter the Night" have modernized the spectacle, and illusionists, who started out as brief breaks for the major action, have elevated their status to exalted heights. Female and superstar impersonators, "dirty" dancers, comedians—all perpetuate the original style of entertainment that Las Vegas has popularized for the world.

Some traditions have changed in recent years, however. Several hotels have added afternoon performances to their show schedules. Certain hotels have eliminated nudity and foul language in the name of family entertainment, especially at early shows. Some hotels even encourage parents to bring their kids along by offering special prices for youngsters, and many showrooms have banned smoking. And the only hotels that still offer a dinner show today are Excalibur, Rio, and Tropicana.

In the not-so-old days, the shows were loss leaders, much as the buffets and hotel rooms are today: They were intended to draw patrons who would eventually wind up in the casino. Admission prices to shows were dirt cheap, and the programs were fairly short. Nowadays it may cost you $60 to see Wayne Newton, and a ticket to the biggest production, "Siegfried and Roy," will set you back $80. Yet many of the smaller shows have much lower prices; at press time, "Forever Plaid" at the Flamingo Hilton was charging $15.95 (with $3-off coupons available everywhere) and tickets to "American Superstars" at Luxor were $12. Las Vegas publicists are fond of pointing out that tickets, even to the top draws, are cheaper than those for Broadway productions—and two drinks are included.

There are several kinds of shows in Las Vegas. The major stars who appear in the "big rooms" are the headliners who command the $40 to $75 ticket prices and attract audiences of 1,000 to 1,500. The big-production spectaculars—90 minutes of singing, dancing, topless showgirls, specialty acts, and special effects—are revues that are extremely popular with the increasing numbers of international tourists who have descended on the city over the last 15 years. Foreign visitors also seem to love magic shows; the two most popular performers in town are Siegfried and Roy—who make things disappear while saying hardly a word—so you don't have to understand English to enjoy them. The same is true for the revues, of course, which rely less on dialogue than on musical numbers and the ubiquitous topless showgirls, whose blatant charms can be appreciated in any language.

Getting into certain shows has become easier than it used to be. Many hotels now have a policy whereby all seats are reserved (pick up your ticket at a box office near the showroom). On the other hand, tickets to see "Siegfried and Roy" are distributed in a slightly different way. You have to appear at the box office (it opens at 6 AM) up to three days before the show, take a number, and wait. Tickets are distributed on a first-come, first-served basis (with preference given, of course, to high rollers and hotel guests). One strategy to bypass the long lines is to check with the box office just before it closes (around 4 PM); another is to appear a half hour before show time and see if there are any cancellations.

To attend a show that doesn't have tickets, the old rules apply. You need to make a reservation and then stand in line at the front door of the showroom for at least 30 minutes (and at least an hour for a popular show on a busy night). On weekends it can be tough getting in to see the top headliners and production revues. Crowds are large, lines are long, and the prime spots are reserved for comped players. Your chances of getting a seat are usually better when you're staying—and gambling—at the hotel. If you plan on spending a fair amount of time at the tables or slots, call VIP Services and find out what their requirements are for getting a comp, or at least a line pass (that allows you to go straight to the VIP entrance without waiting in line with the hoi polloi). Then be sure to have your play "rated" by the pit boss when you gamble in order to qualify for the privileges.

Once at the showroom door, you enter the frightening realm of maître d's (who assign the seats at the door) and captains (who show you to your seats). Many variables determine the quality of seats from which you'll watch the show: how early it is, how crowded it is, how assertive you are, how aloof the maître d' is, and whether or not you tip the seating personnel. If it's early, the showroom is empty, and the staff is friendly, you can often get the best seats (in the middle of the room, in a booth, on the second or third tier) simply by asking. If it's late, the room is packed, the maître d' has his hand out, and you don't tip, you'll probably be ushered to the corner table on the floor, crammed in with 15 other exiles. To ensure a good seat, arrive early and discreetly toke the maître d' (with bills or chips the denomination of which he can readily see; $15–$20 is usually sufficient); if your seats aren't satisfactory, slip the captain a few bucks and point to better ones. Once you've been seated at a table, before the show begins, you'll be asked to pay your bill, which covers two drinks. So as not to disrupt the show, at most places both drinks—which have to be identical—are brought to the table at the same time. (To get around this oddity, many people order a bottle of wine.) Regardless, don't forget to toke your server.

Information on current shows, including their reservation and seating policies, prices, suitability for children, and smoking restrictions, is available by calling or visiting the particular box offices, or in several local publications. The *Las Vegas Advisor* is available at its office (5280 S. Valley View, Las Vegas, 89119, ☎ 702/597–1884) for $5 ($45 per year); this monthly newsletter is invaluable for its up-to-the-minute information on Las Vegas dining, entertainment, gambling promotions, comps, news, and Top Ten Values. You can also pick up free copies of *Today in Las Vegas* and *What's On in Las Vegas* at hotels.

Las Vegas–Style Revues

Boy-lesque (Sahara Hotel and Casino, 2535 Las Vegas Blvd. S, ☎ 702/737–2515). While this show has been around Las Vegas for more than 15 years, an all new version opened in 1992. The female impersonators, with their elaborate costumes and artful makeup, pay tribute to the leading ladies of Hollywood: Barbra Streisand, Cher, Madonna, Dolly Parton, and Diana Ross.

Crazy Girls (Riviera Hotel, 2901 Las Vegas Blvd. S, ☎ 702/794–9433). This is the dirtiest show in town, and it was created to be that way. Unlike other shows, which feature a mixture of topless and clothed showgirls, "Crazy" has a cast of women who wear practically nothing at all times. The basic formula is a chorus line of topless women who lip-sync songs, gyrate to taped music, sing, and do a little comedy. The show is designed to remind the audience of the Crazy Horse Saloon in Paris, which Crazy Girls' producers claim is dirtier than any Las Vegas show, including their own.

EFX (MGM Grand, 3805 Las Vegas Blvd. S, ☎ 702/8919-1111). MGM Grand spent upwards of $50 million to compete with "Siegfried and Roy" for top-show honors in Las Vegas. "EFX" is designed to combine ferocious special effects with Broadway theater and Las Vegas extravaganza. Michael Crawford, star of *Phantom of the Opera,* is at the center of the 90-minute spectacle, singing, doing stand-up comedy, battling dragons, directing the massive movements of the cast of 70, the giant sets, and mind-boggling effects. Though the Broadway theatrics and Las Vegas costumes are imaginative and diverting, the emphasis here is on the effects: 2,500 fixed and 300 moving lights, 48-channel digital surround sound, a stunning 3-D segment, and gargantuan sets that fill the 100-foot stage. "EFX" opens with a giant Wizard of Oz–type likeness of Crawford's face, and just gets wilder from there.

Enter the Night (Stardust Hotel and Casino, 3000 Las Vegas Blvd. S, ☎ 702/732–6325). This show features Vladimir, the famous Russian aerialist who soars above the audience in a stunning ballet; ice dancers Burt Lancon and Tricia Burton; and 30 showgirls dressed in high-fashion style, performing intricate dance numbers. You'll get a taste of the latest theater technology, including computer-controlled scene changes, lighting, and music.

Folies Bergere (Tropicana Resort and Casino, 3801 Las Vegas Blvd. S, ☎ 702/739–2411). This classic French topless revue is performed in a large showroom, with music from 100 to perhaps 40 years old, played at a ponderous pace. On the whole, it's the same standard stuff that "Folies" has been presenting since 1959: singers, dancers, comedians, jugglers, and a cancan finale.

Jubilee (Bally's Casino Resort, 3645 Las Vegas Blvd. S, ☎ 702/739–4567). Donn Arden, who produced shows in Las Vegas from 1952 until his death in 1994, put together this spectacular stage tribute to Hollywood in 1981 for the old MGM Grand Hotel, now Bally's. "Jubilee" is one of the largest shows in town, with a cast of more than 100 performing in a showroom with 1,100 seats. It offers great special effects: The sinking of the *Titanic* is re-created; Samson destroys the temple, and the wreckage goes up in flames. Showgirls parade about in the largest collection of feathers and bare breasts you've ever seen. The $5,000 headdresses weigh an average of 40 pounds each, and the costumes were designed by Hollywood veteran Bob Mackie, who is perhaps best known for the outrageous dresses he has invented for Cher. As is standard for a Donn Arden show, a tribute to the good old days includes songs made famous by Eddie Cantor, Al Jolson, Bing Crosby, and Judy Garland; a short classical ballet uses the music of Johann Strauss. Between the numbers, jugglers, magicians, and specialty performers do their thing in front of the curtain while the stagehands change the sets. "Jubilee" is one Las Vegas spectacle that may also be a victim of its own size: The show is so large that it loses some of the live, up-close excitement you get with a show such as "Enter the Night."

King Arthur's Tournament (Excalibur Hotel and Casino, 3850 Las Vegas Blvd. S, ☎ 702/597-7600). "King Arthur's Tournament" is one of Las Vegas's most unusual big shows. The musical retelling of the King Arthur legend incorporates a medieval jousting show. Costumed knights, beautiful ladies, and fast horses are preceded by a medieval dinner, which you eat with your fingers. It's a great bargain and a wonderful family show—especially families with pre-adolescents who get to make a lot of noise.

Legends in Concert (Imperial Palace Hotel and Casino, 3535 Las Vegas Blvd. S, ☎ 702/794-3261). For those who like the old-time superstars and aren't content merely to watch them on videocassette, "Legends" features impersonators of Elvis Presley, Marilyn Monroe, Buddy Holly, Judy Garland, Louis Armstrong, Hank Williams, and, more recently, Liberace and Roy Orbison. (The rule used to be that only nonliving "legends" could be depicted in the show—the Liberace impersonator was added a few days after Mr. Showmanship died, and Roy Orbison was cloned in April 1989, four months after his death. But as of 1989 that rule was changed, clearing the way for impressions of Neil Diamond, Dolly Parton, and Madonna.) The show is basically wall-to-wall music (enlivened by multimedia images of the real stars and some showgirls and boys dancing in the background); the finale features Elvis in his white jumpsuit, singing "Viva Las Vegas."

Melinda, the First Lady of Magic (Lady Luck Casino and Hotel, 206 N. 3rd St., ☎ 702/477-3000). Beautiful blonde Melinda Saxe is the First (and only) Lady of Magic working in Las Vegas. Formerly a showgirl in the old Siegfried and Roy extravaganza, Melinda aspired to create her own revue and succeeded. She's a pretty good magician, and the act features jugglers and unicyclists in addition to the magic. The early show is geared toward families.

Mystere (Treasure Island Hotel and Casino, 3300 Las Vegas Blvd. S, ☎ 702/894-7722). This New Age circus is the premier family show in town, a uniquely memorable experience bound to please all ages. From the moment you enter the big top, you are intimately involved with this show. "Flounes" (clowns) mingle and fool with the audience as they're seated, and roving "devils" make trouble even before the show begins. The music is rousing and haunting, the acrobatics chilling, and the dance numbers inspiring. With only a single ring, the usual circus-type distractions are kept to a minimum, and there are no animals in the show. Except for "Siegfried and Roy" and "EFX," this is the most expensive show ticket in town (half price for children), but it's worth every penny.

Spellbound: A Concert of Illusion (Harrah's Hotel and Casino, 3475 Las Vegas Blvd. S, ☎ 702/369-5222). As do most revues in Las Vegas, this one gives you a large dose of magic and illusion, along with comedy, dancing, and juggling. The headliners are Mark Kaylin and Ginger, who specialize in transformation illusions and work with some big cats; other acts include Sherry Lukas, who turns playing cards into doves and then the doves into poodles.

Splash (Riviera Hotel, 2901 Las Vegas Blvd. S, ☎ 702/794-9301). This isn't a traditional Vegas T & A show in any sense. First of all, the large number of female dancers are clothed. Secondly, instead of wearing the usual showgirl costume of headdress, fishnet stockings, and feather boas, the "Splashgirls" dress as sea serpents, clams, mermaids, and other amphibious creatures. In time to the music, they jump into a 65,000-gallon water tank, climb out, dry off, and dance in front of fountains that spout from various parts of the stage. Not only do the dancers get wet, so do show goers in the front seats. The music in "Splash" is more contemporary than that of any other Vegas revue production; producer

Jeff Kutash deliberately presents a Top-40 sound, hoping to appeal to younger audiences and create a new wave, as it were, of Strip entertainment. "Splash" also features Shimada the Magician and motorcycle daredevils who whirl around inside a giant steel "Globe of Death." The finale is a 23-minute salute to Broadway and Hollywood, with medleys from *Cats, Little Shop of Horrors, A Chorus Line, Phantom of the Opera,* and *Dirty Dancing.*

Showroom Stars

It used to be that contemporary stars, such as Elton John, the Rolling Stones, Van Halen, Whitney Houston, and REM, eschewed appearances in Las Vegas, which they felt was beneath them culturally. In addition, the headliner and concert scene in Las Vegas suffered through several years of doldrums in the late 1980s and early 1990s, as headliner rooms were transformed into showrooms, and the performers were booked to play to middle-age and senior crowds nostalgic for a golden oldie. But those days are over. Las Vegas is again a hotbed of up-to-the-minute entertainment, thanks to the local population exceeding a million, the baby boomers finally discovering the joys of a Las Vegas vacation, and the opening of the 15,000-seat MGM Grand Arena and the 1,200-seat Joint at the Hard Rock Hotel. All the above stars, along with Bette Midler, Barbra Streisand, Sheryl Crow, and Melissa Etheridge, performed in Las Vegas in the past year. Las Vegas has become a mandatory stop on the circuit for most major acts that now go on the road. Headliner and concert halls are now found at the Aladdin, Bally's, Caesars Palace, Desert Inn, the Hard Rock, and MGM Grand. Performance schedules vary with the star and the season, but most performers appear at least Thursday through Sunday nights. The giveaway tourist magazines in hotels and gift shops will tell you what stars are in town and where and when they're performing during the week. The headliners who command the most attention in Las Vegas these days are:

Ann-Margret. In 1960 she was discovered in Las Vegas by George Burns, who hired her to open his show at the Sahara Hotel. Hollywood talent scouts saw her act there and signed her for starring parts in the films *Bye-Bye Birdie* and *Viva Las Vegas,* in which she costarred with Elvis Presley. Over the years, she has developed a must-see act that features many male dancers and irresistible energy. One of the highest-paid performers today (earning a reported $285,000 a week), Ann-Margret, now in her fifties, puts on a fast-paced show combining lasers, film, and music.

Engelbert Humperdinck. When you go to see "The Hump" at Bally's, where he performs frequently, you'll notice a large group of women up front. This is his fan club, a pack of women who travel all over the West to see him, no matter where. When he plays Las Vegas, they come for the weekend, they're first in line, and they see three or four shows, sitting together in the frônt row. Such is the devoted following for a man whose last hit, "After the Lovin'," was way back in 1977. On stage he delivers a friendly show, pleasing his audiences with such past hits as "Release Me," "There Goes My Everything," "The Last Waltz," and "Am I Easy to Forget?" Over the years, Humperdinck has seasoned into a fine performer, and recently he added a tap-dance segment, donning a top hat to sing Fred Astaire tunes.

Tom Jones. Another Las Vegas veteran, Tom Jones is suddenly a red-hot ticket—the voice, the moves, and the charm have been rediscovered by a new generation of Las Vegas tourists. Jones may still split his pants to please the blue-haired ladies, but he refuses to sing only his hits. Sure, he'll throw in "Green, Green Grass of Home" and "It's Not Unusual," but he also performs such current tunes as his own remake of Prince's "Kiss," Robert Cray's "Ain't Nothing but a Woman," and Paul Simon's "You Can Call Me Al."

Wayne Newton. Mr. Las Vegas, the Midnight Idol, the King of the Strip, Wayne Newton is in many ways the epitome of the Las Vegas headliner. A homegrown phenomenon, he has been performing here since his teens, when he did an act with his brother Jerry at the Fremont's Carnival Lounge. On stage, Newton gives it the Al Jolson treatment, working and sweating his way through two hours of show—singing, telling jokes, playing the guitar, violin, and trumpet. Whatever one thinks of the kind of music (and questionable financial decisions and libel lawsuits) Newton is known for, no one would dispute the fact that, after all these years, he knows how to entertain his audience. Seeing a Wayne Newton show is as much a part of the experience of visiting Las Vegas as gambling and the Hoover Dam. For all that, the Wayner is only in Las Vegas occasionally, splitting his time with Branson, Missouri.

Siegfried and Roy. A trip to Las Vegas isn't truly complete until you've seen the master illusionists Siegfried and Roy strut their stuff. As the stars of "Beyond Belief" at the Frontier from 1981 to 1988, they sold out every show over a seven-year run. They left to tour for a year and a half, but Steve Wynn then signed them to a $55.5 million contract to star at his new Mirage Hotel, where they opened with an entirely new show in February 1990. In their act, Siegfried and Roy have made elephants and motorcycles disappear and have levitated each other as well as the lions and tigers who are their roommates in Las Vegas. The current show includes a fire-breathing dragon, lasers, music written and recorded by Michael Jackson, plus a home video of the stars' pet tiger cubs.

Lounges

The lounges of the Las Vegas casino hotels were once places where such headliners as Frank, Dean, and the gang would go after their shows, taking a seat in the audience to laugh at the comedy antics of Shecky Greene or Don Rickles or to enjoy the music of Louis Prima and Keely Smith. Now the lounges have been reduced to small bars within the casino, where bands play Top-40 hits in front of small crowds pie-eyed from the slots. Virtually every casino has such a spot; all you need to do is buy a drink or two and you can listen to the music all night long. Two of the nicest lounges are at the Las Vegas Hilton and the Tropicana. And local, off-Strip casinos, such as the Rio and Arizona Charlie's, often feature hot lounge acts.

Comedy Clubs

Since the demise of the days when comedians reigned in the casino lounges, comedy has suffered. It's thriving again, however, in the 1990s version of the Las Vegas lounge: the comedy club. There are five in town, and all are doing big business.

Catch a Rising Star (MGM Grand Hotel, 3805 Las Vegas Blvd. S, ☎ 702/891–7777). This comedy club relocated from Bally's to MGM Grand's 400-seat Center Stage Lounge, for two shows nightly. Drinks are not included in the admission price.

Comedy Max (Maxim Hotel and Casino, 160 E. Flamingo Rd., ☎ 702/731–4300). Typical comedy-venue format: three stand-up comedians who take the stage one after another in an intimate showroom with stools around tables. The price of admission includes two drinks.

Comedy Stop (Tropicana Resort Casino, 3801 Las Vegas Blvd. S, ☎ 702/739–2714). Three comedians play two shows nightly at this 400-seat showroom. The price of admission includes two drinks.

Comedy Club (Riviera Hotel, 2901 Las Vegas Blvd. S, ☎ 702/794–9433). There are three shows a night at the 375-seat Comedy Club, which used to be An Evening at the Improv. Admission includes two drinks.

An Evening at the Improv (Harrah's Hotel, 3475 Las Vegas Blvd. S, ☎ 702/369–5222). This club moved from the Riviera to occupy a new 300-seat showroom in the old bingo hall on the second floor of Harrah's. The Improv is dark Monday; drinks are not included in the admission fee.

Dancing

Cleopatra's Barge offers dancing to rock bands on a big boat in the Caesars Palace casino. *Caesars Palace, 3570 Las Vegas Blvd. S,* ☎ *702/731–7110. Live band Wed.–Sun. 10 PM–4 AM.*

The Metz is right on the Strip in the shadow of the MGM Grand. It has a half-million-dollar laser lighting system and state-of-the-art sound system and is very popular with both locals and visitors—despite the mind-numbing disco spun by the DJ. *3765 Las Vegas Blvd. S,* ☎ *702/736–2228.* ⏲ *Nightly from 9 PM.*

Shark Club is a dark, trendy, young club on three levels, each with a dance floor and live music. *75 E. Harmon Ave.,* ☎ *702/795–7525.* ⏲ *Nightly 7 PM–dawn.*

Fine Arts

If your tastes in shows tend toward the low key and cultural, you can call the **Allied Arts Council** (3750 S. Maryland Pkwy., ☎ 702/731–5419) for the local theater, dance, music, and fine arts performances scheduled for the dates of your trip.

Movies

A lot of movies play Las Vegas—there are 12 theaters and 67 screens in town—but you won't see film marquees on the Strip. The easiest cinemas to find are the **Gold Coast Twin** (4000 W. Flamingo Rd., ☎ 702/367–7111), which is at the Gold Coast Hotel and Casino, a couple of blocks west of the Strip, and the **Parkway 3** (3768 S. Maryland Pkwy., ☎ 702/734–8151), near the Boulevard Shopping Mall, roughly 3 miles east of the center of the Strip.

Caesars Palace Omnimax Theatre (3570 Las Vegas Blvd. S, ☎ 702/731–7900) shows movies every day in a big, shiny dome outside its casino; the immense screen shows 70mm movies. Films available in this format usually have appealing scientific or natural-history subjects such as travel on a space shuttle or exploring the Grand Canyon. If you've never seen a film this way, you owe it to yourself to have a look, for the larger-than-life images are breathtaking.

Deep Earth Exploration (MGM Grand Adventures, 3805 Las Vegas Blvd. S, ☎ 702/891–1111) takes intrepid travelers on a high-tech haunted mine ride. You board private cars for a tour of a mine; the cars rock and roll in synchronization with the action on the video screen in front. The car jumps the track and sends you on a wild ride into the very bowels of the molten earth.

Luxor Attractions Level (Luxor, 3900 Las Vegas Blvd. S, ☎ 702/262–4000). This is a three-part motion, video, 3-D, and movie extravaganza, a must-see for high-tech fans. "Search for the Obelisk" (Theater 1) features two sophisticated high-impact motion simulators; "Luxor Live?" (Theater 2) delivers a two-part thrill: large-screen high-resolution video and an astonishing 3-D segment; "Theater of Time" presents an IMAX computer-assisted movie on a 70-foot-tall screen. The three experiences are held together by a plot involving an archaeological discovery of a lost temple directly below Luxor, and the efforts of the archaeologist, the government, and a mad scientist to control its secrets.

Music

Concerts

A number of large stadiums in town host individual artists or groups whose audience can't be contained in a club: The Grateful Dead and Paul McCartney, for example, are among those who have performed at the 31,000-seat outdoor **Sam Boyd Silver Bowl** (off Boulder Hwy. on Russell Rd., ☎ 702/895–3900). The **Thomas and Mack Center** (Tropicana Ave. at Swenson St., ☎ 702/895–3900) is the indoor equivalent of the Silver Bowl. The **MGM Grand** (3805 Las Vegas Blvd. S, ☎ 702/891–7777) has added the 630-seat Hollywood Theater, which hosts performers such as Sheena Easton, Tom Jones, and Manhattan Transfer; the 1,700-seat Grand Theater, which now hosts "EFX"; and the 15,000-seat Grand Garden arena, where Barbra Streisand performed on New Year's Eve 1994, and other superstars like Phil Collins, Whitney Houston, and the Rolling Stones have appeared. The 10,000-seat **Aladdin Theatre for the Performing Arts** (in the back of the Aladdin Hotel, 3667 Las Vegas Blvd. S, ☎ 702/736–0250) occasionally features major artists and touring companies that don't generally work Las Vegas showrooms—like Fleetwood Mac, Tina Turner, and *Phantom of the Opera.*

Country and Western

Dance Hall and Saloon offers live country-and-western music every night except Tuesday, when big-band tapes play. Country-and-western dance lessons are given free on Sunday, Monday, Wednesday, and Thursday at 6:30 PM. *Gold Coast Hotel, 4000 W. Flamingo Rd., ☎ 702/367–7111. ⏲ Weeknights till 1 AM, weekend nights till 3 AM.*

Western Dance Hall is another spot for country-and-western dancing to live bands. You can expect to hear renditions of recent country hits by George Strait, Randy Travis, and Garth Brooks. *Sam's Town Hotel and Casino, 5111 Boulder Hwy., ☎ 702/456–7777. ⏲ Nightly 7:30 PM–5 AM.*

Jazz

The French Quarter room in the **Four Queens Casino** (202 E. Fremont St., ☎ 702/385–4011) has live jazz Monday and many other evenings as well. New Orleans jazz plays nightly in the lounge of the **Bourbon Street Casino** (120 E. Flamingo Rd., ☎ 702/737–7200).

Strip Club

Olympic Gardens (1531 Las Vegas Blvd. S, ☎ 702/385–8987), open 24 hours, is by far the swankiest strip joint in town. The dancers are real crowd pleasers and the patrons are out for good (more or less) clean fun. And women oglers get equal time here: A separate entrance in the rear leads to a back room with male strippers.

11 Reno and Lake Tahoe

RENO

SMALLER, SLOWER, PRETTIER, AND LESS CROWDED than Las Vegas, Reno is one of the great lesser-known vacation destinations in the West. Like Las Vegas, Reno was first put on the map as a railroad station; unlike Las Vegas, most of the action remains downtown, on either side of the famous Arch that proclaims Reno THE BIGGEST LITTLE CITY IN THE WORLD. Only a handful of hotel-casinos are outside the narrow corridor defined by the railroad station and the Truckee River, which runs through town roughly parallel to the tracks.

Reno and its sister city, Sparks (elevation: roughly 4,500 feet), preside over Truckee Meadows, a large valley blocked on the west and north by the mighty Sierra Nevada and on the east and south by the Virginia Range of Comstock Lode fame. Lake Tahoe, one of the largest and most beautiful mountain lakes in the world, is only 45 minutes from Reno. A score of world-class ski resorts are within an hour of Reno, as are Virginia City, one of the best-preserved mining ghost towns in the west; Carson City, capital of Nevada; and Pyramid Lake, a stunning watery apparition in the high desert.

The climate of Reno and the surrounding area is characteristic of the Great Basin Desert in which they lie: mild, dry, breezy. The average annual high temperature is just under 70°F; the low is just over 32°F. Rarely does the temperature climb as high as the upper 90s in the summer or fall as low as the single digits in the winter. The sun shines more than 300 days a year.

This small section of what is now Nevada was the remote western edge of Utah Territory, known for little more than its hot deserts and high mountains, until June 1859, when gold was found in the Virginia Range. The Comstock Lode, one of the richest bodies of gold and silver ore ever discovered, drew so many people to the area that a mere two years later, a huge chunk of Utah Territory was carved into Nevada Territory, and only three years after that, Nevada entered the Union as the 37th state.

Reno's humble beginnings were in 1859, when Charles Fuller built a toll bridge across the Truckee River. Two years later Myron Lake bought the bridge and built a trading station, inn, and tavern. Lake's Crossing, as the bridge was originally known, was only a few yards upriver from today's Virginia Street crossing. The Central Pacific Railroad came through Lake's Crossing in 1868, promised Lake a depot in return for a right-of-way, and renamed the settlement in honor of General Jesse Reno, a northern Civil War hero.

Reno remained a rough-and-tumble railroad stop until a little after the turn of the century, when a New York lawyer discovered Nevada's liberal divorce laws (requiring, at that time, only a six-month residency) and publicized Reno as a divorce haven. For the next 40 years, Reno was known as the divorce capital of the country, where unhappily married women (mostly) came to "take the cure," staying in rooming houses and out at dude ranches, and returning home newly single. In 1928, the residency requirement was lowered to three months and in 1931 to a scandalous six weeks—in conjunction with the legalization of wide-open casino gambling.

For the first few years of legalized gambling, it remained the disreputable activity that it had always been. But then Raymond "Pappy"

Smith, a carnival entrepreneur, came to Reno in 1935 and called upon his carny experience to usher gambling from the back room to the front. He opened Harold's Club right on Virginia Street: brightly lit, inviting, legitimate. Among his many innovations, most of which are still standard operating procedure for casinos today, were free drinks and other liberal complimentaries, a never-ending variety of gambling promotions, eye-in-the-sky catwalks, women dealers, and a massive national advertising campaign that went a long way toward making casinos palatable to the masses. William Harrah copied Pappy's techniques, but upped the ante by sparing no expense toward creating an impeccable, classy atmosphere.

Many casinos opened in the wake of the success of the Smiths and Harrah, and Reno in the 1940s and early '50s came to be known as the gambling capital of the country. By the mid-1950s, however, Las Vegas was expanding at a phenomenal pace. Reno took one look at the growth, shuddered, and installed a "red line" around downtown beyond which no casinos could be built—thus limiting the expansion of gambling for another 25 years. It was only in 1979 that the line was erased and Reno began to look the way it does today. Del Webb's Reno Sahara (now the Flamingo Hilton), Circus Circus, Sundowner, Comstock, Peppermill, and MGM Grand (now Reno Hilton) were all built in that one heady year.

Nowadays, Reno attracts roughly 4.5 million visitors a year, many from northern California, the Pacific Northwest, and western Canada. After years of neglect and stagnation, downtown Reno is undergoing some improvement: Two high-rise parking structures have been built; the National Bowling Stadium, the only one of its kind in the country, opened in January 1995; and a joint venture between Circus Circus and the Eldorado called Silver Legacy, Reno's first Las Vegas–style megaresort, opened downtown in the summer of 1995.

Exploring

Numbers in the margin correspond to points of interest on the Reno map.

Reno's climate, much milder than that of Las Vegas, lures visitors year-round. In winter people come to the area to ski and gamble; in summer they come to enjoy the scenery and gamble. No matter what the season, laying a bet is the number-one activity in downtown Reno, and a tour of the city is principally a tour of the casinos, which are located on and near Virginia Street.

Casinos

1 **Club Cal-Neva** (38 E. 2nd St. at Virginia St., ☎ 702/323–1046). Cal-Neva is a raucous, rambling, two-story gambling hall (there's no hotel) with an emphasis on slots surrounded by large railroad-car facades. The gaming tables have some of the lowest minimums in Nevada, and feature Top Deck Blackjack, a blackjack variation that can pay 17 to 1. The Reno Cal-Neva, which has no relation to the lodge of the same name at Crystal Bay at north Lake Tahoe, also houses Reno's largest and busiest race and sports book (the managers also run books at four other casinos) and its biggest keno game. Warren Nelson, owner of Cal-Neva, modernized the ancient Chinese game of keno by adding horse-race terminology and Ping-Pong balls.

2 **Harrah's** (219 N. Center St., ☎ 702/786–3232 or 800/648–3773). Opened by Bill Harrah in 1937 as the Tango Club, Harrah's is the second-oldest casino in Reno. This is one of the snazziest joints in town,

Reno

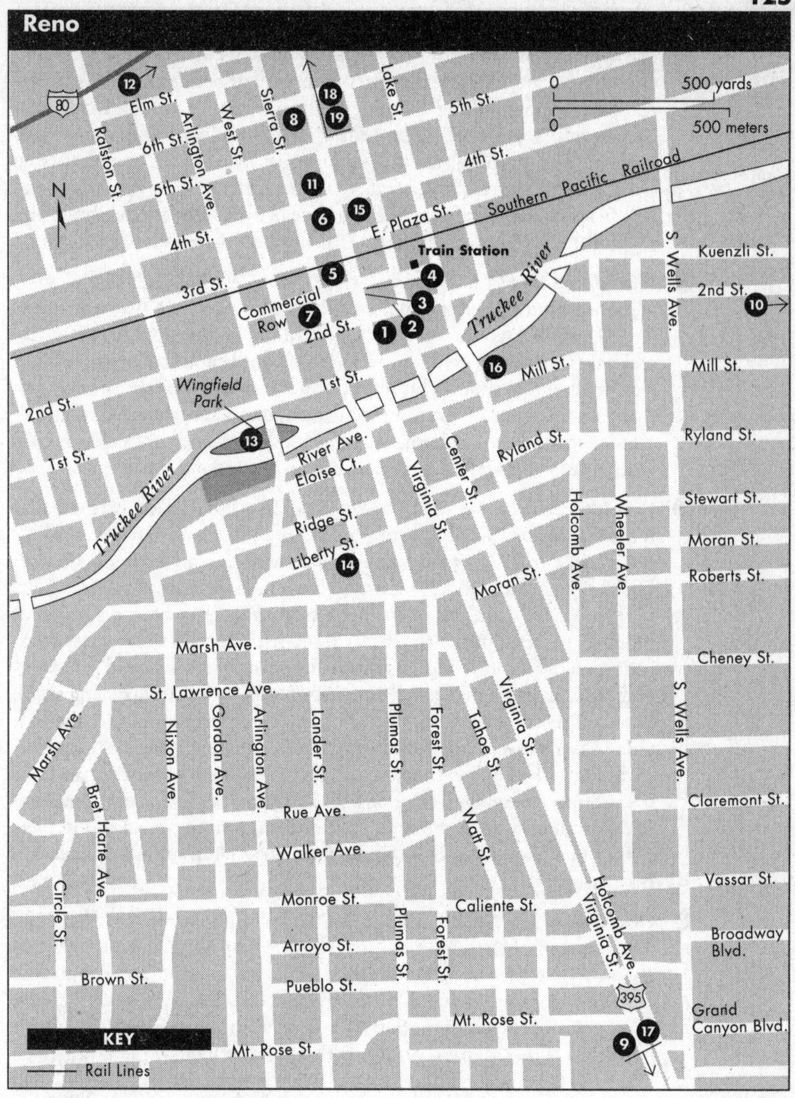

Circus Circus, **8**
Club Cal-Neva, **1**
Eldorado, **6**
Fitzgeralds, **5**
Flamingo Hilton, **7**
Fleischmann Planetarium, **18**
Harold's, **4**
Harrah's, **2**
John Ascuaga's Nugget, **12**
Liberty Belle Saloon, **17**
The National Automobile Museum, **16**
National Bowling Stadium, **15**
Nevada Club, **3**
Nevada Historical Society, **19**
Nevada Museum of Art, **14**
Peppermill, **9**
Reno Hilton, **10**
Silver Legacy, **11**
Wingfield Park, **13**

the house where the wealthy come for upscale treatment. To Harrah's credit, you can still find the occasional $3 blackjack table, nickel slot, friendly people, and friendly service here. Large and sprawling, Harrah's is composed of two buildings—one to the east and one to the west of Center Street—that cover almost two city blocks and house three casinos. The building east of Center Street features the Sports Casino (with a large sports book), a children's arcade, a high-rise hotel, and a 420-seat showroom, plus Harrah's Steak House, one of the city's best restaurants. A branch of Planet Hollywood opened in early 1995.

3 **Nevada Club** (224 N. Virginia St., ☎ 702/329–1721). If you want to step into a time machine that can show you what life was like in the 1940s, you'll love the Nevada Club. Many of the slots here are reel classics from the GI generation. Pull the handle and line up three cherries or three bells, and you might win a classic hot rod. The Nevada Club's minimums at the table games are consistently among the lowest in town, and fans of burgers, flapjacks, shakes, and penny slots should enjoy the 1940s-style diner, Kilroy's, on the second floor.

4 **Harold's** (250 N. Virginia St., ☎ 702/329–0881). This was the first major casino in Nevada, begun by Raymond "Pappy" Smith and his son Harold in 1935. It was the establishment that advertised HAROLD'S CLUB OR BUST on billboards around the world, even at the North Pole. Out front you'll see one of the prettiest murals in town, a portrayal of pioneers camped out in the mountains, with flowing blue water separating them from the Indians on the opposite bank. Harold's, the legend says, is dedicated in all humility to those who blazed the trail. Harold's has no hotel rooms, just casino space, restaurants, a slot-machine sales showroom, and Dick Clark's American Bandstand nightclub. Harold's Club is the best place in the state to shoot craps, since it's the only casino with the Long Hands Meter, a kind of dice "odometer" that counts the number of rolls and amount of time a shooter has going. The "Long Hands" rolls of the day, week, month, and year win big prizes.

5 **Fitzgeralds** (255 N. Virginia St., ☎ 702/785–3300 or 800/648–5022). The concept of the Fitz, now extended to Las Vegas, had its start in Reno, where the original stands proudly on Virginia Street opposite Harold's and the Nevada Club (both owned by the Fitzgeralds Group). The center of the city's St. Patrick's Day celebration (when the Arch's hundreds of bulbs are replaced with all-green lights), the large green casino is the home of good luck, Irish themes, and leprechauns. On the second floor, in the Lucky Forest, patrons can walk wishing steps, rub the belly of Ho-Tei (the god of good fortune), kiss the only Blarney stones to leave Ireland, and touch a lucky horseshoe. But don't be conned—more people lose here than win every day, or the Fitz would have closed long ago.

6 **Eldorado** (345 N. Virginia St., ☎ 702/786–5700 or 800/777–5325). This property has been in the Carano family for three generations, and the Eldorado Hotel and Casino has grown into one of the two ritziest downtown establishments, competing with Harrah's for top honors. The casino is always rammin' and jammin', the restaurants are among the best in Reno, and the buffet is consistently voted number one; Choices, a food court extraordinaire, even puts most of the ones in Las Vegas to shame. The Caranos own their own California winery, and Greg Carano, the marketing director, was a quarterback for the Dallas Cowboys in the 1980s. The Eldorado has just completed an expansion of a new wing of suites, a swimming pool, and more dining options. They also own half of Silver Legacy next door.

7 **Flamingo Hilton** (255 N. Sierra St., ☎ 702/322–1111 or 800/648–4882). What was originally Del Webb's Sahara in the 1970s, and the Reno Hilton for much of the 1980s, was transformed into the Flamingo Hilton in 1989. A multimillion-dollar remodeling brought a carbon copy of the Las Vegas Flamingo to the Biggest Little City in the World. The large, pink-feather neon signs that hang outside cast a bright-pink neon glow in the casino, and the tables include a few $3 minimums, but mostly $5 or more. The Flamingo has a small wing on Virginia Street, with some slots, a bar, and a fine Chinese restaurant, but the main operation is a block west on Sierra Street. The Sunday brunch at the Top of the Hilton, the bar and Continental restaurant on the 24th floor, is the most popular in town.

8 **Circus Circus** (500 N. Sierra St., ☎ 702/329–0711 or 800/648–5010). At the northern end of Virginia Street stands the familiar large neon clown, Topsy. This version of Circus Circus (both sign and casino) is smaller than that in Las Vegas, but it's just as kitschy and crowded. For visitors with children, Circus Circus is a required stop. Complete with circus acts, clowns, games, fun-house mirrors, a snack bar, and a cheap buffet, the midway (overlooking the casino floor) is open from 10 AM to midnight.

9 **Peppermill** (2707 S. Virginia St., ☎ 702/826–2121 or 800/648–6992). Those who prefer the gaudy, glitzy craziness of Las Vegas to the more sedate Reno scene will love the Peppermill. In terms of both noise and decor, this is the loudest casino in town. Neon signs sit atop each section of the room, the dealers wear shiny vests that sparkle in the neon light, and the Peppermill's trademark silk plants, flowers, and trees appear in profusion, especially in the buffet.

10 **Reno Hilton** (2500 E. 2nd St., ☎ 702/789–2000 or 800/648–5080). To get the full effect of a grand casino, walk through the doors of the newest Hilton. Built as the MGM Grand and sold to Bally's in 1986, this 2,001-room monster was taken over by Hilton Hotels in 1992. The 100,000-square-foot casino would be a giant in Las Vegas, so it's doubly overwhelming in Reno. The 2,000-seat Hilton Showroom is the largest in town, and hosts the big Las Vegas production revue, "Splash." A ritzy shopping arcade is on the lower floors, along with an intimate movie theater left over from the original Grand, and a large kids' arcade complete with indoor batting cage. The bowling alley and big ballrooms are on the second level. Tennis courts, a big swimming pool, a spa, a 452-space RV park, parking for 6,000 cars, and a large concrete-based reflecting pool (with a driving range where you aim golf balls at floating greens) occupy the rest of the property.

11 **Silver Legacy** (407 N. Virginia St., ☎ 702/329–4777 or 800/687–7733). The first full-scale themed hotel in northern Nevada, the Silver Legacy is a joint venture between the Eldorado (situated on one side of it) and Circus Circus (on the other), built around the fable of Sam Fairchild, aka "Old Silver," a fictional 19th-century silver baron and eccentric collector who returned 100 years later to build the Silver Legacy. Three hotel towers, the tallest 37-stories high, contain 1,720 rooms and suites, making it the second-largest hotel north of Las Vegas. The centerpiece is the giant dome, its 180-foot diameter is the largest in the country, that houses a 120-foot-tall automated mining machine that produces souvenir silver coins good in the casino. There are also five themed restaurants and a 30,000-square-foot special-events center.

12 **John Ascuaga's Nugget** (1100 Nugget Ave., Sparks, ☎ 702/356–3300 or 800/648–1177). John Ascuaga's Nugget is the anchor of Sparks,

Nevada, Reno's sister city, founded in 1905 as a railroad maintenance town. John A's, as it's locally known, was one of four Nuggets opened in western Nevada in the mid-1950s by Dick Graves, an Idaho restaurateur. The Sparks Nugget, eventually purchased by one of Graves's general managers, John Ascuaga, has expanded continually since it opened. There are now 1,000 rooms, a beautiful indoor recreation area (fifth floor), complete with an Olympic-size pool, a 750-seat headliner room that features the Nugget's own two elephants, and five restaurants. The Nugget also boasts one of the largest exotic tropical-fish tanks in the world outside of a museum, set up behind the extremely long casino bar. While you're here, take a stroll around Victorian Square on the street out front, which has an Olde England theme.

Other Attractions

For a breath of fresh air and relief from the casinos and crowds, walk
13 about four blocks west along the Truckee River until you reach **Wingfield Park.** From here you can catch a glimpse of the river and its environs.

14 South of Wingfield Park, the **Nevada Museum of Art** features an array of traveling exhibits, from the Old Masters to contemporary lithographs, and usually has one show featuring Nevada artists or history. The museum also has a nice gift shop. *160 W. Liberty, ☎ 702/329–3333. ☛ $3 adults, $1.50 students and visitors over 49. ⏲ Tues.–Sat. 10–4, Sun. noon–4.*

15 Two blocks north of the train station is the **National Bowling Stadium.** This $35 million stadium has succeeded in making Reno the Bowling Capital of the World. It features 80 lanes with a massive video scoring system, a 100-seat Omnimax dome theater (made to look like a stainless steel bowling ball), a row of pro shops selling bowling products and services, and a bright, airy '50s-style diner. Ten major national bowling tournaments (each of which can last up to six months) will be held here in the next 10 years, which will pump an estimated billion dollars into the Reno-Sparks economy. *300 N. Center St., Reno, ☎ 702/334–2695. ☛ Free into building, $4 to watch tournaments from grandstand. ⏲ Tournament hrs; call for schedule.*

16 At Mill and Lake streets, you'll find the **National Automobile Museum.** Only a shell of what it once was, when William Harrah was alive and owned it, this collection still features more than 220 antique and classic automobiles. Harrah began buying vintage autos in 1948 with the purchase of a 1911 Maxwell and a 1911 Ford. When Holiday Inn bought the company in 1986, many of the jewels were sold, a number of them to Ralph Engelstad of the Imperial Palace in Las Vegas, where they are now displayed at its Auto Collection. Among those that remain are Elvis Presley's 1973 Cadillac Eldorado, John Wayne's 1953 Corvette, and Al Jolson's Cadillac. All the cars are displayed in clever period-piece galleries inside a gorgeous $10 million museum building. There's also a 22-minute multimedia presentation in the theater, a café right on the Truckee River, and a gift shop full of automobile paraphernalia. *Mill and Lake Sts., ☎ 702/333–9300. ☛ $7.50 adults, $6.50 senior citizens over 62, $2.50 children 6–18. ⏲ Daily 9:30–5:30; closed Thanksgiving, Dec. 25.*

If your Great American Love Affair is not with cars, but with slot ma-
17 chines, be sure not to miss the **Liberty Belle Saloon** (4250 S. Virginia St., in front of the Convention Center, ☎ 702/825–1776). This popular bar and grill is owned by the Fey brothers, grandsons of Charlie Fey, who invented the modern-day slot in the late 19th century, and

authors of the definitive reference book on the history of the machines. Exhibits here display antique machines, including Fey's first, along with descriptions of the evolution of the technology. The Liberty Belle is not only fascinating, but it's also a fine place to eat and drink. It's open Monday through Friday for lunch and dinner, on weekends for dinner only. The bar generally stays open till 11:30 PM.

To explore Reno further, head north on Virginia Street until you reach the University of Nevada's Reno campus. The university, founded in Elko, Nevada, in 1874, moved to Reno in 1885 and now enrolls more than 11,000 students. Best known for its business and mining schools, the Reno campus occupies more than 200 acres.

18 On the campus is the **Fleischmann Planetarium,** with a 6-foot-diameter model of the earth and moon, computer-based exhibits, an observatory, a telescope, and science quiz games. In the meteorite collection is one meteor that you can handle. The planetarium programs special shows that change periodically. *1650 Virginia St., ☎ 702/784–4812. ☛ $5 adults, $3.50 senior citizens and children under 13. Children under 6 not admitted to evening shows. ⏲ Weekdays 9 AM–10 PM, weekends 11–10.*

19 At the northern end of the university grounds, the **Nevada Historical Society** has much to satisfy the visitor interested in Nevada's past. A permanent exhibit surveys mining activities, gambling, the Victorian era, and Native Americans. Additional special exhibits change regularly. Native American artifacts, beadwork, and basketry are also on display, and a research library that specializes in Nevada and the Great Basin is open to the public. *1650 N. Virginia St., ☎ 702/688–1190. ☛ Free (donations accepted). ⏲ Museum: Mon.–Sat. 10–5; research library: Tues.–Sat. noon–4.*

What to See and Do with Children

Circus Circus. This is one of Reno's big kiddie attractions. Styled like its sister hotel in Las Vegas, the mezzanine midway is the place for free circus acts and carnival games. Grab a couple of rolls of quarters downstairs in the casino, then set the older children loose (the younger kids get quickly overwhelmed), and hope that they don't win one of the huge stuffed-animal prizes, which you'll have to carry till you get home! *500 N. Sierra St., Reno, ☎ 702/329–0711. ⏲ Midway: daily 10 AM–midnight.*

Great Basin Adventure. A covered children's history park, the Great Basin has seven exhibits that include a mining area, log flume ride, dinosaur pit, and children's petting zoo. The whole complex is surrounded by Rancho San Rafael Park, the largest in the metropolitan area. *1502 Washington St., Reno, ☎ 702/785–4064. ☛ $2.50 adults, $1.50 senior citizens over 62 and children (doesn't include pony or flume rides). ⏲ Memorial Day–Labor Day, Tues.–Sun. 10–5.*

Idlewild Park. One of the oldest parks near downtown, dating back to 1926 when the first Reno Arch was installed on Virginia Street, Idlewild has lots of big trees, ducks and geese, a rose garden, picnic areas, and a small amusement park with a mini–roller coaster and other kiddie rides. *Idlewild Dr. (take W. 1st or 2nd to Riverside, then cross river and head right on Idlewild), Reno. ☛ $4 for 5 rides. ⏲ May–Sept., daily 11–6; Oct.–Apr., 11–6 on weekends and holidays only.*

Oxbow Nature Study Area. Do the kids' legs need stretching? Take them to this unusual city park by the river. A series of paths meanders through and around an oxbow (former channel) of the Truckee River.

Decks, overlooks, narrative signs, and an interpretive center make this a great place for learning about Reno's river and water system. *Dickerson Rd. (head out W. 2nd, bear left on Dickerson, follow it to the end), Reno,* ☎ *702/785–4319.* ⏲ *Park: during daylight hrs; interpretive center: call ahead for hrs.*

Wilbur May Museum. Next door to the Great Basin Adventure, the May Museum has a fine display of wild animals and exotic artifacts from around the world. An exhibit displays life-size robotic dinosaurs. The gift shop has a fine collection of educational kids' stuff, everything for under $20. *1500 Washington St., Reno,* ☎ *702/785–5961.* ☛ *$2.50 adults, $1.50 children 3–12.* ⏲ *Daily 10–5; closed Mon. Oct.–Mar.*

Wild Island. This 11-acre water park features slides and body flumes, and there's a kiddie wading area. A 36-hole miniature golf course includes a haunted house and a 41-foot castle. There are also kids' racing cars. *250 Wild Island Ct., Sparks,* ☎ *702/359–2927.* ☛ *$14.95 adults (48" or taller), $10.95 for children less than 48" tall.* ☛ *Golf course: $5.95 for 36 holes, $3.95 for 18 holes; Racing cars: $2.50.* ⏲ *Water park: Memorial Day–Labor Day, daily 11–7; golf and racing: year-round.*

Wedding Chapels

Like Las Vegas, the Reno area is flush with wedding chapels that take advantage of Nevada's liberal marriage laws. A marriage license can be obtained in the state of Nevada without a blood test or waiting period. Get one for $35 (cash only) at the **Marriage Bureau in the Washoe County Courthouse** (S. Virginia and Court Sts., ☎ 702/328–3275) for anyone 18 years of age or older. Legal ID with proof of age is required. Couples age 16–18 can obtain marriage licenses with their parents' or a legal guardian's consent, given in person or in writing (and notarized) to the county clerk. The bureau is open daily 8 AM to midnight.

Civil marriages in Reno and Sparks are performed at the office of the **Commissioner of Civil Marriages** (195 S. Sierra St.). Witnesses are provided for the couple as part of the $35 package.

Many wedding chapels in Reno offer quick weddings that cost approximately $45 for the service (photos, music, and food are extra), plus a $10 filing fee and a $35 donation to the minister. Three wedding chapels on Virginia Street are: **Cupid's Chapel of Love** (629 N. Virginia St., ☎ 702/323–2930), **Reno Wedding Chapel** (655 N. Virginia St., ☎ 702/323–5818), and **Wedding Bells Chapel** (642 N. Sierra St., ☎ 702/329–0909).

Shopping

Harold's Club Antique Slots (250 N. Virginia St., ☎ 702/329–0881). Want to take home a classic slot machine? That can be arranged on the mezzanine level of Harold's, where prices begin at around $600.

Meadowood Mall (Virginia St. at McCarran Blvd., ☎ 702/827–8450). Located in fast-growing southwest Reno, Meadowood is anchored by Macy's and JCPenney. More than 100 stores run the gamut from clothing to sporting goods, candy to luggage. A mall shuttle runs to and from the hotels in Reno and Sparks; the $2 round-trip is redeemable for a canvas shopping bag and a coupon book.

Parker's Western Wear (151 N. Sierra St., ☎ 702/323–4481). This is the oldest and certainly the largest Western shop in town. Established in 1919, Parker's is an old-fashioned shop with hardwood floors, autographed celebrity photos on the wall, and large stocks of jeans, boots, shirts, jackets, and other cowboy and cowgirl duds.

Park Lane Mall (310 Plumb La. at Virginia St., ☎ 702/825–7878). The closest mall to downtown Reno, Park Lane is anchored by Sears and Weinstock's. There are 92 stores, selling toys, jewelry, men's and women's apparel, and books; an interesting Nevada store carrying only locally related items; and fast-food restaurants.

Southwest Pavilion (8100 block of Virginia St., ☎ 702/852–6111). A bit of a drive from downtown, this boutique-style shopping center is worth the trip if you're looking for upscale clothing, shoes, jewelry, or gifts. A number of shops here also feature Southwestern clothing and jewelry.

Sports and Fitness

Ballooning

Reno hosts one of the biggest hot-air balloon races in the country in early September. One company that provides rides and weddings is **Zephyr Balloons** (552 N. McCarran, ☎ 702/329–1700).

Biking

This being the land of big hills and mountains, mountain biking seems to be the preferred mode of cycling, yet one can take leisurely rides through Reno along the paths that follow the Truckee River. Bicycle and Rollerblade rentals are available at **Bobo Sheehan's Ski Co.** (1200 S. Wells Ave., ☎ 702/786–5111) and **Reno Bicycle Center** (809 W. 4th St., ☎ 702/329–2453).

Golf

When it comes to teeing off, Reno cannot match the year-round sunny desert terrain of Las Vegas, yet several 18-hole courses are in the area. These courses operate seasonally, most of them closing in the winter, so it would be wise to phone ahead before planning a visit to **Lakeridge Golf Course** (1200 Razorback Rd., Reno, ☎ 702/825–2200), **Wildcreek Golf Course** (3500 Sullivan La., Sparks, ☎ 702/673–3100), or **Glenbrook Golf Course** (Hwy. 50, Glenbrook, ☎ 702/749–5201).

Hiking

Many hiking trails have been established in the Sierra Nevadas. Detailed information about hiking in the Reno–Carson City area is available from the **Carson Ranger District, U.S. Forest Service** (1536 S. Carson, Carson City, ☎ 702/882–2766).

TRAILS

Mt. Rose. One of the highest peaks hereabouts, Mt. Rose offers panoramas of Lake Tahoe, the Sierra Nevadas, and Reno. The trailhead of the 5-mile summit trail is located at the Mt. Rose pass on the right side of Highway 431, en route to Lake Tahoe from Reno, where you'll find a dirt road next to the maintenance building.

Jones Creek, Whites Creek. This 8-mile, moderate-to-difficult loop ascends to two creeks along a fire road and a Jeep trail. You can pick up the trail at Galena Creek Park's north picnic area along Highway 431, about 15 miles from Reno.

Skiing

Most of the good skiing is in the Lake Tahoe area. **Mount Rose Ski Area** (22222 Mount Rose Hwy., off Hwy. 431, Reno 89511, ☎ 702/849–0704), the closest resort to Reno—only 25 minutes by car—has 43 runs. Its summit is 9,700 feet, its base 8,260 feet.

Ski rentals are available at **Bobo Sheehan's Ski Co.** (1200 S. Wells Ave., Reno, ☎ 702/786–5111) and **Galena Ski Rentals** (16795 Mount Rose Hwy., ☎ 702/849–0111).

Tennis

Lakeridge Tennis Club (6000 Plumas St., Reno, ☎ 702/827–3300) has 14 outdoor courts and four indoor courts open to the public; there's a $15 court fee for all-day use. The Reno Hilton (2500 E. 2nd St., Reno, ☎ 702/789–2000) has three outdoor courts and five indoor courts; rates are $6 an hour for outdoor courts, $20 an hour for indoor courts.

Windsurfing

One of the thrills of coming to the Reno and Lake Tahoe area is partaking in the sport of windsurfing. Near Reno, the most popular spot for this activity is on Little Washoe Lake. Lessons and rental equipment are available at **High Sierra Sports** (6431 S. Virginia St., Reno, ☎ 702/851–0200).

Dining

The number of restaurants in the Reno area is certainly smaller than that in Las Vegas, but the kinds of dining opportunities are similar: hotel restaurants, buffets, and coffee shops, in addition to some independent steak houses and ethnic eateries. Restaurants are listed in order of their price category.

CATEGORY	COST*
$$$$	over $25
$$$	$18–$25
$$	$10–$18
$	under $10

**per person for a three-course meal, excluding drinks, service, and 7% sales tax*

$$$$ **19th Hole Restaurant.** One of the top rooms in town, the 19th Hole gets raves from locals as much for its outstanding setting as for its well-prepared Continental fare. This upscale, special-occasion restaurant is located right on the Lakeridge Golf Course, atop a hill: At night, seated in the plush red chairs, you can see the lights of Reno through picture windows; at lunchtime you can watch golfers at play, the mountains in the background. The lunch menu consists of sandwiches and burgers; seafood, steaks, and chicken are featured at dinner. All entrées come with the soup du jour or salad and a vegetable. ✕ *1200 Razorback Rd.,* ☎ *702/825–1250. Reservations advised. AE, MC, V.*

$$$ **Harrah's Steak House.** Located in the basement of the busy Harrah's casino, this dark, romantic restaurant has no view of slot machines to disrupt the warm ambience of the luxurious red booths and candlelight. Burgers, BLTs, and chicken sandwiches are available for lunch; veal steaks, chops, chicken, and fish are offered at dinner. ✕ *219 N. Center St.,* ☎ *702/786–3232. Reservations advised. AE, D, DC, MC, V.*

$$$ **Rapscallion Seafood House & Bar.** Steaks and pastas are available at this clubby restaurant, with lots of dark wood and private booths, but the specialty here is fish: Up to 30 varieties of fresh seafood appear on the menu daily. Among the popular dishes are calamari Rapscallion, deep-fried squid served with scallions and mushrooms, and Rapscallion stew, a concoction that includes a variety of shellfish as well as fish fillets, leeks, tomatoes, garlic, and white wine. Salads, burgers, fish, and steak sandwiches are available at lunch. The service is extremely efficient, with impeccable timing. ✕ *1555 S. Wells Ave.,* ☎ *702/323–1211. Reservations advised for dinner. AE, MC, V.*

$$ ★ **La Strada.** This exceptional Italian restaurant, located in the Eldorado casino, is designed to reflect its name, which means a small street in an Italian market. The Carano family, which owns the casino, imported a special wood-fired brick oven from Italy for baking and an Italian chef who knows his stuff. His wild-mushroom ravioli is especially good, all the pastas are handmade, and the pizza is perfect. ✕ *345 N. Virginia St. at 4th St.,* ☎ *702/786–5700. Reservations advised. AE, D, DC, MC, V.*

$$ **Louis' Basque Corner.** The Basque tradition is very strong in northern Nevada; every good-size town north of Tonopah has at least one family-style Basque restaurant (and rooming house). The Basque hotel is a remnant of a time when tough solo shepherds roamed the mountains with their flocks during the summer, then spent the winters in the towns. At Louis', the hearty peasant fare typical of the Basque region is served at long tables (you'll probably sit with strangers). The dinner price is all inclusive and you'll find yourself facing huge portions of soup, salad, Basque beans, french fries, and a choice of beef, lamb, or seafood entrées—along with a glass of wine and dessert. Be sure to try the Basque special cocktail, Picon Punch, a potent mix of liquors that'll quickly put you into the lively spirit of this place. ✕ *301 E. 4th St.,* ☎ *702/323–7203. Reservations accepted for 10 or more. AE, DC, MC, V.*

$$ **Presidential Car.** The gourmet comp room for the high rollers of Harold's Club, the Presidential Car is another dining room with a view: Large picture windows look right out over Virginia Street and the Reno Arch. Although it's primarily a steak house, this restaurant also does veal, fish, and chicken well. It's known above all for its desserts, luring local chocoholics with a fatally rich Death By Chocolate. ✕ *Harold's Club, Commercial Row and N. Virginia St.,* ☎ *702/329–0881. Reservations advised. AE, D, MC, V.*

$$ **Rivoli's.** Here is another Italian restaurant, but with a difference—the owner sings opera as he dishes up his specialties. The restaurant is small and intimate, right downtown but not in a hotel, and the food is terrific, with pasta, veal, and seafood specialties. The Rivoli has been a successful little trattoria since 1965. ✕ *221 W. 2nd St.,* ☎ *702/784–9792. Reservations advised. MC, V. Closed Sun., Mon. No lunch.*

$–$$ ★ **Café de Thai.** What the Café de Thai—a fancied-up hole-in-the-wall in a strip mall—lacks in atmosphere, it more than makes up for in food. Everything cooked up by Sakul Cheosakul, a Thai national who trained at the Culinary Institute, is exquisitely prepared. His creative menu includes excellent satay and papaya salad appetizers, tom kha kai soup, and Oriental sausage salad. Traditional rice noodle dishes (pad Thai and the like) are also offered. The wok preparations are superb and reasonably priced: Try the garlic pepper pork, peanut beef, or basil chicken. The curries are spicy, but not incendiary. Service is attentive yet unobtrusive. ✕ *3314 S. McCarran Ave. (Mira Loma Shopping Center),* ☎ *702/829–8424. Reservations advised. AE, DC, MC, V.*

$–$$ ★ **Palais de Jade.** The ritziest Chinese restaurant in Reno is in a tasteful black-and-white room, understated and elegant. The dishes tend toward fancy Cantonese, with the moo shu, cashew, and kung pao you've come to know, along with some scallop and lobster preparations and Szechuan specials. The food is delicious, and the servers seem genuinely happy to see you—and treat you accordingly well. ✕ *960 W. Moana Ave.,* ☎ *702/827–5233. Reservations advised. AE, DC, MC, V.*

$–$$ **Rotisserie Buffet.** Although this buffet, at John Ascuaga's Nugget in Sparks, is slightly more expensive than usual ($7 for lunch and $11 for dinner), it's consistently voted the best in town in local polls. There's a nice variety of fresh steam-table dishes, as well as an abun-

Reno Dining and Lodging

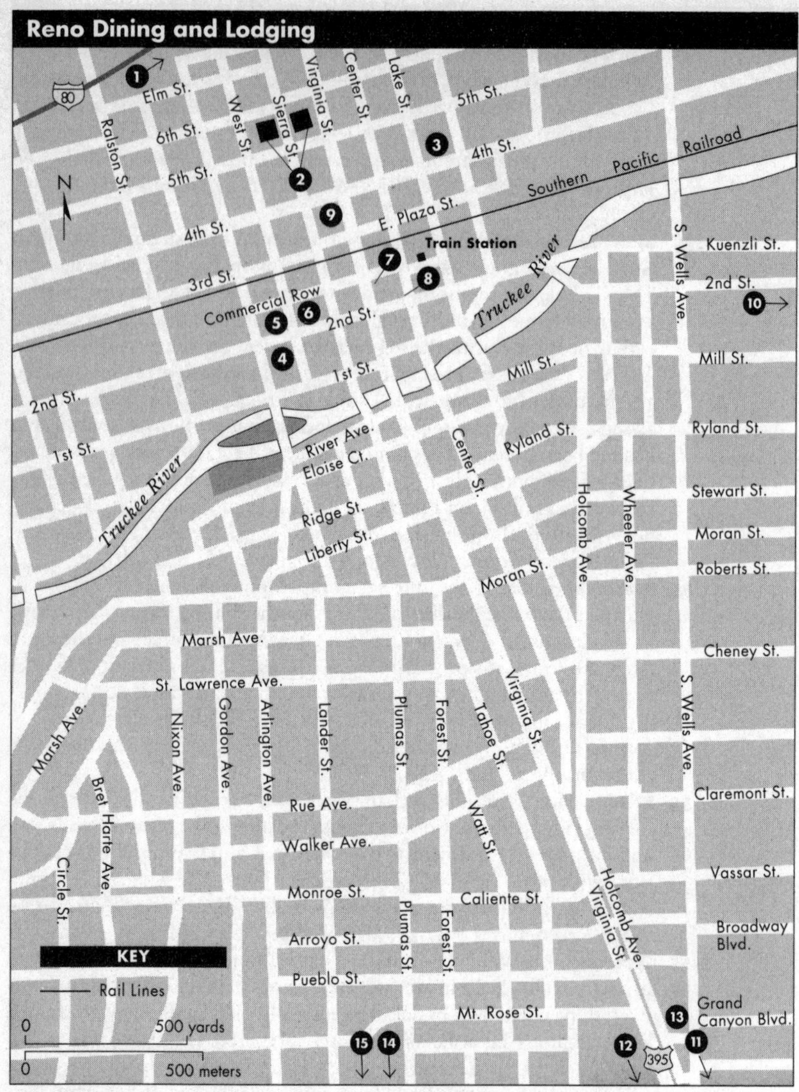

Café de Thai, **11**
Circus Circus, **2**
Comstock Hotel, **4**
Eldorado, **9**
Flamingo Hilton, **6**
General Store (Nugget), **1**
Harrah's, **8**
Harrah's Steak House, **8**
John Ascuaga's Nugget, **1**
La Strada, **9**
Louis' Basque Corner, **3**
19th Hole Restaurant, **14**
Palais de Jade, **15**
Peppermill Hotel, **12**
Presidential Car, **7**
Rapscallion Seafood House & Bar, **13**
Reno Hilton, **10**
Rivoli's, **5**
Rotisserie Buffet, **1**

dance of salads and desserts baked on the premises; the bread is particularly tasty. ✕ *1100 Nugget Ave., Sparks,* ☎ *702/356–3300 or 800/648–1177. Reservations advised 1 hr before buffet begins. AE, D, MC, V. Lunch served 11–2, dinner 5–10.*

$ **General Store.** One of the better coffee shops in town is also at the Nugget. In a large, Barbary Coast–style setting and open 24 hours, the General Store offers an extensive children's menu along with your basic coffee-shop fare: burgers, chicken-fried steak, Jell-O salads. The fine fresh-baked bread is a plus. ✕ *1100 Nugget Ave., Sparks,* ☎ *702/356–3300 or 800/648–1177. No reservations. AE, D, DC, MC, V.*

Lodging

Reno's 22,000 hotel and motel rooms serve roughly 4.5 million visitors a year. However, unlike Las Vegas, only a few of the hotels in Reno are huge: The Reno Hilton, the largest by far, has 2,000 rooms, the Silver Legacy has 1,700, Circus Circus has 1,625, and John Ascuaga's Nugget has 1,000; the room count at other hotels tends to be in the hundreds. Generally speaking, high season is the summer, low season is the winter. Rooms can be especially difficult to book on short notice between May and October, when local events such as Hot August Nights, the Reno Air and Balloon races, the Reno Rodeo, and the Reno State Fair take place one right after another. On the other hand, on weekdays in winter, hotels and motels practically give away their rooms; they're still not as inexpensive as Las Vegas's lodgings during slow times, but almost. Any time of year, however, it's always best to call as far ahead as possible and ask about any package deals that the large hotels may be offering.

CATEGORY	COST*
$$$$	over $100
$$$	$75–$100
$$	$50–$75
$	under $50

**All prices are for a standard double room, excluding service charge and 8% tax.*

$$$–$$$$ **Eldorado.** Recently expanded to compete with the best of Reno's big hotel casinos, the family-owned Eldorado is known for its fine food and attention to detail. Although it's located right in the central gambling district, the hotel offers rooms that overlook the mountains on all sides. Valet parking is available, and self-parking is convenient at a 10-story parking structure across Sierra Street, with an overhead walkway into the hotel. 🏨 *345 N. Virginia St., 89501,* ☎ *702/786–5700 or 800/648–5966,* FAX *702/322–7124. 1,045 rooms. 6 restaurants, lounge, pool. AE, D, DC, MC, V.*

$$$–$$$$ **Flamingo Hilton.** When the old Reno Hilton became the Flamingo Hilton in 1990, it was spruced up and given a new casino, new neon signs, new restaurants, and remodeled rooms. The green-and-white accommodations are medium-size and have mountain views from either side of the hotel. On July 4, 1993, a new million-dollar neon sign lit up the entryway to this hotel, which is one block west of Virginia Street. 🏨 *255 N. Sierra St., 89501,* ☎ *702/322–1111 or 800/648–4882,* FAX *702/785–7086. 604 rooms. 4 restaurants, lounge. AE, D, DC, MC, V.*

$$$–$$$$ **Harrah's.** One of the most luxurious hotels in downtown Reno, Harrah's has large rooms decorated in blues and mauves, with king-size beds and quilted bedspreads. Both sides of the hotel offer picture windows with views of the mountains. Because the lobby is on the second floor, you'll have to lug your bags through the casino. Full-scale pro-

duction revues with showgirls and comedians are staged in Harrah's showroom. *219 N. Center St. at Virginia St., 702/786–3232 or 800/648–3773, FAX 702/788–2815. 565 rooms. 4 restaurants, pool, health club, showroom. AE, MC, V.*

$$$–$$$$ **John Ascuaga's Nugget.** Don't let the out-of-the-way location in downtown Sparks put you off; the Nugget has a lot going for it, including some of the largest and most luxurious rooms in town—and at lower rates than Harrah's. Also, the stunning recreation area on the fifth floor of the tower provides indoor swimming and hot-tubbing year-round. Another nice touch is that the elevators are between the front desk and the casino, thereby eliminating long, baggage-laden treks through the slot-machine area. Kids will enjoy seeing Bertha and Angel, the elephants who live in a habitat in front of the employee parking lots; the "girls" parade between the showroom and their home each night, and sun themselves at various times during the day outside their house. The ELEPHANT CROSSING sign at the street is a good photo op. *1100 Nugget Ave., Sparks 89431, 702/356–3300 or 800/648–1177, FAX 702/356–3434. 983 rooms. 6 restaurants, lounge, indoor pool, showroom. AE, DC, MC, V.*

$$$–$$$$ **Reno Hilton.** While most of Reno's hotels are downtown (only the Peppermill, Clarion, and John A's Nugget are not), the Hilton is out near the airport, thrust up in the middle of the metro area, alone and proud, surrounded by a huge parking lot and little else of interest. The former Bally's was bought by Hilton in 1992 for a bargain-basement $82 million and received a new paint job and face-lift. Hilton subsequently invested another $82 million worth of renovations, including redecorating every hotel room, expanding the sports book into a Las Vegas Hilton–size Superbook, and redoing the restaurants. Some picture windows offer spectacular views of the mountains. The tallest (27 floors) hotel in Reno, the Hilton also has the largest casino, 100,000 square feet of tables and slots, and a large shopping arcade downstairs. *2500 E. 2nd St., 89595, 702/789–2000 or 800/648–5080, FAX 702/789–2418. 2,001 rooms. 4 restaurants, lounge, pool, driving range, tennis courts, health club, shops, showroom, theater, wedding chapel. AE, DC, MC, V.*

$$–$$$ **Peppermill Hotel.** The home of Reno's most colorful casino has plush, sedate rooms upstairs in various color schemes. While the Peppermill is 3 miles south of downtown, it's near the shopping centers, and local residents love it. The fireside lounge and the slots regularly win top honors in the *Reno Gazette-Journal*'s "Best of Reno" awards. *2707 S. Virginia St., 702/826–2121 or 800/648–6992, FAX 702/826–5205. 633 rooms. 4 restaurants, lounge, pool. AE, D, DC, MC, V.*

$$ **Comstock Hotel.** Two blocks west of Virginia Street is one of the many Nevada casinos that aim to re-create the Old West. Here the subject is the 19th-century mining activity in nearby Virginia City. The small and conservative rooms have Victorian-style furnishings and views of the mountains or the city. *200 W. 2nd St., 89501, 702/329–1880 or 800/648–4866, FAX 702/348–0539. 310 rooms. 2 restaurants, deli, lounge, pool. MC, V.*

$ **Circus Circus.** Although this is a smaller version of the giant Las Vegas property, it still has two sprawling towers, connected by a monorail. The marquee promises: ROOMS AVAILABLE. IF NOT, WE'LL PLACE YOU. If you do get a room here—and these are easily the most inexpensive rooms in a major downtown Reno hotel—you'll find the small, orange-walled accommodations, with two queen beds, as garish as those at the Las Vegas Circus Circus; here, though, some have views of the mountains. *500 N. Sierra St., 89503, 702/329–0711 or 800/648–5010, FAX 702/329–0599. 1,625 rooms. 3 restaurants, lounge. AE, DC, MC, V.*

Nightlife

Reno's nightlife is much less frenzied than that of Las Vegas. There are only four showrooms. The **Hilton Showroom** at the Reno Hilton (2500 E. 2nd St., ☎ 702/789–2000) is the biggest, with seating for 2,000. Las Vegas producer Jeff Kutash fills the Hilton Showroom with his "Splash" revue, a clone of the long-running "Splash" that plays at the Riviera. The 750-seat **Celebrity Room** at John Ascuaga's Nugget (1100 Nugget Ave., Sparks, ☎ 702/356–3300) features country stars, such as Michael Martin Murphy, Juice Newton, and the Bellamy Brothers, and nostalgia acts like the Drifters and the Lettermen. **Sammy's Showroom** at Harrah's (219 N. Center St., ☎ 702/788–3773) is the place for minirevues in Reno, which change about twice a year. The 600-seat **Showroom** at the Flamingo Hilton (255 N. Sierra St., ☎ 702/322–1111) currently is presenting "American Superstars," a high-glitz impersonator show.

Just for Laughs (Reno Hilton, ☎ 702/789–2285), the only comedy club in town, has one show (8:30 PM) on weekdays, two shows (8:30 and 10:30) Friday and Saturday.

Popular nightclubs for drinking and dancing to rock music with the locals include **Dick Clark's American Bandstand** (Harold's Club, 2nd Floor, ☎ 702/786–2222) and **Delmar Station** (700 S. Virginia St., ☎ 702/322–7200). The best place to dance to country music is at **Baldini's Casino** (865 S. Rock Blvd., Sparks, ☎ 702/358–0116); **Boots Bar and Grill** (above the Horseshoe Club downtown, ☎ 702/323–7900) is the most convenient.

Excursions

A rewarding side trip from Reno, Virginia City is one of the largest and best-preserved 19th-century mining towns anywhere, attracting hundreds of thousands of visitors a year. Clinging precariously to the steep eastern slope of Mt. Davidson, the little town is a time capsule of the Wild West, complete with boardwalks, saloons, and mine barons' mansions. Similarly, Carson City, one of the smallest state capitals in the country (and one of the few with no scheduled airline service), is well worth a visit. Among its attractions are fine 100-year-old stone buildings, the best museum in the state, several casinos, the State Capitol, a number of handsome 19th-century mansions on shady backstreets, and the governor's residence.

Virginia City

GETTING THERE

From Reno, head 8 miles south on U.S. 395. Then take the Highway 341 turnoff and proceed 20 miles through the scenic Virginia Range to Virginia City. Geiger Overlook just before the summit provides a spectacular view of Truckee Meadows.

EXPLORING

Numbers in the margin correspond to points of interest on the Virginia City map.

The Comstock Lode remains one of the largest gold and silver deposits ever discovered; in today's dollars, with today's technologies, the Comstock would be worth in the billions. The boomtown of Virginia City was built right atop the lode, which was mined from the hard rock under Mt. Davidson. Hundreds of miles of shafts and tunnels honeycombed the Lode, reaching a depth of 3,500 feet. The heyday of the boom lasted nearly 20 years, from 1860 till 1880. At its peak, Virginia City boasted 30,000 residents, six churches, 110 saloons, and the only elevator between Chicago and San Francisco. Half the town burned to the ground in 1875; only a few buildings still standing originate from an earlier date.

Unlike thousands of boomtowns throughout the American West, Virginia City was never rendered a total ghost town. Its die-hard residents, proximity to Carson City and Reno, and on-again off-again mining kept it alive for the forgotten 75 years between final borrasca (bust) and its rediscovery in the 1950s. Though only 800 people now call Virginia City home, the town's proud citizens, some of them descendants of the first settlers, preserve their Wild West heritage like a treasured family heirloom.

The town is small, with only one commercial business street, and ideal for walking. Most visitors will stroll for a couple of hours on C Street, take a 35-minute railroad ride, look for souvenirs, and grab a bite to eat before going on to Carson City. But do explore a bit of B Street (uphill) and D Street (downhill) for the town behind the town.

1 To orient yourself, you might well begin at the Virginia City **Chamber of Commerce** (C St., across from post office, ☎ 702/847–0311). Here you can pick up brochures, maps, and tips on what to see.

Samuel Clemens, then in his twenties, lived in Virginia City for a couple of years and reported on the local excitement for the Territorial Enterprise, often utilizing the techniques of frontier journalism—wild exaggeration, satire, and ribaldry. It was here that he first used the name "Mark Twain," and later he wrote of those early days in *Roughing It.*
2 His memory lives on in the **Mark Twain Museum,** where you'll find his copy desk, typewriter, an original printing press, and other artifacts. *C St., ☎ 702/847–0525. ☛ $1 adults, 50¢ children, children under 12 free. ⌚ Daily 10–5.*

One block south, at the corner of C and Taylor streets, a second mu-
3 seum devoted to the writer, the **Mark Twain Museum of Memories,** commemorates Twain's time in Virginia City through many period items and exhibits on Virginia City history. *C and Taylor Sts., ☎ 702/847–0454. ☛ $2 adults, children free. ⌚ Daily 10:30–4.*

For a thirst quencher and a taste of Old West "hospitality," consider
4 the **Bucket of Blood Saloon** (C St., ☎ 702/847–0322), the host to many a Friday night brawl back in 1876 (which is how it got its name). Today it offers drinks and gaming, a wonderful view of the mountains, and a piano-banjo duo that plays the old tunes. The original 30-foot wood bar still stands, along with old pictures, guns, bottles, and swords. The world's largest dice machine (a $1 slot that flips and reads the dice, then pays off according to the odds) is not only one of a kind, but the best gambling experience in Virginia City, which has no tables, only slots. The Bucket of Blood T-shirt is a classic.

5 Another Old West establishment, the **Delta Saloon** (C St., ☎ 702/847–0789), is home to the "suicide table," a faro table later converted to blackjack. Three of the various owners of this item were said to have taken their lives when they were wiped out financially in the games played on it. The suicide table is at the same time the most hyped and humdrum sight in town. The nearby shrine to the Bonanza Kings, who unearthed the largest and richest vein of them all, is far more interesting. The rest of the joint is nicely remodeled, especially the upstairs hallway and ballrooms.

Bucket of Blood Saloon, **4**
The Castle, **12**
Chamber of Commerce, **1**
Delta Saloon, **5**
Fourth Ward School, **10**
Mackay Mansion, **9**
Mark Twain Museum, **2**
Mark Twain Museum of Memories, **3**
Piper's Opera House, **11**
Ponderosa Saloon, **6**
Virginia and Truckee Railroad, **8**
The Way It Was Museum, **7**

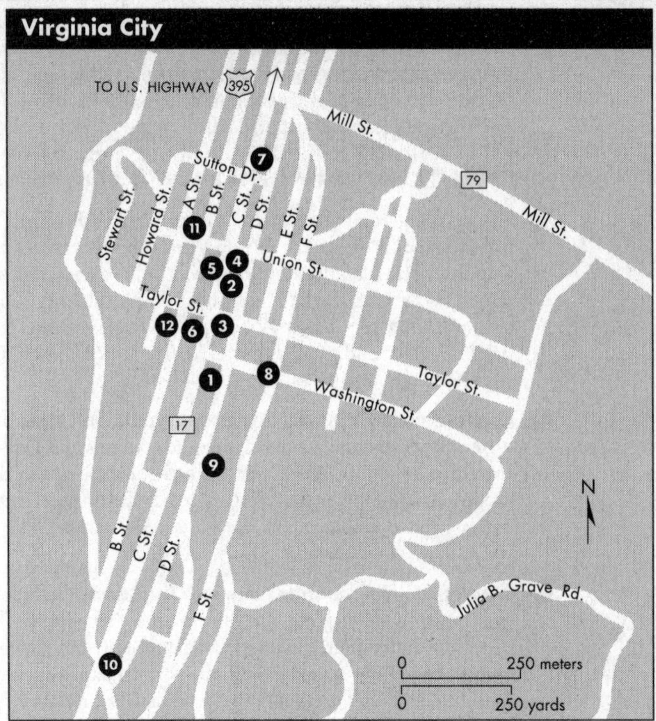

6 Another historic Old West watering hole, the **Ponderosa Saloon** hosts a rear tunnel that meanders more than 300 feet into a restored portion of the Best and Belcher mine. A guided tour through this passageway offers a graphic display of the horrendous working conditions under which the Comstock miners labored. It's now a constant 52°F in the tunnel, around 60°F lower than the searing temperatures to which the men were subjected—along with steam, poison gases, and primitive technology—when they descended into the mine. The tour lasts 30 minutes, so if you chill easily, bring a sweater. *C St., ☎ 702/847–0757. ☛ $3 adults, $1.50 children. ⏲ Daily 10–5.*

For further insight into local history, walk north to the intersection of
7 C Street and Sutton Drive, where you'll find **The Way It Was Museum.** A 16-minute color video describes the history of the Comstock Lode, and the museum holds an extensive collection of mining artifacts, among them a working model of an early water-powered stamp mill (used to crush the ore from which silver and gold was extracted), costumed mannequins, mining equipment, and a blacksmith shop. *C St. and Sutton Dr., ☎ 702/847–0766. ☛ $2. ⏲ Daily 10–6.*

Turn now, and walk southeast toward F and Washington streets and
8 the celebrated old **Virginia and Truckee Railroad.** In its heyday, as many as 45 trains arrived and departed daily between Virginia and Carson cities and Reno. Completed in 1869, the line hauled millions of dollars in gold and silver ore from the Comstock mines. Today the steam-powered train makes 35-minute rail trips nine times a day down the hill to Gold Hill, Virginia's bedroom community. Passengers have the choice of riding in the open car or in the partially covered car. *Washington and F Sts., ☎ 702/847–0380. ☛ $4 adults, $2 children 5–12, $8 all-day pass. ⏲ Memorial Day–Sept., daily; Oct., weekends only; 1st ride at 10:30, last ride at 5:45.*

9 Head over to D Street to visit the history-rich **Mackay Mansion,** built in 1860 by the Gould and Curry Mining Co. John Mackay (pronounced *mak*-kee), one of the Comstock's richest mining barons, took control of Gould and Curry and this house in 1874. The mansion is one of the area's oldest homes and includes an old mine vault. Tours of this beautifully restored Victorian-style home are offered. *129 D St., ☎ 702/847–0173. ☛ $3, children under 8 free. ⏲ Daily 10–6.*

10 Now go south on D Street until it joins C Street. Built in 1876, the **Fourth Ward School** is one of the nation's few schools of this size and type left standing. The four-story building was built to accommodate 1,026 students, and it remained a school until 1936. Visitors can now enjoy an exhibit called "A Comstock Lesson," two classrooms restored to their original state, and a gift shop. *C St., ☎ 702/847–0975. ☛ Donation requested. ⏲ May 15–Oct., daily 10–5.*

11 On the corner of B and Union streets, you'll find **Piper's Opera House,** host to such legendary actors as Maude Adams and David Belasco. Restored in 1969 by John Piper's great-granddaughter, the theater still retains many of the original features, such as round-backed chairs, chandeliers, and the balcony. *B and Union Sts., ☎ 702/847–0433. ☛ $2, children under 10 free. ⏲ Daily 11–4:30.*

12 A block south of the Opera House is **The Castle,** the best-restored mansion not only in Virginia City but in all of Nevada. Built in 1868 by a mine superintendent, the Castle was untouched by the big fire of 1875, and was sold only twice, with all its furnishings included. Thus, the museum part of the house (the rear half is occupied by the owners) has a fine collection of the original European antiques, including furniture, lamps, mirrors, wallpaper, shutters. *D St., just south of Taylor, no ☎. ☛ $2.50. ⏲ Daily 11–4.*

Carson City

GETTING THERE

For the trip to Carson City, head south on Highway 341 from Virginia City, turn west on U.S. 50, and continue for about 3 miles until you come to U.S. 395. You can also get to Carson directly from Reno by traveling south for 40 miles on U.S. 395.

EXPLORING

Carson City was founded in 1858 by Abraham Curry, one of Nevada's great pioneers and visionaries, who bought Eagle Valley, a large patch of desert and a small trading post, for $1,000. Curry immediately laid out a town site for a state capital, even though "Nevada" was not yet a state, nor even a territory. In fact, it was still part of the Latter-day Saints' vast Utah Territory and had only a few hundred people living in it. Curry's amazing foresight was validated less than a year later when silver was discovered nearby in the Virginia Range. Within four years, Nevada had become a state. Curry's town site, named Carson City after famed western explorer Kit Carson, was indeed its capital.

Today, Carson City, a beautiful old town with 40,000 residents, has a vitality beyond its population numbers. Because two major highways—U.S. 50 and U.S. 395—both pass through the center of town, the streets are always lively. This is the place where gambling and easy divorces were legalized in 1931, where brothel prostitution has never been declared fully illegal (except in Clark, Washoe, and Douglas counties), and from where Nevada has fought its numerous battles with the federal government over the regulation of gambling, wilderness areas, and a high-level nuclear-waste repository. If Reno is the Biggest Little City in the World, then Carson City might just be the Biggest Little Town in the World.

A visit to the **Nevada State Museum**—the former Carson Mint, across from the Carson Nugget Casino—will brief you on local history. During the Civil War era, in an attempt to raise money for the Union, Congress authorized the hasty construction of this mint, where some $50 million in silver and gold was coined from 1870 to 1893. A complete set of Carson City–minted coins is now on display, reflecting this financial period in the building's history. Also featured are exhibits on early mining days; complete silver service from the U.S.S. *Nevada,* an early 20th-century battleship; the handiwork of Dat So La Lee, a Washoe Indian whose willow baskets are considered the finest in the world; and a maze of mining tunnels and exhibits in the basement. The gift shop is well stocked with Nevada books and souvenirs. *600 N. Carson St., ☎ 702/687–4810. ☛ $3 adults, children under 18 free. ⌚ Daily 8:30–4:30; closed Thanksgiving, Dec. 25, Jan. 1.*

While you're in the town center, be sure to take a self-guided tour of the **State Capitol.** With its impressive dome, large green lawn, Alaskan-marble halls, and interesting murals, this is easily one of the prettiest capitols in the country. Portraits of Nevada's governors line the walls. A small museum on the second floor has the finest and most eclectic display of artifacts in the state, including a photographic history of the building itself and an exhibit of all the state symbols. While the governor still maintains an office here, most governmental activity takes place across the street, in the newer legislative building. *101 N. Carson St., ☎ 702/687–5030. ☛ Free. ⌚ Daily 8–5 for self-guided tours.*

About 2 miles south of the capital complex, off U.S. 395, the **Nevada State Railroad Museum** features beautifully restored antique rolling stock of the Virginia & Truckee Railroad. Once or twice a month during the summer, the steam train travels the loop around the property; when it's not operating, a regular motorcar does this fun little joyride. *2180 S. Carson St., ☎ 702/687–6953. ☛ $2 adults, children under 18 free. Steam train rides: $3 adults, $1 children over 4. Motorcar: $1 adults, 50¢ children over 4. ⌚ Wed.–Sun. 8:30–4:30.*

The **Carson City Chamber of Commerce** maintains its office nearby, and sells souvenirs, T-shirts, and maps for self-guided tours of local sites, government buildings, and 26 historically significant or interesting homes in the area. *1900 S. Carson St., ☎ 702/882–1565. ⌚ Year-round, weekdays 8–5; May–Dec., also open weekends 10–3.*

Reno Essentials

Arriving and Departing

BY BUS

Greyhound Lines (155 Stevenson St., ☎ 702/322–2970 or 800/231–2222) offers nationwide service, with frequent runs to the San Francisco Bay Area and other points in California.

BY CAR

To reach downtown Reno from the airport, take Route 395N to Interstate 80, head west on I–80, and get off at the North Virginia exit.

BY PLANE

Reno-Tahoe International Airport (☎ 702/328–6400), on the east side of the city, serves western Nevada. The airport is a 10-minute drive from downtown. There is no commercial airline service to Carson City, the state capital.

America West (☎ 800/235–9292), **American** (☎ 800/433–7300), **Delta** (☎ 800/221–1212), **Reno Air** (☎ 800/736–6247), **Southwest** (☎ 800/435–9792), and **United** (☎ 800/241–6522) are the principal airlines that fly into Reno.

Between the Airport and Downtown. Citifare Bus 24 runs between the airport and the downtown bus center every 25 minutes. **Bell Limousine** (☎ 702/786–3700) has service to Reno and surrounding areas. All major hotels offer courtesy shuttles from the airport.

Getting Around

Reno, accessible by air, rail, and road, has a small central visitor core. Most major hotels are on or near Virginia Street, and the majority of the gambling action is within a four-block radius of downtown (with the notable exceptions of the Reno Hilton, Peppermill, Clarion, and John Ascuaga's Nugget in Sparks). A car will come in handy for those who want to hike, ski, or visit Virginia City, Lake Tahoe, or Pyramid Lake. A number of bus companies serve the area, making it easy to arrange nearby excursions.

BY BUS

Citifare (4th and Center Sts., ☎ 702/348–7433) operates local buses in Reno 24 hours a day. The fare is $1.

BY TAXI

Reno-Sparks Cab Co. (☎ 702/333–3333), **Whittlesea Checker Taxi** (☎ 702/322–2222), and **Yellow Deluxe Cab Co.** (☎ 702/355–5555) serve the Reno area. The base charge is $1.50 plus $1.40 per mile.

BY TRAIN

Amtrak (☎ 800/872–7245) provides daily service on the *California Zephyr,* westbound to San Francisco in the morning and eastbound toward Chicago in the evening. The passenger trains stop at 135 East Commercial Row, right in the middle of downtown, snarling traffic—an amusing reminder that Reno is Reno thanks to the railroad.

Guided Tours

Sierra Nevada Stage Lines/Gray Line Tours (2050 Glendale Ave., Sparks, ☎ 702/331–1147 or 800/822–6009) has daily tours in Reno and from Reno to Virginia City and Lake Tahoe. Passengers are picked up at, and returned to, their hotels.

Important Addresses and Numbers

EMERGENCIES

Police, fire, ambulance (☎ 911).

HOSPITAL EMERGENCY ROOMS

Washoe Medical Center (77 Pringle Way at Mill St., ☎ 702/328–4140) and **St. Mary's Regional Medical Center** (235 W. 6th St., ☎ 702/789–3188) have 24-hour medical service.

PHARMACY

Shopko (6139 S. Virginia St., ☎ 702/852–0700) is open weekdays 9–9, Saturday 9–6, Sunday 10–6.

VISITOR INFORMATION

Reno-Sparks Convention and Visitors Authority (4590 S. Virginia St., Reno, NV 89502, ☎ 702/827–7366 or 800/367–7366).

LAKE TAHOE

An oasis amid Nevada's arid deserts, Lake Tahoe's vast expanse of crystal-blue water surrounded by rugged mountain peaks and dense forests of Ponderosa pines has become a favorite playground for natives and tourists alike. Tahoe offers some of the country's best downhill ski resorts in the winter, boating and fishing in the summer, and casino entertainment 24 hours a day, every day of the year.

Although the California–Nevada border officially divides the lake from north to south, Lake Tahoe's character also reflects an east–west split. The woodsier north shore has a few scattered casinos on the Nevada side and rustic condominiums on the California side, whereas the more-developed south shore has 18-story luxury casinos clustered on the Nevada state line and blocks of small motels and restaurants on the California side. A scenic road circling Tahoe offers stunning vistas of lake, forest, and mountain.

Exploring

This tour covers the Nevada side of Lake Tahoe, traveling from north to south.

Numbers in the margin correspond to points of interest on the Lake Tahoe map.

To reach Lake Tahoe from Reno, drive south on U.S. 395 to Highway 431 (the Mt. Rose road), and take it over the summit (8,911 feet) and down to Highway 28.

1 Two miles north on Highway 28, **Crystal Bay** is Nevada's northernmost community on Lake Tahoe's shores. Don't expect the flash of Las Vegas or the "biggest little city" atmosphere of Reno. Crystal Bay has more of a small-town, outdoorsy feel. The **Cal-Neva Lodge** (2 Stateline Rd., Crystal Bay, ☎ 702/832–4000) is one of the area's most popular casinos. In the 1950s, Frank Sinatra co-owned this casino/hotel, until he was seen in the company of a prominent gangster. The Nevada Gaming Control Board forced Sinatra to sell his share in the property, on the grounds that it was illegal for gaming licensees to hobnob with known mobsters. Today, the exterior of the Cal-Neva has a dated, '50s look, but the interior has undergone a complete renovation. A spacious, mountain-lodge sitting room with an immense stone fireplace and a stuffed deer and elk create an Old West feel.

2 Just a few miles south on Highway 28 is **Incline Village,** one of Tahoe's most attractive communities, with affluent lakeshore homes, contemporary redwood condominiums, and inviting shopping areas, as well as plenty of outdoor diversions—hiking and biking trails and the area's greatest concentration of tennis courts. A **Recreation Center** (980 Incline Way, ☎ 702/832–1300) features an eight-lane swimming pool, a cardiovascular-fitness area, a basketball court, and a snack shop. The **Hyatt Lake Tahoe** (Country Club Dr. at Lakeshore, ☎ 702/832–1234 or 800/233–1234), Incline's only hotel-casino, offers gambling in an elegant setting, first-rate guest rooms, and a lakeshore dinner restaurant.

3 Fans of the longtime television series *Bonanza* can visit the **Ponderosa Ranch,** at the southeast edge of Incline Village on Highway 28. The Cartwrights' home is set in a Hollywood-style Western town, complete with a Pettin' Farm, Moonshine Shootin' Gallery, and Hossburgers. There's also a self-guided nature trail, free pony rides for children, and, if you're here from 8 to 9:30 in the morning, a breakfast hayride. ☎ *702/831–0691.* ☛ *$8.50 adults, $5.50 children 5–11, hayride $2.* ⏲ *Mid-Apr.–Oct., daily 9:30–5.*

4 Traveling south along the east side of the lake, you'll come across **Sand Harbor Beach,** a popular recreation area that often reaches capacity

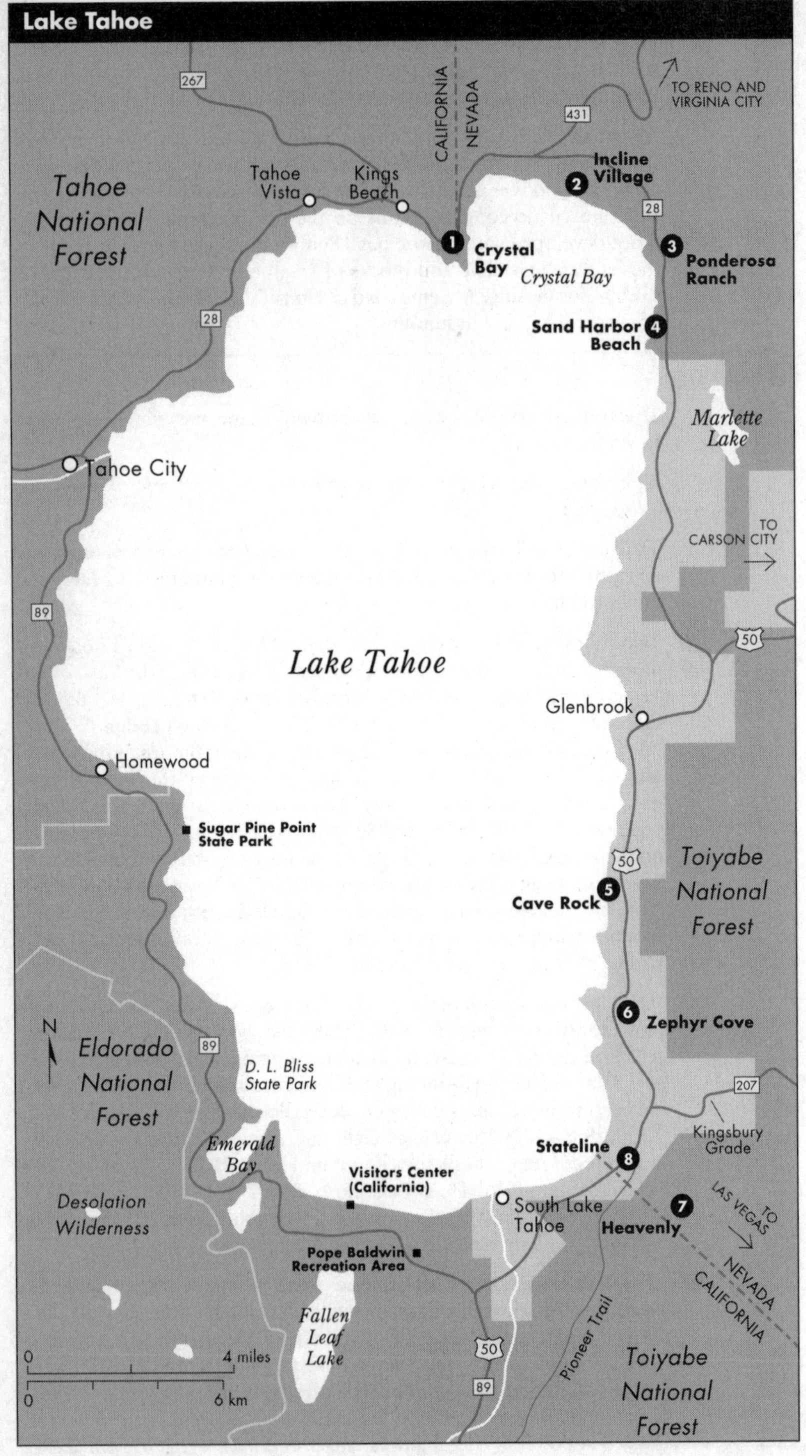
Lake Tahoe
267
CALIFORNIA
NEVADA
TO RENO AND VIRGINIA CITY
431
Tahoe National Forest
Tahoe Vista
Kings Beach
Incline Village
28
Crystal Bay
Crystal Bay
Ponderosa Ranch
28
Sand Harbor Beach
Marlette Lake
Tahoe City
TO CARSON CITY
89
50
Lake Tahoe
Glenbrook
Homewood
Sugar Pine Point State Park
50
Toiyabe National Forest
Cave Rock
Zephyr Cove
N
Eldorado National Forest
89
D. L. Bliss State Park
207
Kingsbury Grade
Emerald Bay
Stateline
Visitors Center (California)
Desolation Wilderness
South Lake Tahoe
Heavenly
TO LAS VEGAS
Pope Baldwin Recreation Area
NEVADA
CALIFORNIA
Fallen Leaf Lake
Pioneer Trail
0
4 miles
0
6 km
50
89
Toiyabe National Forest

by 11 AM on weekends. In July the beach hosts a pop-music festival; in August it's the site of a Shakespeare festival (☎ 702/832–1606) in which performances take place on the beach under the stars.

5 Next you will meet U.S. 50 and wind through the forests along the
lakeshore. The road passes through one of Tahoe's landmarks, **Cave**
Rock, a tunnel cut through 25 yards of stone (it's one of only three tunnels in all of Nevada). Tahoe Tessie, the local version of the Loch Ness
monster, is reputed to live in a cavern below. About 6 miles south of
6 Cave Rock, you'll come to **Zephyr Cove,** a tiny resort with a beach,
marina, campground, picnic area, historic log lodge, and nearby riding stables. From late April to early November, the MS *Dixie II* sails
from here to Emerald Bay, one of the most beautiful spots on the lake.
☎ *702/588–3508.* ☛ *$14–$35 adults, $5–$10 children 4–12; food*
is additional. Lunch and dinner cruises.

A short distance past Zephyr Cove, just before the towering casinos and
neon lights of Stateline, Kingsbury Grade (Route 207) goes off to the
left (east). This was originally a toll road used by wagon trains to get
7 over the Sierras' crest. Now it leads to the Nevada side of **Heavenly** (☎
916/541–1330 or 800/243–2836), America's largest ski resort, with
all levels of terrain on both the California and Nevada sides of the mountain. Whether you're a skier or not, you'll want to ride 2,000 feet up
on the 50-passenger **Heavenly Tram,** which runs part way up the mountain, to 8,200 feet. There you'll find a memorable view of Lake Tahoe
and the Nevada desert. ☎ *702/586–7000.* ☛ *Round-trip tram fare: $12*
adults, $6 senior citizens and children under 12; after 6 PM, adults $8.
⏲ *Tram runs June–Sept., daily 10–10; Oct.–May, daily 9–4.*

Past Heavenly, Kingsbury Grade continues east. It's a steep and winding road down to Carson Valley, with spectacular views all along the way. At the bottom of Route 207, turn left on Foothill Road (Route 206), which leads past **Walley's Hot Springs Resort** (2001 Foothill Rd., ☎ 702/782–8155), a small lodge with natural hot-spring pools (☛ $12, no children under 12). Beyond the resort you'll soon come to **Genoa,** the oldest settlement in Nevada, which hosts two good museums, Mormon Station State Park, and the state's oldest saloon, the Genoa Bar—all on the main street.

8 If you don't turn off at Kingsbury Grade, when you arrive in **Stateline** **Park** in one of the hotel lots, and walk. Five casinos are clustered together within one long block just east of the California–Nevada state border.

Harvey's Resort Hotel and Casino (☎ 702/588–2411 or 800/553–1022) is where gambling in Lake Tahoe all began. The hub of this towering casino is the original Wagon Wheel Saloon and Gambling Hall, established in 1944 by Harvey Gross. At the time, it was a six-stool counter with three slot machines and a 24-hour gas pump, the only service between Placerville and Carson City. Today, Tahoe's largest resort offers well-appointed rooms, eight restaurants, 10 cocktail lounges, and a complete health spa. Games include blackjack, craps, pai gow, roulette, baccarat, and many slot machines.

A pedestrian tunnel beneath Highway 50 connects Harvey's to **Harrah's Casino/Hotel Lake Tahoe** (☎ 702/588–6611 or 800/648–3773). This luxurious hotel offers spacious rooms with views of the lake and the mountains. Top-name entertainment is offered in the South Shore Room and Center State lounge. Gamblers will enjoy the more than 150 table games, including blackjack, craps, baccarat, keno, roulette, poker, big six, pai gow, and bingo, as well as more than 1,500 slot machines.

Harrah's also offers free classes in the table games. While parents gamble, kids can play video games in the supervised children's arcade downstairs.

Harrah's operates a second casino, **Bill's** (☎ 702/588–2455), next door. Open to the street, Bill's is comparatively low-key, with generally lower table minimums, a McDonald's restaurant, and 10¢ popcorn. Bill's is strictly a fun gaming house, not a hotel, and may be less intimidating to novice gamblers.

Caesars Tahoe Resort (Hwy. 50, ☎ 702/588–3515 or 800/648–3353), on the other hand, attracts the high rollers. Roman details are subtle but prevalent in the casino, from laurel-wreath designs in the carpet to the waitresses' toga-style dresses. Games include craps, 21, roulette, big six, baccarat, sic bo, pai gow, and, of course, hundreds of slot machines. Caesars also offers a race and sports book. Top-name entertainment is featured in the 1,500-seat Circus Maximus and the Cabaret.

Tahoe Horizon Casino Resort (☎ 702/588–6211 or 800/322–7723) is across the street from Caesars, and has shaken off its dated Western interior for a rich, contemporary look. In a bid to attract upscale patrons, the $15 million renovation follows a French beaux-arts design, with cream-color marble and mirrors. Games include blackjack, craps, roulette, keno, minibaccarat, and many slot machines. The Golden Cabaret features adult revues and production shows.

What to See and Do with Children

With its wealth of outdoor recreation, Lake Tahoe is an easy place to keep children and teenagers entertained. All the ski areas offer children's ski programs and most have child-care facilities. Although children are not allowed in the casinos' gambling areas, all these establishments have game arcades and some, like the Hyatt Regency in Incline Village, offer special youth-oriented activities all day. Among the lake's attractions, the **Ponderosa Ranch** (*see* Exploring, *above*) is usually a big hit with kids.

Commons Beach in the middle of Tahoe City has a playground for children. The **North Tahoe Beach Center** has a 26-foot hot tub, open year-round; in summer, the heat is turned down until 1 PM for youngsters. The beach has an enclosed swim area and four sand volleyball courts. This popular spot for families has a barbecue and picnic area, a fitness center, horseshoes, boat rental and tours (summer only), a snack bar, and a clubhouse with games. *7860 N. Lake Blvd., Kings Beach,* ☎ *916/546–2566.* ☛ *Daily fee: $7 adults, $3.50 children.*

In summer the **Lake Tahoe Visitors Center** (*see* Important Addresses and Numbers *in* Lake Tahoe Essentials, *below*) sets up discovery walks and nighttime campfires, with singing and marshmallow roasts.

Off the Beaten Track

Donner Memorial State Park (off I–80, 2 mi west of Truckee) commemorates the Donner Party, a group of 89 westward-bound pioneers who were trapped here in the winter of 1846–47 in snow 22 feet deep. Only 47 survived, some by cannibalism and others by eating animal hides. The Immigrant Trail Museum offers a slide show hourly about the Donner Party's plight. Additional displays relate the history of other settlers and of railroad development through the Sierras. ☎ *916/582–7892.* ☛ *$2 adults, $1 children 6–17.* ⏲ *Sept.–May, daily 10–4; June–Aug. daily 10–5. Closed Dec. 25, Jan. 1.*

Old West facades line the main street of nearby Truckee, a favorite stopover for people traveling from the San Francisco Bay area to the north shore of Lake Tahoe. Fine-art galleries and upscale boutiques are plentiful, but you will also find low-key diners, discount skiwear, and an old-fashioned five-and-dime store. For a map outlining a walking tour of historic Truckee, stop by the information booth in the Amtrak depot.

Shopping

In South Lake Tahoe there's some good shopping south of town at the intersection of Routes 50 and 89, at the **Factory Outlet Stores.** In Tahoe City, try **Boatworks Mall** (780 N. Lake Blvd.), Cobblestone Mall (475 N. Lake Blvd.), and the **Roundhouse Mall** (700 N. Lake Blvd.).

Participant Sports

For most of the popular sports at Lake Tahoe, summer or winter, you won't have to bring much equipment with you. Bicycles and boats are readily available for rental at Lake Tahoe. Golf clubs can be rented at several area courses. All of the major ski resorts have rental shops.

Boating

Lake Tahoe draws boat, water-ski, and Jet Ski enthusiasts. Keep in mind that the water at Lake Tahoe is always cold—you'll need a wet suit. **North Tahoe Marina** (7360 N. Lake Blvd., Tahoe Vista, ☎ 916/546–8248) rents powerboats, ski boats, water-ski equipment, and private party boats. It also offers fishing charters. **Zephyr Cove Resort** (4 mi north of the south shore casinos, in Zephyr Cove, ☎ 702/588–3833) features powerboats, ski boats, Jet Skis, parasailing, and fishing charters.

Golf

These courses in the Lake Tahoe area have food facilities, pro shops, cart rentals, and putting greens.

Edgewood Tahoe (U.S. 50 and Lake Pkwy., behind Horizon Casino, Stateline, ☎ 702/588–3566) is an 18-hole, par-72 course with a driving range. Greens fees include carts.

Incline Championship (955 Fairway Blvd., Incline Village, ☎ 702/832–1144) is another 18-hole, par-72 course with a driving range. Carts are mandatory.

Incline Executive (690 Wilson Way, Incline Village, ☎ 702/832–1150) has 18 holes but is much easier: Par is 58.

Lake Tahoe Golf Course (U.S. 50, between South Lake Tahoe Airport and Meyers, ☎ 916/577–0788) has 18 holes, par 70, and a driving range.

Northstar-at-Tahoe (Rte. 267, between Truckee and Kings Beach, ☎ 916/562–2490) has 18 holes, par 72, with a driving range.

Old Brockway Golf Course (Rtes. 267 and 28, Kings Beach, ☎ 916/546–9909) is a nine-hole, par-35 course.

Resort at Squaw Creek Golf Course (400 Squaw Creek Rd., Olympic Valley, ☎ 916/583–6300) is an 18-hole par-71 championship course designed by Robert Trent Jones, Jr.

Tahoe City Golf Course (Rte. 28, Tahoe City, ☎ 916/583–1516) is a nine-hole, par-33 course.

Tahoe Paradise Golf Course (Rte. 50 near Meyers, South Lake Tahoe, ☎ 916/577–2121) has 18 holes, par 66.

Hiking and Camping

Desolation Wilderness, a 63,473-acre preserve of granite peaks, glacial valleys, subalpine forests, the Rubicon River, and more than 50 lakes, offers hiking, fishing, and camping. Trails begin outside the wilderness preserve; Meeks Bay and Echo Lake are two starting points. Permits (free) are required for access and can be obtained from the **U.S. Forest Service's Lake Tahoe Visitors Center** (*see* Important Addresses and Numbers *in* Lake Tahoe Essentials, *below*), the **Desolation Wilderness** headquarters (870 Emerald Bay Rd., Suite 1, South Lake Tahoe, CA 96150, ☎ 916/573–2600 or 916/573–2674), and the **El Dorado National Forest** (☎ 916/644–6048).

D. L. Bliss State Park (☎ 916/525–7277), near Emerald Bay, has 168 family campsites; the fee is $14 per campsite. There's a $5 day-use fee for entering the park; the park is closed in winter.

Skiing

The Tahoe Basin ski resorts offer the largest concentration of skiing in the country: 15 downhill ski resorts and 11 cross-country ski centers, with more cross-country skiing available on thousands of acres of public forests and parklands. The major resorts are listed below, but other, smaller places also offer excellent skiing. To save money, look for ski packages offered by lodges and resorts; some include interchangeable lift tickets that allow you to try different slopes. Midweek packages are usually lower in price.

DOWNHILL SKIING

Alpine Meadows Ski Area is a ski cruiser's paradise, with skiing from two peaks—Ward, a great open bowl, and Scott, for tree-lined runs. All main runs are groomed nightly. Alpine has some of Tahoe's most reliable skiing conditions and an excellent snowmaking system; it's usually the first in the area to open each November and the last to close, in May or even June. The base lodge contains rentals, a cafeteria, restaurant-lounge, bar, bakery, sports shop, ski schools for skiers of all skill levels and skiers with disabilities, and a children's snow school; there's also an area for overnight RV parking. Beginner runs are close to the base lodge. Ski from every lift; there are no "transportation" lifts. *6 mi northwest of Tahoe City off Rte. 89, 13 mi south of I–80, Box 5279, Tahoe City, NV 96145,* ☎ *916/583–4232, snow phone 916/581–8374, information 800/441–4423;* FAX *916/583–0963.*

Diamond Peak has a fun, family atmosphere with many special programs and affordable rates. A learn-to-ski package, including rentals, lesson, and lift ticket, is $32; a parent-child ski package is $40, with each additional child's lift ticket $6. There is a half-pipe run just for snowboarding. Snowmaking covers 80% of the mountain, and runs are well groomed nightly. The ride up mile-long Crystal chair rewards you with one of the best views of the lake from any ski area. Diamond Peak is less crowded than some of the larger areas, and it offers free shuttles to lodging in nearby Incline Village. There's Nordic skiing here, too (*see* Cross-Country Skiing, *below*). *1210 Ski Way, Incline Village, NV 89450, off Rte. 28 (Country Club Dr. to Ski Way),* ☎ *702/832–1177 or 800/468–2463,* FAX *702/832–1281.*

Heavenly Ski Resort gives skiers plenty of choices. Go up the Heavenly Tram on the California side (*see* Exploring, *above*) to ski the imposing face of Gunbarrel or the gentler runs at the top, or ride the Sky Express high-speed quad chair to the summit and choose wide cruising runs or steep tree skiing. Or drive over the Kingsbury Grade to the Boulder or Stagecoach lodges and stay on the Nevada-side runs, which are usually less crowded. Snowmaking covers both sides, top to bottom, for generally good conditions. The ski school, like everything else at Heavenly, is large and offers a program for everyone, beginner to expert. *Ski Run Blvd., Box 2180, Stateline, NV 89449,* ☎ *916/541–1330 or 800/243–2836, snow information 916/541–7544;* FAX *916/541–2643.*

Kirkwood Ski Resort lies 36 miles south of Lake Tahoe in an Alpine-village setting, surrounded by incredible mountain scenery. Most of the runs off the top are rated expert only, but intermediate and beginning skiers have their own vast bowl, where they can ski through trees or wide-open spaces. This is a destination resort, with 120 condominiums, several shops, and restaurants in the base village; overnight RV parking; and a shuttle bus to Lake Tahoe. There's snowboarding on all runs, with lessons, rentals, and sales available. (For Nordic skiing, *see* Cross-Country Skiing, *below.*) *Rte. 88, Box 1, Kirkwood, NV 95646,* ☎ *209/258–6000, lodging information 209/258–6000, snow information 209/258–3000;* FAX *209/258–8899.*

Northstar-at-Tahoe is the Sierras' most complete destination resort, with lots of activity in summer and winter. The center of action is the picturesque Village Mall, a concentration of restaurants, shops, recreation facilities, and lodging options from hotel rooms to condos and houses. Two northeast-facing, wind-protected bowls offer some of the best powder skiing around, including steep chutes and long cruising runs. Top-to-bottom snowmaking and intense grooming assure good conditions. There are also lessons, rentals, and sales. (For Nordic skiing, *see* Cross-Country Skiing, *below.*) *Off Rte. 267, between Truckee and North Shore, Box 129, Truckee, NV 96160, lodging reservations* ☎ *916/562–1010 or 800/533–6787, snow information 916/562–1330;* FAX *916/562–2215.*

Squaw Valley USA was the site of 1960 Olympics. The immense resort has changed significantly since then, but the skiing is still first class, with steep chutes and cornices on six Sierra peaks. Beginners delight in riding the tram to the top, where there is a huge plateau of gentle runs. At the top of the tram you can reach the High Camp Bath and Tennis Club in the lodge with impressive views from its restaurants, bars, and outdoor ice-skating pavilion. Base facilities are clustered around the Village Mall, with shops, dining, condos, hotels, and lodges. The valley golf course doubles as a cross-country ski facility. On the other side of the golf course is the Resort at Squaw Creek, with its own run and quad chairlift that runs to Squaw's ski terrain. *Rte. 89, 5 mi northwest of Tahoe City, Squaw Valley USA, NV 96146,* ☎ *916/583–6985, reservations 800/545–4350, snow information 916/583–6955;* FAX *916/581–7106.*

CROSS-COUNTRY SKIING

With 11 areas to choose from on mountaintops and in valleys, this is a Nordic skier's paradise. For the ultimate in groomed conditions, there is America's largest cross-country ski resort, **Royal Gorge** (Box 1100, Soda Springs, CA 95728, ☎ 916/426–3871), which offers 317 kilometers of 18-foot-wide track for all abilities, 88 trails on 9,172 acres, two ski schools, and 10 warming huts, as well as four cafés, two hotels, and a hot tub and sauna.

Diamond Peak at Ski Incline (☎ 702/832–1177) has 35 kilometers of groomed track with skating lanes. The trail system goes from 7,400 feet to 9,100 feet with endless wilderness to explore. The entrance is off Route 431.

Kirkwood Ski Resort (*see* Downhill Skiing, *above*) has 80 kilometers of groomed-track skiing, with skating lanes, instruction, and rentals.

Northstar-at-Tahoe (*see* Downhill Skiing, *above*) gives cross-country skiers access to Alpine ski slopes for telemarking and also provides 65 kilometers of groomed, tracked trails with a wide skating lane. There's a ski shop, rentals, and instruction.

Skiers who want to tour the backcountry should check with the **U.S. Forest Service** (☎ 916/587–2158) prior to entering the wilderness.

Sledding and Snowmobiling

There are five public **Sno-Park** areas in the vicinity, some for snowmobiling and cross-country skiing, as well as sledding. All are maintained by the California Department of Parks and Recreation; an advance permit is required. Call the parks department at 916/653–8569 or contact the Lake Tahoe Visitor Center (*see* Important Addresses and Numbers *in* Lake Tahoe Essentials, *below*).

Several companies in the area offer snowmobile tours. **Snowmobiling Unlimited** (Box 460, Carnelian Bay, CA 96140, ☎ 916/583–5858), one of the area's oldest operators, offers guided tours and rentals, as well as a track to zoom around on, for $25 per half hour.

Swimming

There are 36 public beaches on Lake Tahoe. Swimming is permitted at many of them, but since Tahoe is a high mountain lake with fairly rugged winters, only the hardiest will be interested, except in midsummer. Even then the water warms to only 68°F. Lifeguards are on duty at some of the swimming beaches, and yellow buoys mark safe areas where motorboats are not permitted. Opening and closing dates for beaches vary with the climate and available park-service personnel. There may be a parking fee from $1 to $4.

Dining

At all Tahoe restaurants, make advance reservations for weekends, and plan to wait for the coffee shops and buffets that don't take reservations. Because Tahoe is a resort area, dress tends to be casual, even in the more expensive restaurants.

CATEGORY	COST*
$$$$	over $30
$$$	$20–$30
$$	$12–$20
$	under $12

**per person for a three-course meal, excluding drinks, service, and 7% sales tax*

North Tahoe Area

$$$–$$$$ **Lone Eagle Grille.** A Hyatt restaurant, this is the best place on the north shore to come for dining with a view. Located on the lakeshore in a wooded setting, it is a short downhill walk from the hotel. Specialties are rotisserie duck and chicken, prime rib, and mesquite-broiled fish and steaks. ✕ *Country Club Dr. at Lakeshore, Incline Village,* ☎ *702/832–1234. Reservations advised. AE, D, DC, MC, V. No lunch. Sun. brunch.*

$$–$$$ ★ **Soule Domain.** A cozy, romantic, 1927 pine-log cabin with stone fireplace is the setting for some of Lake Tahoe's most creative and delicious dinners. Chef-owner Charles Edward Soule IV uses fresh foods and herbs to create such specialties as filet mignon with shiitake mushrooms, Gorgonzola, and brandy or tuna grilled with papaya-mango salsa. ✕ *On Cove St. across from Tahoe Biltmore, Crystal Bay, ☎ 916/546–7529. Reservations advised. AE, DC, MC, V. No lunch.*

$ **Lake View Dining Room.** Eggs, burgers, salads, and steaks are served 7 AM–11 PM before a wide lakeside view in the Cal-Neva Casino. ✕ *2 Stateline Rd., Crystal Bay, ☎ 702/832–4000. AE, D, DC, MC, V.*

$ **Sierra Cafe.** Located downstairs in the Hyatt, this coffee shop has a touch of elegance. Padded, burgundy-leather booths, upholstered chairs, a large brick fireplace, and an abundance of greenery add to the ambience. You can order from the menu, or go for the Sierra's buffet. This is the place to bring the kids if you're staying at the Hyatt. ✕ *Country Club Dr. at Lakeshore, Incline Village, ☎ 702/832–1234. No reservations. AE, D, DC, MC, V. ⏲ Daily 24 hrs.*

South Tahoe Area

$$$$ **The Summit.** On the 16th floor of Harrah's, in the former Star Suite (once the home-away-from-home of visiting royalty and celebrities), this intimate, restaurant with balcony offers romantic dining with spectacular views of Lake Tahoe. A tuxedo-clad pianist plays the grand by candlelight while a fire crackles in the immense hearth. The creative menu includes quail with prune sauce for an appetizer; artfully presented salads; lamb, wild game, or seafood entrées with delicate sauces; and such sensuous desserts as soufflé with vanilla cream sauce. ✕ *Harrah's Hotel/Casino, Stateline, ☎ 702/588–6606 or 800/648–3773. Reservations advised. Jacket and tie. AE, DC, MC, V.*

$$$–$$$$ **Empress Court.** Plush velvet booths, etched-glass partitions, and linen tablecloths prove that "elegant Chinese" is not an oxymoron. Empress Court serves traditional Chinese dishes as well as such specialties as grilled squab salad, seasoned deep-fried pork ribs, and satay beef. Even the fortune cookies—dribbled with sweet chocolate—look impressive. ✕ *Caesars Tahoe Resort, Stateline, ☎ 702/588–3515 or 800/648–3353. Reservations advised. AE, DC, MC, V.*

$$–$$$ **Sage Room Steak House.** In the center of Harvey's casino, this romantic restaurant is far removed from the flashing lights and slot machine jangles. Elegant but unpretentious service is the rule, with steak Diana and bananas Foster flamed table-side. Specialties include Dungeness-crab cocktail, black-bean soup, mesquite-broiled quail and ragout of boar or venison, and an award-winning wine list. ✕ *Harvey's Resort Hotel/Casino, Stateline, ☎ 702/588–2411 or 800/648–3361. Reservations advised. AE, D, DC, MC, V.*

$–$$ **El Vaquero.** Harvey's Mexican restaurant is downstairs, in the hotel's shopping arcade, far from the slots and gaming tables. Decorated with wrought iron, a fountain, and tiles, giving an authentic Old Mexico feel, El Vaquero serves traditional Mexican fare, such as carne asada, enchiladas, and chimichangas. ✕ *Harvey's Resort Hotel/Casino, Stateline, ☎ 702/588–2411 or 800/648–3361. Reservations advised. AE, D, DC, MC, V.*

$ **Sierra.** Harrah's casual coffee shop is pleasantly decorated with upholstered booths, brass lanterns on the walls, and lots of greenery. Hearty dinners—most less than $10—include old-fashioned meat loaf, Cajun catfish, ravioli, and sandwiches. Asia, a dimly lit section at the back, offers Chinese, Vietnamese, Korean, and other Pacific Rim specialties. ✕ *Harrah's Casino/Hotel, Stateline, ☎ 702/588–6611 or 800/648–3773. No reservations. AE, D, DC, MC, V.*

Lodging

In addition to the Nevada casino-hotels described here, many small, less-expensive motels are clustered on the California side of Lake Tahoe's south shore. Free shuttle buses provide convenient access between south shore motels and casinos. Some inexpensive choices in the area include **Lakeside Inn** (Hwy. 50 at Kingsbury Grade, ☎ 702/588–7777 or 800/624–7980), the only low-rise casino in Stateline, and a short car ride from the main hotels at the border; **Tropicana Lodge** (4132 Cedar Ave., off Stateline Ave., ☎ 916/541–3911 or 800/447–0246), the quintessential California resort motel, clean and cheap; and **Day's Inn** (3530 Lake Tahoe Blvd., 1 mi west of Stateline, ☎ 916/544–3445 or 800/350–3446), which offers good rates and no surprises.

CATEGORY	COST*
$$$$	over $100
$$$	$75–$100
$$	$50–$75
$	under $50

**All prices are for a standard double room, excluding 8% tax and service charge.*

North Tahoe Area

$$$$ **Hyatt Lake Tahoe.** At this elegant, four-star resort, all of the guest rooms have a view of the lake. Blond-wood furniture, oversize beds with lots of extra pillows, warm color schemes, and minibars lend the guest rooms an understated luxury. The hotel is a block from a private beach, where guests can enjoy Jet Ski and speedboat rentals and a lakeside restaurant. The casino is classy, not flashy, offering all the traditional games plus a sports book and live entertainment. Camp Hyatt (for ages 3–12) and Rock Hyatt (for ages 13–17) offer supervised indoor and outdoor games, meals, movies, and sightseeing throughout the summer and on weekends and holidays year-round. *Country Club Dr. at Lakeshore, Incline Village 89450, ☎ 702/832–1234 or 800/233–1234, FAX 702/831–7508. 460 rooms. 3 restaurants, pool, tennis courts, health club, beach. AE, D, DC, MC, V.*

$$$–$$$$ **Cal-Neva Lodge Resort Hotel/Casino.** Cal-Neva is the oldest hotel on the lake and the only casino in Nevada that qualifies as a "lodge." Rooms are upscale, with Country French armoires and dressers and floral bedspreads. All rooms have lake views. This hotel-casino is a five-minute walk from Lake Tahoe's shores. *2 Stateline Rd., Crystal Bay 89402, ☎ 702/832–4000 or 800/225–6382, FAX 702/831–9007. 220 rooms. 2 restaurants, pool, massage, spa, tennis courts, health club. AE, DC, MC, V.*

$ **Tahoe Biltmore.** Across the street from the Cal-Neva Lodge, the Biltmore is a bargain for those seeking an alternative to the bustle of South Lake Tahoe and the expense of the Hyatt. Room rates average $65 in the high season (and can get as low as $27 in the low season), and the lake isn't far off. Built in 1946, this '50s-style resort features dark wood and has a rustic-lodge feel, but don't expect it to be as nice or well kept as its more expensive neighbor. The large, smoky casino offers table games such as poker and keno, and lots of slots. *5 Hwy. 28, Crystal Bay 89402, ☎ 702/831–0660 or 800/245–8667, FAX 702/832–7675. 86 rooms. Restaurant, pool. AE, D, DC, MC, V.*

South Tahoe Area

$$$$ **Caesars Tahoe.** For easy access to the registration desk, enter through the doors nearest valet parking. Once upstairs, you'll find faux Corinthian columns in the hallway, and plush rooms in gray, mauve, and mint green. Most rooms have round Roman tubs. The pool is indoors, with a waterfall and a swim tunnel through a man-made rock. *Box 5800, Stateline 89449, ☎ 702/588–3515 or 800/648–3353, FAX 702/586–2050. 440 rooms. 5 restaurants, lounge, indoor pool, tennis courts, health club, nightclub, showroom. AE, DC, MC, V.*

$$$$ **Harrah's Casino/Hotel Lake Tahoe.** The most ostentatiously luxurious hotel on the south shore, Harrah's provides spacious, comfortable rooms, most offering superb views of the lake and mountains. Each guest room comes with a minibar and two full bathrooms—and each bathroom has its own color TV and telephone. Downstairs are a heated indoor pool, two hot tubs, and a complete health club. ☒ *Box 8, Stateline 89449,* ☎ *702/588–6611 or 800/648–3773,* FAX *702/586–6607. 534 rooms. 7 restaurants, pool, health club, kennel. AE, DC, MC, V.*

$$$–$$$$ **Harvey's Resort Hotel/Casino.** This family-owned hotel is Tahoe's largest resort. The reception area is one flight down from the casino, completely removed from the frenetic gaming atmosphere. The rooms are elegantly but comfortably furnished in "American traditional" with Colonial and French Provincial accents, featuring soft color schemes and marble-tiled baths. Most rooms have excellent lake and mountain views. Llewellyn's, Harvey's four-star, 19th-floor restaurant, offers fine dining with panoramic views. ☒ *Box 128, Stateline 89449,* ☎ *702/588–2411 or 800/648–3361,* FAX *702/588–6643. 740 rooms. 9 restaurants, pool, health club, tennis courts, convention center. AE, DC, MC, V.*

$$–$$$$ **Horizon Casino/Resort.** Formerly the Old West–style High Sierra, this hotel underwent a $15 million renovation in a bid to attract upscale patrons; the casino and lobby now sport a beaux-arts look, with Italian-marble floors, brass highlights, and lots of mirrors. Games include blackjack, craps, roulette, keno, mini-baccarat, and slot machines. The Grand Lake Theater offers top-name entertainment, and the Golden Cabaret features revues, magicians, and smaller-scale production numbers. The hotel's restaurants include Le Grande Buffet, Continental cuisine at Josh's, and bistro sandwiches and specialty coffees at the 24-hour Four Seasons cafeteria. ☒ *Box C, Stateline 89449,* ☎ *702/588–6211 or 800/322–7723,* FAX *702/588–3110. 539 rooms. 3 restaurants, pool, wading pool, 3 hot tubs. AE, DC, MC, V.*

Nightlife

You will find top-name entertainment and production shows at the casinos. The **Circus Maximus** at Caesars Tahoe, **Emerald Theater** at Harvey's, and the **South Shore Room,** a 950-seat theater at Harrah's, are as large as some Broadway houses. Typical headliners include David Copperfield, the Moody Blues, and Diana Ross.

Sometimes there are two performances a night in the big showrooms, and reservations are almost always required for superstars. Cocktail shows usually run $20–$40, including tax and one drink. Smaller casino cabarets sometimes have a cover charge or drink minimum. Casino lounges have no cover charges, and they feature jazz and pop musicians; the last set usually ends at 2:30 or 3 AM.

Lounges around the lake often offer pop and country music singers and musicians, and in winter the ski resorts do the same. **Turtles** (☎ 916/544–5400) is a fun spot for dancing in the luxurious Embassy Suites, just across the state line from Harrah's; a DJ spins Top 40 tunes and oldies. Summer alternatives are outdoor music events, from chamber quartets to jazz bands and rock performers, at **Sand Harbor** (Hwy. 28, 5 mi south of Incline Village, ☎ 702/832–1606) and the **Lake Tahoe Visitors Center amphitheater** (Hwy. 89, 6 mi north of junction of Hwy. 89 and Hwy. 50, ☎ 916/573–2674 in summer, 916/573–2600 rest of the year); summer at Sand Harbor also includes the Sand Harbor Shakespeare Festival (☎ 702/832–1606).

Lake Tahoe Essentials

Arriving and Departing

BY BUS

Greyhound (☎ 800/231–2222) stops in Truckee and Stateline.

BY CAR

The major route is I–80, which cuts through the Sierra Nevada about 14 miles north of the lake; from there CA 89 and CA 267 reach the north shore. U.S. 50 is the more direct highway to the south shore. U.S. 395 runs 35 miles south from Reno to Carson City; U.S. 50 to the lake intersects with U.S. 395 at the south end of town. NV 431 connects the south end of Reno to the north end of the lake in 35 miles.

BY PLANE

Tahoe Casino Express (☎ 702/785–2424 or 800/446–6128) provides service from the Reno airport (*see* Reno Essentials *in* Reno, *above*) to Lake Tahoe's south shore casinos; **Aero-Trans** (☎ 702/786–2376) and **Reno-Tahoe Connection** (☎ 702/825–3900) serve the north shore.

BY TRAIN

There is an **Amtrak** station in Truckee (☎ 800/872–7245).

Getting Around

BY BUS

South Tahoe Area Ground Express (STAGE, ☎ 916/573–2080) runs 24 hours along U.S. 50 and through the neighborhoods of South Lake Tahoe. On the lake's west and north shores, **Tahoe Area Regional Transit** (TART, ☎ 916/581–6365 or 800/736–6365) runs between Tahoma (from Meeks Bay in summer) and Incline Village daily 6:30–6:30. Free shuttle buses run among the casinos, major ski resorts, and motels of South Lake Tahoe.

BY CAR

The scenic 72-mile highway around the lake is marked Route 89 on the southwest and west, Route 28 on the north and northeast shores, and U.S. 50 on the southeast. It takes about three hours to drive, but allow plenty of extra time—heavy traffic on busy holiday weekends can prolong the trip, and there are frequent road repairs in summer.

In winter, sections of Route 89 may be closed, making it impossible to complete the circular drive—call 702/793–1313 to check road conditions. I–80, U.S. 50, and U.S. 395 are all-weather highways, but there may be delays during major storms. Carry tire chains from October to May (car-rental agencies provide them with rental cars).

BY TAXI

Sierra Taxi (☎ 916/577–8888) serves the south shore. **Yellow Cab** (☎ 916/546–3181) serves all of Tahoe Basin. On the north shore, try **Tahoe Taxi** (☎ 916/583–8294).

Guided Tours

BOAT

The ***Tahoe Queen*** (☎ 916/541–3364 or 800/238–2463) is a glass-bottom stern-wheeler that makes 2½-hour lake cruises year-round from Ski Run Marina off U.S. 50 in South Lake Tahoe; sunset and dinner cruises are also offered. Fares are $16–$20 adults, $6–$10 children; in winter, the boat shuttles skiers to north-shore ski areas on weekdays for $20 round-trip.

AIR

CalVada Seaplanes Inc. (☎ 916/525–7143) provides rides over the lake for $45–$81 per person, depending on the length of the trip.

ORIENTATION

Gray Line (☎ 702/331–1147 or 800/822–6009) runs daily tours to South Lake Tahoe, Carson City, and Virginia City. Another good tour provider is **Tahoe Limousine Service** (Box 9909, South Lake Tahoe 96158, ☎ 916/544–2220 or 800/334–1826).

Important Addresses and Numbers

EMERGENCIES

Dial 911 for police or ambulance in an emergency, or call the **California Highway Patrol** (☎ 916/587–3510) or the **Nevada Highway Patrol** (☎ 702/687–5300).

VISITOR INFORMATION

Lake Tahoe Visitors Authority (1156 Ski Run Blvd., South Lake Tahoe, CA 96150, ☎ 916/544–5050 or 800/288–2463) provides information and lodging reservations for the south shore.

For those who are driving a car around the lake, **Lake Tahoe Visitors Center** (Taylor Creek, ☎ 916/573–2674 in season; 916/573–2600 off-season), operated by the U.S. Forest Service, offers a free cassette player and a tape that tells about points of interest along the way. It's open daily June–September, weekends in October.

Tahoe North Visitors and Convention Bureau (Box 5578, Tahoe City, CA 96145, ☎ 916/583–3494 or 800/824–6348, FAX 916/581–4081) provides information and lodging reservations for the California north shore.

Incline Village/Crystal Bay Chamber of Commerce (969 Tahoe Blvd., Incline Village, NV 89451, ☎ 702/832–1606 or 800/468–2463) stocks information on the Nevada north shore.

Lake Tahoe Hotline (☎ 916/542–4636).

Ski Phone (☎ 415/864–6440) offers around-the-clock ski reports and weather information.

Road Conditions (☎ 702/793–1313 or 415/557–3755 or 800/427–7623).

INDEX

✕ = restaurant, 🏨 = hotel

D

E

M

N

O

T

NOTES

NOTES

NOTES

NOTES

NOTES

NOTES

NOTES

NOTES

Fodor's Travel Publications

Available at bookstores everywhere, or call 1–800–533–6478, 24 hours a day.

Gold Guides

U.S.

Alaska
Arizona
Boston
California
Cape Cod, Martha's Vineyard, Nantucket
The Carolinas & the Georgia Coast
Chicago
Colorado
Florida
Hawaii
Las Vegas, Reno, Tahoe
Los Angeles
Maine, Vermont, New Hampshire
Maui
Miami & the Keys
New England
New Orleans
New York City
Pacific North Coast
Philadelphia & the Pennsylvania Dutch Country
The Rockies
San Diego
San Francisco
Santa Fe, Taos, Albuquerque
Seattle & Vancouver
The South
U.S. & British Virgin Islands
USA
Virginia & Maryland
Waikiki
Washington, D.C.

Foreign

Australia & New Zealand
Austria
The Bahamas
Bermuda
Budapest
Canada
Cancún, Cozumel, Yucatán Peninsula
Caribbean
China
Costa Rica, Belize, Guatemala
Cuba
The Czech Republic & Slovakia
Eastern Europe
Egypt
Europe
Florence, Tuscany & Umbria
France
Germany
Great Britain
Greece
Hong Kong
India
Ireland
Israel
Italy
Japan
Kenya & Tanzania
Korea
London
Madrid & Barcelona
Mexico
Montréal & Québec City
Moscow, St. Petersburg, Kiev
The Netherlands, Belgium & Luxembourg
New Zealand
Norway
Nova Scotia, New Brunswick, Prince Edward Island
Paris
Portugal
Provence & the Riviera
Scandinavia
Scotland
Singapore
South America
South Pacific
Southeast Asia
Spain
Sweden
Switzerland
Thailand
Tokyo
Toronto
Turkey
Vienna & the Danube

Fodor's Special-Interest Guides

Branson
Caribbean Ports of Call
The Complete Guide to America's National Parks
Condé Nast Traveler Caribbean Resort and Cruise Ship Finder
Cruises and Ports of Call
Fodor's London Companion
France by Train
Halliday's New England Food Explorer
Healthy Escapes
Italy by Train
Kodak Guide to Shooting Great Travel Pictures
Shadow Traffic's New York Shortcuts and Traffic Tips
Sunday in New York
Sunday in San Francisco
Walt Disney World, Universal Studios and Orlando
Walt Disney World for Adults
Where Should We Take the Kids? California
Where Should We Take the Kids? Northeast

Special Series

Affordables

Caribbean

Europe

Florida

France

Germany

Great Britain

Italy

London

Paris

Fodor's Bed & Breakfasts and Country Inns

America's Best B&Bs

California's Best B&Bs

Canada's Great Country Inns

Cottages, B&Bs and Country Inns of England and Wales

The Mid-Atlantic's Best B&Bs

New England's Best B&Bs

The Pacific Northwest's Best B&Bs

The South's Best B&Bs

The Southwest's Best B&Bs

The Upper Great Lakes' Best B&Bs

The Berkeley Guides

California

Central America

Eastern Europe

Europe

France

Germany & Austria

Great Britain & Ireland

Italy

London

Mexico

Pacific Northwest & Alaska

Paris

San Francisco

Compass American Guides

Arizona

Chicago

Colorado

Hawaii

Hollywood

Las Vegas

Maine

Manhattan

Montana

New Mexico

New Orleans

Oregon

San Francisco

Santa Fe

South Carolina

South Dakota

Southwest

Texas

Utah

Virginia

Washington

Wine Country

Wisconsin

Wyoming

Fodor's Español

California

Caribe Occidental

Caribe Oriental

Gran Bretaña

Londres

Mexico

Nueva York

Paris

Fodor's Exploring Guides

Australia

Boston & New England

Britain

California

Caribbean

China

Egypt

Florence & Tuscany

Florida

France

Germany

Ireland

Israel

Italy

Japan

London

Mexico

Moscow & St. Petersburg

New York City

Paris

Prague

Provence

Rome

San Francisco

Scotland

Singapore & Malaysia

Spain

Thailand

Turkey

Venice

Fodor's Flashmaps

Boston

New York

San Francisco

Washington, D.C.

Fodor's Pocket Guides

Acapulco

Atlanta

Barbados

Jamaica

London

New York City

Paris

Prague

Puerto Rico

Rome

San Francisco

Washington, D.C.

Rivages Guides

Bed and Breakfasts of Character and Charm in France

Hotels and Country Inns of Character and Charm in France

Hotels and Country Inns of Character and Charm in Italy

Short Escapes

Country Getaways in Britain

Country Getaways in France

Country Getaways Near New York City

Fodor's Sports

Golf Digest's Best Places to Play

Skiing USA

USA Today The Complete Four Sport Stadium Guide

Fodor's Vacation Planners

Great American Learning Vacations

Great American Sports & Adventure Vacations

Great American Vacations

National Parks and Seashores of the East

National Parks of the West